KT-221-535

Happy Birthday!
28ᵗʰ May 1970.
with love from
Peter. xox.

The Reality of Monarchy

THE REALITY
OF MONARCHY

ANDREW DUNCAN

HEINEMANN : LONDON

William Heinemann Ltd
LONDON MELBOURNE TORONTO
JOHANNESBURG AUCKLAND

First published 1970
Copyright © Andrew Duncan 1970
434 21655 0

Printed in Great Britain by
Cox & Wyman Ltd, London, Fakenham and Reading

Contents

Foreword

Writing about the reality of an institution that thrives to a large extent on make-believe and irrational attitudes requires the help of people who would not normally talk about their work in any but the most nebulous terms.

In spite of recent developments, the British Monarchy is still an extraordinarily closed institution. The reality is often camouflaged. I have spoken to nearly five hundred people, from members of the royal family to minor officials. To them, my gratitude. As this is not a book of which all would want to approve – in public – I shall not embarrass them now, or in the future, by disclosing their names where they are not specifically mentioned.

Endless help has been given by the Queen's Press Secretary, William Heseltine, C.V.O., and his assistants.

But it must be stressed this book is in no way 'officially' inspired. The interpretation of events is entirely my own. The only pressure, and that of a polite nature, came from the London Embassy of a European country. It was ignored.

Prologue

'What angle are you going to take?' the Queen asked at a cocktail party in Santiago, Chile, one sunny November evening.

A good question. What is left to be said about a moderately attractive, middle-aged woman pursued unwillingly through life by every branch of the communications industry intent on recounting in breathless detail every remark, every hat, every dress? Queen Elizabeth the Second, forty-second monarch since William the Conqueror, descendant of George Washington, Mohammed, Egbert of Wessex, and anyone else you care to mention. By grace of her position, doyenne of the cult of personality: an exposed, lonely woman forced to fulfil an astonishing round of engagements and symbolic duties, that make little concession to the twentieth century, in order to sustain an institution that, rationally, should have as much relevance to the modern world as other ancient British customs such as rolling the waffle.

It is one of the curious phenomena of the late twentieth century that such an eccentric institution can not only survive, but apparently thrive. Millions of the Queen's gloom-laden subjects, wincing with all the rivetingly documented withdrawal symptoms of power, sink comfortably into the past, raise their glasses, and say, 'Well, thank God we've got her.'

If nothing else, the British are world champions at the Monarchy game, producing competitors who are less drab than the Dutch, less pompous than the Scandinavians, and more sophisticated than the most devious President. 'My sister,' says Princess Margaret, in her inimitable tone of throwaway haughtiness, 'copes very well with Presidents.'

It is a long-running theatrical production that is well-entrenched, even if audience reactions are occasionally conditioned more by appeals to the past than the present or future, and even if amongst a majority of those under thirty the attitude is not, 'Will they continue?' but 'How long *can* they continue?' A show for the middle class, produced with *élan* by the aristocracy for the benefit of all. Or so it seems.

But who knows the reality of Monarchy? Who knows its true cost? This was going to be one of the ill-informed subjects of debate during the early seventies. In isolation, it was meaningless. It had to be assessed in relation to the Queen's actual work. And what is her job, as opposed to theoretical make-believe and vague historical justification? What is her relationship to apparently decaying or disillusioning institutions like the Church, the Commonwealth, and Parliament. Or vice versa?

One of the Queen's most influential religious advisers said to me: 'Five years ago, constitutional Monarchy in this country was dead from the neck up. It's now becoming popular again.' Is it?

A senior member of her staff, discussing preliminary plans for the State visit to Australia in March 1970, said: 'Of course, I shouldn't think Australia will stay in the Commonwealth for more than another ten years . . .'

Who knows what members of the royal family really think about their work? It is endlessly repeated that the Queen is a pleasant mother with a reasonable sense of fun who works hard, buys ice-lollies for the children, and is a cornucopia for trivial domestic chit-chat re-told by erstwhile servants. She also has a pretty enjoyable life at times – or why else would she be sipping gin and tonic at the Hilton Hotel in Santiago while her subjects in Britain, about to embark on yet another economic squeeze, were grizzling under the burst-pipe rigours of the sixty-eighth 'unexpectedly severe' winter of the century?

Why indeed? That was part of the angle. But, most important, how does an integral yet archaic aspect of British society like Monarchy operate during a vital transition period? Is it a blockade against the stumbling of Western civilization? Or a convenient middle-aged hallucination disguising reality?

Fundamental changes are taking place, and the Queen is the pivot, although her role and influence are blurred too often by sentimentality. The witless sycophancy that quivers from the maudlin pens of most royal sob sisters, probably devalues the institution more than the most devastating criticism. A television film,[1] designed to show her at work, was a cosy glimpse at nothing very much, and worried at least three members of her family. 'It succeeded in making us more popular in the short term,' said one, 'but the long term results could be very harmful.' 'Should be locked in a vault and never seen more than once every ten years,' said another.

Still, no other nation has managed for so long to keep the façade of Monarchy stimulating, the appearance immaculate. The gentle, harmless hypocrisy necessary to maintain it is a unique British characteristic. Yet the very advantages of having a supposedly non-controversial Head of State have their own problems. Often, the Monarchy can appear to be little more than a soporific for a geriatric society, an international vaudeville, or a focal point for complacency. Again, this is a fact often better appreciated by royalty themselves than their apologists.

Initially, there was astonishment that Prince Charles, in his first public interview, could talk sense. 'That's crazy,' Lord Harewood told me. 'People think that even if you're only a peer in this country you must be tolerably moronic, and almost certainly unprofessional. Charles himself was bound to be at least as intelligent as the average undergraduate.'

[1]*Royal Family* (see p. 211 et seq.)

It is futile to be over-critical, thus missing one of the potent advantages of Monarchy: the fun it provides. Nevertheless, it should not be free from objective observation. In Britain today, away from the fetid atmosphere of a hypercynical capital city, any attempt to treat royalty as an important institution that is not above politics (which it is not and never has been) is still as socially dangerous as suggesting on Vatican Radio that the Pope has a mistress. In many quaint, post-imperial redoubts, fury is evoked by saying the Queen stamped her size four and a half shoe in a tantrum, or looked bored, or made a dreadful speech. Queen Victoria never had such protection.

Most criticism of the Monarchy is uninformed. Most information sprinkled with regal goo. Comment is secondhand and many people who write about the royal family have never even seen them, let alone spoken to them or their advisers. How often one longs for a chink of realism to slip between the unctuous posturings, rumours, or backstairs prattle staked along the royal progress.

For one year, from the Opening of Parliament in Autumn 1968, I decided to follow the Queen everywhere, a trail that led from a blackout in Northern Brazil, to a languid tour of the family farms in Dorset; lunch in the QE2 to a stroll past bidets in Glasgow; from the Derby to Ascot, to Goodwood, and other Queenly horse pursuits; from an extraordinary party at the British Embassy in Rio de Janeiro to champagne on a London underground platform; from Buckingham Palace to Windsor, to Balmoral, to Sandringham; from a dire operetta in Vienna to the maternity wing of a South London hospital; from a Windsor council flat to cocktail parties and champagne in half a dozen different parts of the world; from an exuberant crush in Valparaiso to a tree-planting ceremony in Cambridge drizzle; from a shivering parade ground where she paid some sort of obeisance to guns, to a cruise down the Norwegian fjords; from the Opening of Parliament to Trooping the Colour, to the garden parties, to the showpiece of a royal year – the Investiture of Charles as Prince of Wales at Caernarvon (Appendix).

It was a year of exhilaration, surprise, chaos, boredom, mismanagement, success, gossip, tactlessness, tiredness and some failures. It was bonanza year for European Monarchy. None were deposed, deported, beheaded and one was even promised a new throne: Prince Juan Carlos, 31, who shared Queen Victoria as a great-great grandmother with our own Queen, was named successor to Generalissimo Franco – although it is true that the sight of an elderly dictator proclaiming to a puppet parliament the future coronation of a young aristocrat who had been disloyal to his father was not the happiest augury for the club. Africa lost one king when Idris I of Libya was deposed by the Army, reducing the Arab monarchies to three, and pushing republicanism even further into that world. The Indian cabinet continued plans to abolish 'Anachronistic' privileges, such as tax-free privy purses, enjoyed by their princes. And in Britain, the year was climaxed by an incredible few weeks of brilliantly stage-managed regal adoration, the like of which had never been seen since the Queen's Coronation.

As Monarchy is a family profession, I watched the supporting cast at work, and spoke to many of them – with varying degrees of co-operation. Memories remain, Prince Philip in tetchy mood, on a settee in his office. Princess Margaret, hospitable and charming, lunching off what appeared to be a card table while her daughter, Sarah, played with the Queen's youngest, Edward. Princess Alexandra plaintively looking for her husband at a party. Charles examining the new Royal Mint at a small village in Wales. Anne drinking schnapps at ten o'clock in the morning on a Tyrolean railway station. Lord Snowdon discussing money with the man who came to mend the stereo. Lord Harewood in a cramped, tatty office. Angus Ogilvy in something more splendid giving his chauffeur a reference . . .

Then, there were the Cabinet Ministers who, uncomfortable

xiii

in morning dress, parade with the Queen and speak to her privately afterwards. Their attitude is sometimes schizophrenic to say the least, as must be expected. The Church leaders, scarlet clad and pious, on the lawns of Buckingham Palace for a tea-time chat, but cunning when there is a chance to use the Queen as a mouthpiece . . .

It became generally acknowledged as the most critical year for the British Monarchy since the Queen ascended the throne. In retrospect it may be seen as the most decisive since Edward VIII's abdication. Changes were beginning that could dramatically alter the Queen's position. It was, above all, the year the royal family tip-toed from the cloisters, peeped from behind the mystical shroud and decided to show they were real people. Well almost. And this is what happened.

The Royal Vaudeville - I

'The streets are lined by that good-humoured, loyal crowd which is characteristic of London'. *How the Queen Reigns* by Dorothy Laird, Hodder and Stoughton, 1959, p. 94.

'The State Opening of Parliament may be a splendid tourist spectacle, but if it can't be planned better it ought to be scrapped. The traffic in London on Wednesday was murder. My normal trip takes 10–15 minutes. On Wednesday, it took an hour and 40 minutes' – letter in *Daily Express*, 3 November, 1968.

THE CEREMONIAL YEAR, that was to end in triumph, began inauspiciously for the Queen with ironic hints of a difficult future. Opening of Parliament, on Wednesday, 30 October, was as always, an example of the British genius for amalgamating historical significance and elegant eccentricity with the purposeful present, in order to produce the most irate traffic jam of the year.

Autumn, when the tourists have slunk home with their polaroid mementoes, when the King's Road dollies discard their exuberant conning, and when the Guards change at Buckingham Palace with scarcely a spectator in sight, is the close season for pageantry. Paradoxically, the city is often at its most beautiful. A pale evening sun speckles the buildings with iridescent softness, turning the Houses of Parliament to gentle brown-grey. The parks, bereft of hippie campers, become acres of tangible green memories to a feudal

I

Monarchy that preferred hunting to the profitable philistinism of speculators.

It is the time, too, when the Queen performs her most important constitutional duty of the year. She finishes her summer holiday at Balmoral, and starts the ceremonial treadmill by being dragged from Buckingham Palace to the House of Lords by four Oldenburg bays in the rickety Irish State Coach, bought by Queen Victoria from a Dublin coach builder in 1852 and now providing anxiety every time it is used. Disaster, if it fell to pieces on the way to Parliament.

By tradition two hostages for the Queen's safe return remain at the Palace. A courtier and a politician. The Lord Chamberlain, Lord Cobbold, head of the Household, educated at Eton and King's College, Cambridge, a former Governor of the Bank of England, aged sixty-five. The Vice-Chamberlain, Charles Morris, M.P., educated at Brookdale Park Secondary School, Manchester, a member of the Post Office Workers' Union, aged forty-three. His job was created in order to ensure that politicians had access to the Court, a function he now accomplishes by spending one and a half hours in the House of Commons library writing in longhand a six hundred word personalized report of the day's proceedings that is delivered to the Queen before dinner wherever she is in Britain. In the eighteenth century, this was done by the Prime Minister, then the chore was passed down to the Home Secretary. Now it's Mr Charles Morris, Labour Member of Parliament for Openshaw, who sits in the equerrys' room sipping coffee with Lord Cobbold, awaiting the Queen's return.

More than anything else, the two men symbolize the intriguing relationship between Crown and Parliament, a relationship that must remain a polite charade, except in extreme circumstances, and whose pantomime aspect was about to be illustrated.

The Queen was apprehensive as she rode to Parliament with Prince Charles, granted special leave from Cambridge, and Princess Anne, taking the day off from learning French at a language school. She had managed to have some of the sentences in the speech re-worded so it wasn't too stuffed with the banal phrases of her Ministers. 'Why can't you give me something more readable. It's so difficult to say,' she had complained, and a few more tortuous Civil Service lines had been expunged. Everyone knew she was, on this occasion, announcing Government plans for the next twelve months.

And the plans were the problem. This year there were fourteen words about reform of the House of Lords. The implication was clear. Once the hereditary system is abolished as an aspect of Government, it may appear ridiculous to continue with the Monarchy. The Queen could become the fairy standing on a crumbling cake.

It was not a new idea. After the Reform Bill of 1832, many people thought it would be only a matter of years before the hereditary system was abolished. But when Britain became successfully imperialist, Queen Victoria, besides adding prestige to her profession, allowed her position to be used ruthlessly in the cause of Empire, flag, and patriotism. Edward VII worried about the House of Lords and, in spite of success in preventing a Cabinet Committee suggesting changes[1] introduced the present Queen's grandfather, George V, as 'the last King of England'.[2]

In 1910, George V himself had to agree to Asquith's demands that more peers should be created if the Lords

[1] *Journals and Letters of Reginald, Viscount Esher,* Ivor Nicholson and Watson, 1934, Vol. 2, p. 228: 'Viscount Esher hears that the Cabinet Committee which is considering the question of the House of Lords, has put aside in deference to Your Majesty's own wishes, all idea of making proposals which involve touching the hereditary principle upon which that House rests.'

[2] *Haldane of Cloan,* Allen and Unwin, 1960, p. 231: 'As they talked, the King asked Lord Haldane if he knew his son (who was later to become George V). "No", said Lord Haldane, he had not had that honour. "Come then," said the King, "and I'll introduce you to him." They walked across the room to where the young prince was standing, and the King said, "Let me present you to the last King of England." '

became troublesome enough to block legislation. Lloyd George had called them 'the last of the litter'. Winston Churchill thought they were a Punch and Judy show . . .

It was a continuous battle, but now the situation was different. Already, the Queen was troubled with undercurrents or republicanism by stealth. The previous year Emrys Hughes,[3] a continuous sniper at royal privilege, had introduced a Bill to abolish titles.

Parliamentary procedure insists on the Queen's consent before anything is discussed that could affect her position, as this did. Her advisers at the Palace were not enthusiastic and hinted that the Bill should be quietly ignored, but a Labour Minister told her: 'It would be a mistake to stop it. If you let the Bill come forward, it will be a flop.' The Queen was sceptical, and even more pressure – of a dinner-party-conversation type – was exerted, unsuccessfully. The debate took place on a Friday lunch-time[4] and was preceded by a statement from the then Home Secretary, Roy Jenkins. 'I have it in command from the Queen to acquaint the House that her Majesty, having been informed of the purport of the Bill, has consented to place her prerogative and interest, so far as they are affected by the Bill, at the disposal of Parliament for the purposes of the Bill.'

As predicted the Bill, a therapeutic joke, attracted hardly any attention.

At Windsor, the following week-end, the Queen remarked there hadn't been much in the newspapers. 'There was something about it in *The Times* and the *Guardian,*' she was told.

'Yes, but I mean the newspapers.'

She knew, too, as the coach and horses clattered towards Westminster, that there was an inverted snobbery about the British that partly explained the enduring success of the Monarchy. Curiously, she had often felt uneasy with Harold Macmillan, patrician, urbanity wrapped in nettles, who tended

[3] Died 18 October, 1969.
[4] 17 March, 1967 from 12.44 p.m. until 2.40 p.m. Titles (Abolition) Bill.

4

to act grand-dad at their weekly audiences, discussing affairs of state while looking directly over her head at pictures on the wall, or a clock. There was also the suspicion he didn't tell her anything. Harold Wilson, on the other hand, had begun their relationship on a note of folksy civility by telephoning a private secretary to ask if he could bring his wife when he kissed hands on appointment as Prime Minister in October 1964. It was an unusual request, particularly as his father and sister also came along in another car. In fact, Palace gossip was so inflamed that one story said Wilson's influential private secretary Marcia Williams, was also present. She wasn't. Colleagues were sceptical. 'The Queen thinks Harold's a prosy old bore, a *petit bourgeois*,' said one.

During the year, the Queen had innumerable opportunities to observe how appearance and reality are, if anything, less compatible for politicians than monarchs. Only two weeks ago there had been Richard Crossman.

Richard Crossman had been made Lord President of the Council in 1966. Like many other high-sounding British jobs, it is of little practical importance, but immense constitutional significance, giving the holder precedence next to the Prime Minister. The Labour Party's resident intellectual, Crossman, was unenthusiastic. He thought it was a waste of time, a sinecure, and didn't want to meet the Queen anyway. The week before he had mentioned at dinner how 'frightfully horsey' he found her, and how he disliked the hocus-pocus surrounding British State occasions. Still, he didn't decline the job, and first time he met the Queen, she said: 'I hear you had dinner with . . . the other evening.' Unknown to Crossman, his companion had been one of the Queen's closest friends. She smiled. Immediately the atmosphere relaxed. In spite of one or two contretemps, he became very impressed with her – so much so that on 15 October, 1968, the eve of his last Privy Council meeting before becoming Minister of Health and Social Security, he asked if he could bring his wife and two children to look round the Palace.

Strange how everyone succumbed in the end.

At the House of Lords, Yeomen of the Guard, accompanied by Special Branch detectives, searched the cellars in remembrance of Guy Fawkes. The Lord Great Chamberlain, Lord Chancellor and Earl Marshal stood waiting to conduct the Queen to her robing room, one of the few parts of the building that still remains under royal control.[5]

For a few years after her accession the Queen had practised wearing the Imperial State Crown, weighing nearly three pounds, but didn't need to any more. It had been taken under guard straight to Westminster from the Tower of London.

She has made only one innovation – changing the time from 11.00 a.m. to 11.30 on the assumption that the later time would cause less inconvenience to rush-hour traffic. Otherwise the ceremonial is the same, historically based on the Norman custom of kings wearing their crowns on three occasions a year: at Gloucester on Christmas Day, at Winchester during Easter, and Westminster at Pentecost. They became known as 'parleys', and the first recorded King's Council was held by William the Conqueror in 1076. The present Palace of Westminster was founded by Edward the Confessor, and declared 'the King's Palace of Westminster – for ever', by Henry VIII in 1536. Technically, the Queen is coming to the House of Lords to take possession, meet with representatives of the Church, Parliament, and Judiciary, and tell them what they are going to do.

In the House of Lords, Lord Montgomery tested the weight of the Sword of State. He had held it, front stage left, on several Openings and wrote early in the year, asking if he could once more have the honour. It was known that, at seventeen days from his eighty-second birthday, he was

[5]On 26 April, 1965, the Queen agreed that the Palace of Westminster should remain royal, but control and occupation should be vested in the Lord Chancellor for the House of Lords, and Mr Speaker for the Commons. The Lord Great Chamberlain remains responsible for the robing room, staircase, anteroom and royal gallery.

perhaps not fit enough, but the Queen didn't want to disappoint him so she agreed. The previous evening, the Duke of Norfolk, hereditary Earl Marshal, who had organized State occasions since 1930, had a rehearsal, with his wife taking the role of Queen. 'My standard is high,' he says. 'In this country we live really on, and by, tradition. If we start letting up on these State occasions we're going to get much cheaper. If we don't consider the dignity of what we do, it will get slipshod, and people won't want to see it. Of course, you have a few days of inconvenience, but I wonder if it inconveniences the public as much as people returning by train from a Manchester football match, and cutting up the seats. Which way would you like to live?'

He is a man of consummate antiquity, too obvious a target for mockery, too obviously competent to deserve it. To watch him puffing through ceremonies, red round cheeks blowing in and out like bellows, skin hooded and wrinkled like a turtle, is to watch a vision of the past. Possibly one of the few men left in England who demonstrably believed every word he said, he had committed his life to his heritage with an intensity that found opposition difficult to understand. When Richard Crossman said he wouldn't take part in State occasions the Duke of Norfolk thought he must be opposed to the Monarchy. Surely that wasn't true? Harold Wilson was told that his senior Minister had been making extraordinary remarks about the Queen. Crossman explained his attitude to Sir Michael Adeane, the Queen's private secretary. Adeane listened, said it would be perfectly all right for Crossman not to attend the Opening. 'But when I tell the Queen you think it's a lot of rubbish, she'll say, "Well, it's still rather unfair of the Lord President to stay away." Think about it.'

Crossman did. Eventually he hired his morning suit from Moss Bros. and attended.

Bernard Marmaduke Fitzalan-Howard, sixteenth Duke of Norfolk, a descendant of Edward I and Margaret of Valois, a man of far more humour and subtlety than he might look in ermine rig, was going to have an interesting year. And he knew it, as he escorted the Queen from the Norman porch into her robing room where she put on her ermine-lined, crimson velvet cape, measuring eighteen feet, four and a half inches long.

In the chamber of the House of Lords, robed peers and their ladies had been gathering for an hour or more. Jewel-encrusted (an unkind commentator said 'glass sequined') bosoms began to sprout below well-powdered faces and above long evening dresses, decorated with the best family diamonds. Lorgnettes were clutched, period piece props in an improbable setting. Ten unattractive chandeliers hung over the room. The judges straggled in together, and sat facing each other on the Woolsack. Diplomats squawked in a sort of pen to the right of the throne.

Princess Margaret entered wearing yellow, with the Duchess of Gloucester in blue. The assembly stood. Margaret felt sorry for the Queen today, because she thought the Government were using her more and more as a skirt to hide behind. She mouthed 'Hello' to her friends, leant forward to speak to her husband, Lord Snowdon, seated in front, opposite the Archbishop of Canterbury.

Candles were lit in front of the throne. Then silence, except for a few aborted coughs. . . .

Trumpets are heard from outside, then voices. House lights dim, and the throne is lit from concealed spots. Enter one of those processions of Englishmen disguised like packs of cards and pantomime dames that would look absurd in any setting that couldn't justify it by a noble past (Appendix). Directly in front of the Queen, the Duke of Norfolk and the Lord Great Chamberlain walk backwards as a mark of respect.

She sits on the throne, with Prince Charles on her right, composed and relaxed; Princess Anne on her left. She sends Black Rod to fetch the Members of Parliament from the House of Commons, and everyone waits a few minutes for them to arrive. Lord Montgomery, standing erect with the sword of state, begins to sway, feeling faint in the close atmosphere. The Queen notices him from the corner of her eye, but doesn't move her head, or betray any emotion, even so much as a heavy swallow or a deep breath.

The Lord Chancellor approaches the throne, bows, then kneels on the top red-carpeted step of the dais to give her a printed copy of proposed Government legislation called the Gracious Speech.

Lord Montgomery stumbles one step forward, clutches for a hand, and is led from the chamber for smelling salts. Lord Tryon, Keeper of the Privy Purse, takes the sword and stands in, as the Queen begins her speech, amplified by four gilt-painted microphones hidden in the canopy of the throne.

'My Lords and Members of the House of Commons. My husband and I look forward with pleasure to the State Visit of the President of the Republic of Italy, and to our own visit to Brazil and Chile . . .

'A Bill will be introduced to effect the change to a decimal currency . . .

'Legislation will be introduced on the composition and powers of the House of Lords.

'My Government will begin consultations on the appoint-ment of a Commission on the Constitution. The Commission would consider what changes may be needed in the central institutions of government in relation to the several countries, nations, and regions of the United Kingdom . . .

'A Bill will be brought before you to reduce to 18 the age for voting and to make other reforms in electoral law . . .

'My Government will carry forward their comprehensive programme for the reform of the law . . .

'My Lords and Members of the House of Commons, I pray that the blessing of Almighty God may rest upon your Counsels.'

Just plans. The reality would appear at the end of the year, in the Prorogation speech. Before that a lot would happen.

Imperturbable, still emotionless, the procession returns to disrobe. If the Bill to reform the House of Lords succeeds there will no longer be such a position as Earl Marshal. The Duke of Norfolk retires to take off his four hundred year old parliamentary robes.

His tailor, standing nearby, tells him not to touch them in case they fall to pieces. The collar is already fraying.

Are you worried, Your Grace, about your job?

'No. They've tried to take it away four times in my lifetime.'

What would you do if they succeed this time?

The short replies are spoken lazily, deep voiced with a confidence that inhibits argument. 'Get a Royal Warrant. To put us all back again.'

Like Humpty Dumpty.

'We're not as easy money as they think, you know.'

The Queen doesn't have to worry as she clip-clops home. Cheers mingle with the sound of the National Anthem, the bells of St Margaret's Church, and the occasional derisive comment. She is off to South America, to meet her husband, leaving the family in charge.[6]

[6]When the Queen goes abroad Councillors of State are appointed. These are usually made up of the four senior members of the family in succession to the throne, not excluded by age. The Queen Mother and Prince Philip are also Councillors of State. In practice, the work is usually done by the Queen Mother and Princess Margaret.

The Road Show-I

'The man who invented the red carpet needed his head examining.' Prince Philip about to disembark from the royal VC10 on to yet another red carpet in Brazil.

'Good luck to a great royal trouper as she sets out on her travels once again.' *The People*, 3 November, 1968.

THERE WERE TWELVE DRAFTS of the arrangements for the Queen's visit to Brazil. Schedules were re-vamped and titivated until the last minute so that the final programme had to be elaborately telegrammed to London for approval instead of being sent by diplomatic bag. Not that it was all done in a rush. Such is the ornate ritual for sending the royal vaudeville on tour that initial planning had started two years previously. The official invitation had been delivered in November 1967, and during the last few months British Embassy officials in Rio de Janeiro had been weaned from their gentlemanly struggles with the most casual nation in the world into the devious bitchery and intricate protocol that only a royal tour inspires. Who would have guessed that in the institutional depths of their conventional souls lurked the machiavellian skills to make a nation believe what they hadn't seen, love what they did not know, admire a legend? 'The Queen is surrounded by an aura that is quite extraordinary. The only other place I've seen it is with the African chiefs. No royal occasion is like a British one, I'm convinced of that,' explained a British Embassy official.

A vast publicity campaign was prepared, special match-boxes inlaid with pictures of the Queen's head were strewn around town, and the first British trade exhibition since 1931 was organized – in addition to the more effete Foreign Office preoccupations that sometimes make any royal tour appear to be a collection of problems invented by diplomats to assuage the fluttering sensibilities of their in-bred community. Who should wear what? And when? Who should meet the Queen? Who deserves what medals? Who first shakes the Queen's hand – the Governor, the Admiral, the Air Marshal, the Brigadier? Which Civil Servants go to the banquet, and which to the less prestigious reception afterwards? The gold-rimmed white cardboard invitation to a royal function, far too large to put in a pocket and far too grand to fold, is more than a passport to join several hundred people for a free booze-up with the Queen. It is status on a universal scale, perhaps the only remaining supreme snob gesture that is respected and admired from Clacton to Calcutta. 'I had a drink with the Queen.' Everyone knows you mean the Queen of England, and not one of those twopenny continental poseurs cliché-ing their images with bicycles. King Baudouin and Queen Fabiola of the Belgians spent twenty-four hours in a DC6 flying to India for a State Visit because the Government thought a Boeing 727 would be too expensive. When King Olav of Norway visited Brazil, officially, the previous year, he took a retinue of eight. The Queen needed five aeroplanes, a yacht with 230 ratings and 21 officers (only 175 and 15 when in harbour, in England), two frigates, fourteen members of the Household, two plain-clothes police officers, seven officials, twenth-four staff including the Royal Pastry Chef and a Page of the Presence, and a twenty-two-piece orchestra. Instructions were relayed ahead that she didn't want to eat oysters or lobster.

Impressed as they were by such style, the Brazilians were none the less pre-occupied with the rumblings of a counter-revolution and four important visits in two months – as befits an immensely desirable country being wooed by every developed nation, a coquettish heiress, luscious and willing who can afford to indulge her caprices when the old men come sniffing around. President Frei of Chile was there for a week from 4 September, and sat in a São Paulo traffic jam for fifteen minutes; Mrs Indira Gandhi, Prime Minister of India, for five days from 22 September; more significantly, Willy Brandt, who was then Foreign Minister of West Germany, for three days from 23 October; and the Rumanian Foreign Minister, Corneliu Manescu, for two days at the end of October. By the start of the Queen's visit, the all-male protocol department of Itamaraty, Brazil's Foreign Ministry, were suffering more than usual from the hazards of international goodwill. Twenty-four people worked on the final plans for a couple of months, and then as a final dilemma, the President abolished summer time, which was to start the day of the Queen's arrival. All the schedules had to be altered. 'They didn't really do much about the Queen until it was nearly time for the visit. They have the philosophy that it will be all right on the day,' said a British official, miffed because such down the table nations should take precedence. But that, alas, was the reality. And the British Queen, elegantly packaged in the glow of political and economic expediency, was being sent to Brazil, then Chile, primarily as a saleswoman.

Before the visit was over, interminable speeches would be read, the Royal Temper lost, the Royal Foot stamped, and the Royal Charm spread, all to great effect. The feed-back from royal mystique wraps everyone in an indefinable mire of sycophantic flapdoodle, and in the wake of Royal Progress, chaos was almost averted, business was transacted, and friendship was achieved. The cost was enormous.

On Friday, 1 November, the Queen inoculated against tetanus, polio, yellow fever; vaccinated and preparing to swallow daily anti-malaria and stomach upset pills because, as Buckingham Palace reassuringly announced, 'the Queen is not a fairy';[1] accompanied by an assortment of politicians, policemen, pages, doctors and secretaries; and having overcome the fear she might catch chicken-pox from her nephew Viscount Linley; once more said good-bye to her four children and, just before nine o'clock in the morning left London airport in a blue and white VC10 piloted by three Squadron Leaders and carrying, amongst other goodies: twenty-four bottles of Liebfraumilch Madonna, thirty-six bottles of Château Latour, twelve bottles of Anjou Rosé, twenty-four bottles of Beaujolais, three tins of Dundee cake, six packets of shortbread, eight boxes of After Eight mints, three jars each of strawberry and raspberry jam, six bottles of soured cream, two tins of chipolatas, one packet of dried parsley, six bottles of Long Life fresh milk, packets of assorted cheese balls, twenty-four tins of Danish cream, three bottles of mint sauce, and three tiaras. And yes, there were the traditional items that are taken everywhere: tea-making equipment of bottled Malvern water, monogrammed electric kettle and China tea; hot-water bottle, special feather pillows, and barley sugar to suck before a speech. Polo sticks, a ton of silver-framed photographs, and assorted presents, two hundred poppies for Remembrance Day, and other regal impedimenta, had gone ahead in *Britannia*. It was, after all, the first time a reigning British monarch had visited South America.

The Queen didn't take a passport. As they are issued in her name, it would seem odd for her to have one.

She was travelling to a continent that provides a massive catalogue of missed opportunities, patronizing attitudes and lack of foresight by the British who once had enormous influence there, with investment during the 1920s reaching £1,200 million. Now it had fallen to £150 million and only the sad mementoes remained; golf clubs, country clubs, Harrods in Buenos Aires, tea-time, the Rio Cricket Association founded in 1872 and visited by the Duke of Windsor

[1] *Evening Standard*, 19 August, 1968.

in 1931 who drank a cup of tea in the 'Bowler's Arms' pub. Ah, nostalgia. What could be done? A lady-in-waiting provided by the Brazilian Government to supplement the two brought by the Queen, was chosen largely because of her virtuosity at muffin-making and her habit of taking tea every afternoon. Secure and cosy. Quaintness, the English narcissism, was lovely.

But the United States, Japan, West Germany, had come clod-hopping in with their banks, their inventiveness, their ruthlessness, their market research, their smart, bi-lingual salesmen, and stolen our prestige and our profit. (Appendix.)

Ten years previously, a leading British car manufacturer had refused to set up a factory in Brazil because he thought the annual sale would never reach thirty thousand. As the Queen flew over the South Atlantic, she knew that Volkswagen were manufacturing with Teutonic randiness three hundred thousand every year, and selling them for £1,000 each. The Americans had a ten billion dollar investment in Latin America which gave only a twelve per cent return, compared with only eight per cent in the Common Market. Since 1964, when the CIA had helped remove President Joao Goulart, who had been careless enough to allow communists to infiltrate the traditionally right wing Army, the Americans had concentrated on Brazil and doubled their AID programme in one year, 1964, to $179 million. They had recently held a mammoth industrial exhibition in São Paulo, and were competing with the British for the sale of submarines to the Brazilian Navy – an attempt the British tried to foil by cunningly sending their host's defence experts on a bibulous cruise down the coast in *Britannia*. It was Sir Michael Adeane's idea that two groups of about one hundred businessmen should have the use of the yacht.

In preparing background information for the Queen, the Foreign Office experts had been reminded they were dealing with an educated woman, and not a schoolgirl, one of the common misconceptions amongst Civil Servants, and politicians, many of whom feel privately she is a rubber ball to be bounced to strategic places with the minimum of real information and the maximum of manufactured charisma. She was annoyed when Harold Macmillan tried to stop her going to Ghana in 1961 because of the danger. 'Danger,' she told him, 'is part of the job.'

So, of course, is confusion, and there would be plenty in Brazil, a country difficult to understand in upper middle class British terms – or, for that matter, in any terms but its own. It covers half of South America, is larger than Western Europe, and includes the devastating potential of Amazonia which itself is half the size of the United States. Fifty million of the hundred million population are under eighteen. A country matured without infancy, accomplishing in three generations the changes Europe achieved after several centuries of dissension, a Reformation and an Industrial Revolution. A scintillating morass of contradictions, slums slinking into all the cities and massive wealth which allows 19,000 Brazilian visitors to Britain to spend nearly the same as 142,000 Italians, a military dictatorship where rival soldiers are more likely to play football, using tanks as goalposts, than shoot each other.[2] The Army's traditional role had been that of a wet nurse to instability rather than a politically ambitious force and there were only 120,000 officers and men. It is a country where after four hundred years there is only one road between Rio de Janeiro, the emotional *de facto* capital, and São Paulo the fastest growing concrete and glass skyscraper excrescence in the world with sixty-five new buildings a day and an estimated population of ten million by 1980. One road, and yet an aeroplane shuttle service every half-hour. A country where indolence creeps around, sanctified by sunshine and using staggering potential as collateral. In 1966 tin ore was imported from Thailand. Then someone

[2]In 1954, after President Vargas committed suicide, soldiers were sent to the Palace – where they found rivals installed. They played football, using the tanks as goalposts.

found a two hundred million ton mountain of it in the interior. In spite of overwhelming inefficiency – Petrobras, the State oil company, had twenty Presidents in seventeen years, and thirty-seven thousand employees for an eight per cent share of the market, compared with Shell's eight thousand employees and thirty-five per cent – Brazil was producing half its oil needs, and would be self-sufficient in five years. 'The land of the future – and always will be,' say the Rio inhabitants about their country. They are wrong, and of all the places the Queen could have visited, Brazil was probably the most sensible and piquant.

Sensible because at last British exporters were overcoming their apathy and had doubled sales in one year – from £19,800,000 in 1967 to £44,000,000 in 1968, although this was half the trade with Portugal.[3] Piquant because at times the visit was to seem painfully like the swan song for a way of life, the maiden aunt (Britain not the Queen) unwilling to learn new tricks and with few imaginative gestures to make, inquisitive about the thrusting, silly, enthusiastic, ribald, disdainful, adolescent. At others, it was impossible not to admire the panache with which the aunt kicked up her skirts to provide a display of breathtaking vulgarity. The Queen, who was to become an entrancing coagulant for all the inconsistencies, was at that moment preparing to arrive in Dakar, Senegal, and the first huffiness of the trip was about to be felt.

She would spend forty hours twenty-seven minutes in the air, covering 17,917 miles – more flying time than on any previous visit of her reign. In February, Air Commodore Archie Winskill, C.B.E., D.F.C., Captain of the Queen's Flight, started preparations that would result in a one hundred and six page, half-inch thick document being passed to four hundred participants in the drama.

[3] In 1969, Britain exported goods worth £74,850,000 to Portugal. Imports were £75,975,000

First, he had to choose an airline. Usually the Queen flies on a plane chartered from BOAC or BEA, but BOAC had relinquished the South American route in 1964 because they couldn't make it pay, and the Government refused a £1,250,000 loan. This apparent ineptitude was fairly typical of the British indifference to South America, but an independent firm, British United Airways, had nearly doubled the traffic, broke even in the third year and were about to make a profit on the route. They, naturally, wanted the prestige of flying the Queen, but it was thought they would have difficulty taking a plane from passenger service. Moreover, it was the RAF's fiftieth anniversary, and they are always anxious to show their skill at VIP travel. They were asked to estimate a cost. The eventual air bill excluding the Chilean part of the trip, was £35,000. BUA, gracefully realizing they could not compete with a subsidized organization, performed their flag waving by sending plaster replicas of the Crown Jewels on a tour of Brazil and Chile accompanied by two genuine, one hundred per cent British bobbies in blue uniforms and bland expressions.

Air Support Command headquarters at Upavon, Wiltshire, planned the route and arranged for two VC10's to be prepared. One, call-sign Ascot 1901 and continuously charted on a map in the control room with red and white diagonally shaped pieces of cardboard, was for the Queen. The other was kept on twenty-four-hour standby at Brize Norton throughout the tour, ready to leave at two hours' notice. Two special interiors were designed, with the unfortunate lack of subtlety that results when the practical military mind collides with the delicacies of interior decoration in an effort to impress. No one won, and the Queen had to walk past the galley and cabin crew's station in order to reach her specially plumbed flush lavatory. The rest of her compartment, in the front of the aircraft, was adequate for a month's holiday: lounge, dining-room, dressing-room, and bedroom with adjacent small lounge. There was no night flying. Behind her, facing backwards, there were two blocks of seats for members of the Household and staff. 'An absurd layout. There won't be many Air Commodores up for medals after this,' commented a Household member.

A Comet from the RAF's VIP Squadron 216 at Lyneham travelled to Brazil and Chile in July on a proving flight with Private Secretary Sir Martin Charteris, Press Secretary Heseltine, and Chief Superintendent Perkins,[4] the Queen's detective, who sat huddled terrified in the back of the official car as Brazilian drivers demonstrated their faith in God and their ability to swerve flamboyantly in and out of traffic, one hand on the wheel, at speed, and apparently looking the other way. Optimistically, in a country where you are considered early if you arrive an hour late for an appointment, they checked timings to the last second, and suggested a few minor alterations in the programme. Planning, according to Heseltine, is a point of departure.

For the actual visit, the Comet left a day before the Queen carrying some staff and luggage (the Queen's labelled in yellow, Prince Philip's mauve, Household members in red and yellow, staff in white). An RAF Hercules and an Andover of the Queen's Flight had started about a week earlier. The Hercules was used for carrying spares, and an air-conditioning unit not provided at Brazilian airports. The Andover was to replace one piloted from Mexico City by Prince Philip who had been there for the last three weeks cheering Britain at the Olympics where we won five gold medals including the clay pigeon shooting. It was thought advisable to overhaul the Andover, although not strictly necessary.

For seven days before take-off, the Queen's VC10 was wax-polished, overhauled, and fitted. Notices to airmen, NOTAM, were posted throughout the route requesting 'purple' airspace, which meant that other planes should keep ten miles away.

Five foreign countries were alerted to co-operate in the

[4]Promoted to Commander during the year. See page 149.

event of an accident. At St Mawgan, Cornwall, a manned helicopter was in readiness and an RAF Shackleton patrolled the route. The United States Air Force provided three Hercules aircraft – one patrolling from Lisbon to the Canaries, and two others at thirty minute readiness at Moron and Lajes. The Spanish Air Force patrolled a few hundred miles of the Sahara, and provided two frigates, and three helicopters, at various points with a 180-mile radius of action and a thirty-minute search plan. The Portuguese Air Force had one Neptune following the route, and a patrol boat in readiness. Senegal provided a Constellation until the royal plane was intercepted by the Brazilian Air Force with two Hercules, one Neptune, two helicopters – and a surface ship from the Navy.

To make quite sure these precautions were not needed, all RAF personnel, including stewards, on the VC10 were from the *élite* five per cent who have an 'A' category pass in written and flying examinations.

But, as with all meticulous plans, the trivial and unexpected happened. Food collected from London airport was wrapped in tin foil and had to be transferred to plastic containers before being heated. This took time, and Miss Margaret ('Bobo') MacDonald, the Queen's dresser, tired after hours arranging clothes, became irritated that she couldn't have a hot breakfast. Not even the lunch of rainbow trout, cold fillet of beef, raspberries and fresh cream, could soften the indignation. She was annoyed. And when 'Bobo' is upset, the entourage trembles. She complained to the Queen. The Queen became cross and asked why couldn't 'Bobo' have her hot breakfast. For the crew, at least, it was an inauspicious start.

Recife, in the State of Pernambuco, North Eastern Brazil, is one of the most poverty-stricken parts of the world. Five thousand babies a year die of malnutrition before they are a year old, and the average life span is thirty-five, compared with fifty-five in the rest of Brazil and about seventy in

England. Unemployment was at fifty per cent and there was an average daily intake of only 1,400 calories – half that of a British housewife. But Recife, the third largest city in Brazil, where 40,000 girls from the 1,200,000 population are said to be registered with the police as prostitutes, was about to give an impressive demonstration that the really poor love the unattainably rich with guileless enthusiasm. A superb advertisement for the seeping mystique of Monarchy.

Prince Philip, about whom much was said and little understood, was circling overhead in his Andover, waiting to land exactly on schedule and substantiate the reputation that fizzles uncomfortably before him, enlivened partly by his own action, partly by diplomatic tut-tuts. 'If anyone asks me, "Is it true that Prince Philip said, or did, such and such a thing?" I immediately answer, "Yes, yes, yes, of course it is," ' said a harassed British Ambassador who had coped with a previous royal visit.

Prince Philip, naturally, had his own ideas about the people he was visiting. 'When God was creating the world and dealing out the resources, every time he came to Brazil he gave them twice as much as anybody else. After this had been going on for some time the Archangels, who were standing around, said, "Now steady on. You know, you are overdoing it. Why are you giving so much to Brazil?" And He said, "You wait." And next He created the Brazilians.'

The confrontation promised to be lively.

Although, with Latin courtesy, the endemic and continuing political crisis had been postponed for the Queen's visit, three people had been killed in street clashes in Rio the previous week, and students had even been arrested for listening to a popular song, *Caminhando* (Walking), deriding the Army:

> There are soldiers who are
> Armed but not loved
> Mostly lost with their
> weapons in their hands

21

> In the barracks they
> learn the old lesson
> Of dying for the country
> and living for nothing.

The previous evening, Recife University had been plundered by gunmen of the C.C.C. (Commando Communist Chasers).

So, as Philip landed, the airport was ringed with machine-gun-toting police. Officials, swathed in the rainbow-coloured dignity of every conceivable medal and uniform, fretted in the ninety-degree sun. Thousands of schoolchildren clutching Union Jacks supplied by the Central Office of Information, waited in a special enclosure. Their parents, curious and excited, watched from behind the glass of the passenger lounge. What were they expecting? The Portuguese Monarchy had once been transferred to Rio de Janeiro, so they had at least a slim traditional and history-book recollection of the system. Officials had advised them to keep their knees covered, not to speak until spoken to, not to kiss the Queen and not to curtsy as it was undemocratic. Newspapers had warned they should call her Queen Mam, Prince Philip 'Her Highness Royal', had referred to 'Sir Perklins' the Queen's bodyguard, and had become lyrical:

> I remember still the girl
> who used to play
> in the flowery parks of England . . .
> and the girl became a woman
> She became Queen
> to conduct the destiny of England;
> how pretty was the girl,
> how pretty is the woman,
> how pretty is the Queen of England!
> Welcome to our land
> charming Queen Elizabeth II.[4]

[4]Haraldo Maranhao, *Times of Brazil*.

Perhaps the Queen would be wearing a crown, and be preceded by a Beefeater or other exotica from the royal caravanserai. Perhaps she would give them a magical smile.

Then, happily tinged by the spectacle, they could return to their *favelas*. What excitement. What anticipation. What a day for Recife.

Her Majesty's languid Ambassador to Brazil, Sir John Russell, kinsman of one of Britain's more exotic aristocrats, the Duke of Bedford, and looking the part, a tall, well-built man in tropical white suit, floppy hat, sun glasses, and somewhat blasé smile, tested the seat of a 1935 Lincoln convertible, the sort of transport used by American hoodlums, and gave a fey, queenly wave of his right hand. The royal standard, one of about a dozen in assorted sizes flown ahead, fluttered back at him from the mudguard pennant. A thin red carpet, indispensable prop to any royal movement, dribbled along the tarmac to the velvet-covered steps leading into the car . . .

And there was the Prince, tanned, tall, wearing a brown suit, coming down the steps of the Andover, being greeted by the Governor of Pernambuco, chatting to Russell. The two men may not have liked each other very much, but they had a wary respect. 'The Ambassador has a flair which must interest the Brazilians to a certain extent, and surprise them to an even greater extent,' said Philip. 'Prince Philip could tend to put people off,' said Russell. He and Prince Philip had similar characteristics, both liked to be the centre of attraction, had the same penetrating way of looking below their listeners' eyes, the easy assumption of superiority, the background to be convincing, the height to inspire trust. There are two types of successful British diplomat. One is safe, dull, predictable, conditioned by pre-war imperial grandeur, living in a cloud-cuckoo land of wishful thinking where the annual cocktail party for the Queen's birthday is considered as a unifying thread for the British way of life and any Foreign Office statement is the modern equivalent of

Holy Writ. They are in the majority. The other type is not too popular with them: an extrovert with a mind uncluttered by the irrelevancies of protocol: dramatic, autocratic, self-assured, with impeccable qualifications that disarm criticism. Such a man was Sir John Wriothesley Russell. Eton, Trinity College, Cambridge, in the diplomatic service for thirty-one years, former head of the Foreign Office news department, married to a Greek beauty queen Aliki Diplarakos with a daughter, Georgiana, who even wowed the surfeited girl-watchers of Rio. Eclectic and astute as only the apparently lackadaisical British aristocrat can be. 'From our point of view, commercial emphasis is important. But of course you cannot overplay it *vis-à-vis* your host.'

As they waited for the VC10 to land after ten hours forty minutes flying 4,940 miles from Heathrow, they talked about a previous royal visit, to Ethiopia in 1965, where Russell had also been Ambassador. Then Prince Philip, casual, elegant, went into the plane to greet his wife. Now the private words, intimate gestures of meeting after a long absence must be sacrificed for the benefit of the crowd, the band, the guard of honour, the Civil Servants, waiting outside. A cough, a re-assuring look, and she steps into the sunshine. Is that the Queen? A small figure in turquoise turban and green and yellow print dress, colours complimentary to the Brazilian flag, looking, well, all right in a Cheltenham-tea-party way, but not really the image composed by a million words a year. Nervous, still, after all this time. And then the feed-back from the cheering crowd begins, and she smiles shyly. Republicans enjoy other people's royalty and automatically upgrade most of their emotions like shyness, nervousness, boredom, and call them 'dignity'.

Two national anthems. One, the Brazilian, is a minute and a half long. A bouquet from the Governor's daughter, the first of many, and now an eight-mile drive into Recife. She can't even travel in the same car as her husband, but goes with

Governor Nilo Coelho and the head of his Military Household, preceded and followed by a security car, flanked by
outriders. Prince Philip is with the Governor's wife.

Past the specially painted pavements, and the shacks that
cannot be embellished, guarded by four thousand police
and a red security helicopter overhead, cheered joyfully by
the ubiquitous crowd that is for ever Queen-watching. 'I'm
surprised they all recognize me,' she said. Round the city
square, and into the ornate Palacio do Campo das Princessas
where one hundred and fifty assorted dignitaries, wives, and
children are lined in two rooms waiting to be presented. It
had been hell for the Governor. Who to invite? Who could
he afford not to? Some of the unlucky ones stood outside, toe
trampling with mere rubbernecks.

Then the lights went out all over town. Panic. Disgrace.
Humiliation. Generals, thrown into burly confusion, and
convinced this was another C.C.C. plot, rushed to the balcony as a cameraman's flash-bulb exploded. Fitfully, with the
teasing indecision of a roulette wheel, the lights came on
again until, like the dying flicker of the Governor's pride,
there was a total blackout for twenty minutes. Why should
such a thing happen while the world watched Recife, and
laughed? The Queen was laughing, anyway, because she
likes nothing better than a minor disaster to start off a tour
on the correct note of homely tension. Perhaps it was even
an advantage. She told her hosts that only a week ago, at
Covent Garden, exactly the same thing happened when the
B.BC-ITV consortium making a television documentary
of her life overloaded the circuit. 'Where's Cawston?'[5] she
said, smiling. In Rio, unfortunately, because of confusion
over Brazilian airline schedules.

Perkins, hands clasped in front of him, watchful, correct,
impervious as if he had known this would happen, looked
heavenwards. A general produced a seven-pronged candelabra and the Queen continued to meet people by its

[5]Richard Cawston, director of the television film, *Royal Family*.

25

light, thankful that the power failure hadn't happened a few minutes earlier, or she would have been trapped in the lift.

After admiring a picture, which she was then given (Prince Philip was presented with a pot), the Queen was driven to the quay where *Britannia* waited, floodlit. 'What a lovely welcome,' she said to the Governor's wife. She was piped aboard by six pipers, followed by Prince Philip, the British Ambassador and assorted officials including Perkins carrying a posy, two umbrellas, and a raincoat. A brass band played, two lights at the foot of the gangplank, decorated with lifebelts saying HMY *Britannia* were carried up, and the Queen sailed for Salvador de Bahia, escorted by four frigates – two Brazilian and two English.

At the airport, two hippies were arriving to see the Queen. She reminded them, they explained, of the fairy stories they read as children.

The Queen enjoyed Recife and stayed up for a long time to talk about it. The captains from the two Brazilian frigates came over by a rope pulley for dinner. Lord Chalfont, Minister in attendance, was so impressed that he went for a ride in it himself afterwards. Lady Fairfax was unfortunately seasick, but there was a delayed crossing the line ceremony when members of the crew known in Navy circles as 'Snotty Yachties' dressed as King Neptune, his Consort and five bears, got on thrones and conducted a performance in excruciating rhyming couplets composed by a sailor. Then they shaved and tossed flour on those who hadn't crossed the line in *Britannia*, and ducked them. The Ambassador suffered. And Lord Chalfont. Heseltine sensibly stood near the Queen, on the sun deck.

The 413-foot yacht, painted Britannia blue with royal coat of arms on the bow, and cypher on the stern, has always been the most controversial item of royal expenditure. Criticism has been parried, first, by the extraordinary suggestion that it would become a hospital ship in wartime,[6] and more recently by the fact that since April 1968, it has been used on NATO manœuvres. The 'hospital ship' assertion is as fanciful as claiming that Buckingham Palace would be used as a sanatorium in a psoriasis epidemic, and is made with far more enthusiasm by Government officials than members of the Household who treat the claim with the same scepticism they reserve for other public excuses for royal expenditure.

At £1,250 a day, or £500,000 a year, it is a somewhat costly indulgence for seventeen weeks' royal duties a year – even though extravagance on board is kept to a minimum, with gin at fourpence a tot. Built for £2,098,000 in 1952, it has cost more than £9,000,000 since then, including a £355,000 re-fit in the autumn of 1969.

It operates with the same hierarchical efficiency as other aspects of royal life, and canvas-shoed sailors give orders by hand signal or walkie-talkie to avoid disturbance . . . Household members have problems – such as how to cope with shirts when there is only a twice-weekly laundry on board and a multitude of white tie receptions ashore. Not that it seemed to matter as they steamed gently into Salvador de Bahia for church on Sunday morning. The Governor, Luiz Vianna Filha, had jovially strewn his desk with Union Jacks, doodled EIIR copiously on his blotter, had 8,000 square metres of roads paved, and imported eight impressive police outriders equipped with red Harley Davidson motorcycles from Rio at £40 each (freight rate) because Salvador was deficient in such matters. He said he hoped, prayed, willed that everything would be successful during the three-hour visit.

Salvador de Bahia, The Saviour Bay of All Saints, one of the most beautiful of Brazil's resorts, and a former capital

[6]Maurice Foley, Under Secretary of State for Defence, replied to a House of Commons question on 12 June, 1968, that *Britannia* cost the minimum necessary to maintain her in readiness for a war-time role as a hospital ship.

during the Portuguese colonial days, with 160 churches gracefully decaying on the assumption that lethargy in time evolves into architectural significance, with candomblé voodoo specialists gently combating threats of modernity inherent in the recent discovery of oil producing 150,000 barrels a day, Salvador de Bahia welcomed the Queen with confetti, hibiscus, curiosity, and a Lincoln convertible three years newer than that provided by Recife. Prince Philip had an older, albeit more glamorous 1926 Isotta Fraschini, custom built as a replica of Rudolph Valentino's by a rich playboy for his fiancée. Now owned by a sixty-year-old vet, Otavio Rodriguez de Sousa, it had been transported, at Government expense, from his home in São Paulo. As no one else could drive it, he was asked to wear chauffeur's uniform and peaked hat and told, delicately, not to talk to Prince Philip because, after all, he was only the chauffeur. Otavio, who would like to have dressed in one of his cowboy hats and hammed it a bit, shrugged and said Okay. He had eleven children, and was, therefore, commendably knowledgeable about the more arcane considerations of civilization. His reward was a leather wallet. The Queen's driver got a wallet and a Royal Victorian Medal (bronze).

Not everyone wanted to, or could, say matins with the Queen. Perkins, in a blue double-breasted pin-stripe, panting and red-faced with the heat, crept behind the railings at the side of the church and pulled a couple of photographers from the bushes. They didn't know who he was. They didn't speak English. He didn't speak Portuguese. They had a tradition for telling officialdom to get stuffed. They complied without a murmur when he said: 'Move away.' Such authority built an empire, and is now puzzled by its loss.

Meanwhile, posing for pictures with admiring American tourists, looking like a caricature of the imperial past in a splendid white uniform draped with gold braid, one hand on his sword, the other clasping a glass of beer, stood Commander Cedric Coxon, R.N., Defence attaché to the British

Embassy. He was waiting at the English Club, founded in 1874 adjacent to the Anglican Church where, also gathered in delightful hats to meet their Queen, were seventy-five 'English' members, some of them English in the same loose way that fourth-generation Californians are 'Irish'. As the Queen arrived, walking past a massive Union Jack punctured with holes like Gruyère cheese, they surrounded her in a general scrum, not quite knowing whether to smile, or indeed how to smile. Does one grin, simper understandingly, give a sympathetic twitch, bow, curtsy? What does one do, if one is a transplanted Britisher in such circumstances?

She stayed a few minutes before driving to a showpiece church of ornate gold carvings, and the inevitable museum, along the packed streets, stopping to collect a posy from a young girl, not having much time to see the slogans 'Fascists close schools' and 'Unite workers against the dictatorship', not being shown the slums and the naked children messing in the streets. She was shaded with a black, London-type umbrella. 'The only way we can cast a shadow over the British Empire,' remarked the Governor.

On to the Mercado Modelo, a local market where they accept Diner's Club cards for the aphrodisiacs, trinkets, carvings sold by Bahian girls, delectable descendants of African slaves with jutting jaws and buck-toothed, disdainful sexiness, and limbs that undulate with perpetual rhythm. Much of the character, the stench of fish, the scruffy yelping for a bargain, had been emasculated by fumigation and rose petals strewn on coconut matting. But a crowd managed to follow the royal party, surrounding the Queen and cutting off the others. 'My God, it's dreadful,' said a panicky Brazilian official. 'This place is far too small. We told the British Ambassador it would be like this, but he wouldn't listen.'

'Queenie, queenie, look up here,' shouted photographers perched on the fragile roof of a stall. A man was yanked from the crowd to present Prince Philip with a berimbau, the Queen was given a silver balanganda. A samba band, with tambourines and drums, paraded in front of her, and immediately she had passed, the crowds swarmed in. Lady Rose Baring, a lady-in-waiting who reads *Flook* before anything else each morning, looked happy and hummed wistfully. 'How lovely,' she said. Lord Chalfont muttered to Lady Fairfax: 'A nice cool drink, I think.' Prince Philip, sweating, looked puzzled. Sir John Russell, his huge arms flailing, forced a way through to the cars at the back of the market. Already the Queen was there, perched ready to wave. Prince Philip mouthed, 'Thank you very much.' The police pushed, shouted, blew whistles. And then the motorcade was off once more, with brass bands, national anthems, church bells, uniformed officials, cheers, goodwill, back to *Britannia*.

And the State Visit hadn't even begun yet.

The Road Show - II

'What rot, and a waste of time, money, and energy all these State visits are.' Edward VIII in his diary while at Oxford. (Quoted in *The Modern British Monarchy* by Sir Charles Petrie, Eyre & Spottiswoode, 1961, p. 168.)

'My husband and I are looking forward to seeing much more of this remarkable State.' The Queen opening Museum of Modern Art, São Paulo, Brazil, on 7 November, 1968. Or almost any other opening.

'Another place for conversation between two heads of State and all the practical good that can follow when two countries put their heads together.' Commentary, *Royal Family*, BBC–ITV Consortium film, 1969.

STATE VISITS, the defeat of the impossible in support of the incredible, should all be approached gently, like any other love affair. This allows time for nervous tantrums (a BBC television producer overturning the breakfast table because of slow service in one of Rio's leading hotels) to exhaust themselves, acclimatization to be leisurely, and sense of humour to develop as the only alternative to dementia. A cacophony of ceremony, present swapping, and high living is about to start. (Appendix.)

The visit was still 'informal' as *Britannia*, serenaded by the Royal Marine band playing 'Marina', named after a former chief of Rio police and sent to England with the suggestion it should be used, sailed with a flotilla of yachts and seven security boats into Guanabara Bay on Tuesday, 5 November.

There were more handshakes, gun salutes, national anthems, a one hundred and ten minute flight in the VC10 to Brasilia, a slight contretemps with the control tower, and confusion about the exit before the Queen was 'officially' in Brazil.

The crew had flown to Brasilia on Sunday to check timings and made sure the plane could land accurately at the military air base. Now, as they approached on schedule to the second, there was a hesitant request from the control tower. Could they circle a couple of times, because the President was late? No, old boy, they could not. Everything was planned to a 'doors open, doors close' efficiency. Oh.

President Artur da Costa e Silva[1] urged his driver to hurry. An aloof man of apparently profound mediocrity, damned with faint praise by his predecessor as 'a good colleague', the President knew the Queen's visit would allow him a few days' unalloyed dignity, maybe, and her presence would by osmosis invest him with responsibility. So, in order to establish his anglophilia, he had just bought two £1,000,000 B.A.C. 1-11s. All successful politicians improve their position by the company they keep, and the President needed an image booster. Although he had successfully tight-roped between the extreme left and right since he took over in 1967, his government was becomingly increasingly authoritarian. American encouraged, and to some extent justified, fear of Communism was reaching the bogies under the bed stage, the Army generals had begun to see national security threats in teaching sex education to girls of seventeen. The disenchanted told of how the President had three secretaries: one who could read, one who could write – and the third to keep her eye on the two intellectuals in the office. The President's wife, Doña Yolanda, a vision of fan-toting dowagerism, was also something of a politician and had recently signed a petition to the Pope asking for lefties to be thrown out of the Roman Catholic church – the only nation-wide organization able to rival the Army in influence.

[1]Died 17 December, 1969.

One of the most militant, Archbishop of Recife Dom Helder Camara, said: 'Brazil does not develop because it is in the hands of a few privileged people.' Those privileged people, would be ubiquitous in the next few days, rent-an-*élite* travelling from party to party in their evening dress hired at five guineas a time from Casa Rolla in Rio. Hairdressers had been booked for months, as had all scheduled flights between Rio and Brasilia.

Brasilia, like the people themselves, was a flamboyant gesture, a confection of monolithic soullessness and architectural haughtiness that had materialized in 1960 after a gestation period of half a century. The overall plan was chosen by an international jury including Sir William Holford from Britain, Stamo Papadachi (U.S), and André Sive (France), and most of the buildings had been designed by Oscar Niemeyer. Its midwife had been ex-President Joscelino Kubitschek, a devious man of superabundant charm, whom the Queen had met previously. She mentioned him many times during the visit, and received back a barrage of silence and muttered non-answers. Kubitschek was in the tradition of Brazilian leaders who are loved in spite of, or because of, their casual attitude to municipal honesty, like the Governor who appointed six hundred different men to the job of State taxidermist and stuffed their salaries in his own bank account, or ex-President Goulart who was said to have accumulated a £40,000 hotel bill in a few weeks, or practically every public official for whom the kick-back was an accepted perk. Kubitschek, though, was the Brazilian entrepreneur par excellence. He had been allowed to exile himself in Paris, but had returned a few years later to a hero's welcome, and public opinion polls at the time of the Queen's visit showed that he would be elected President in a free election. Reputed by his enemies to be the eighth richest man in the world, he watched the visit from a comfortable flat in Copacabana, attended by a bevy of soft-shoed servants who call him 'President', listening to mood music on the

33

stereo, swathed in expensive jewellery, and his features showing the haunted, taut look that comes from two face-lifts, constant phone tapping, and threats of arrest. When I met him a few days after the Queen left South America, he boasted that the government wouldn't dare arrest him because he was too popular. Next day he was in jail, one of President Costa e Silva's 'purged' men, and the protests had a *'c'est la vie'* acceptance. He began the Brazilian car industry, had the vision to coerce a bankrupt nation into building a show-piece capital that may well become the headquarters of the United Nations within a few years, became personally wealthy, and practically wrecked the economy. 'Louis XIV ruined France with Versailles,' said a Brazilian economist. 'Who wouldn't want Versailles today, though?'

Or Brasilia? Maybe in a few years. But, as the Queen landed, there were few people at the airport and not many lining the broad streets.

Of course, it was foolish to expect everything to go right. The plane landed, and taxied to a beautiful standstill several yards from the end of the red carpet. Hurriedly an additional length was found and placed in position, while the Brazilian Air Force vainly tried to manipulate the steps into place. On the Sunday there had been an argument between them and the RAF about this part of the venture. The Brazilians wanted to provide their own steps. The RAF said, 'No' because Varig were handling airport facilities, and even had their manager, Roland Hill, on board the Queen's plane. A compromise was reached: Varig ladder, and Brazilian Air Force personnel, they were unfamiliar with the procedure.

After about five minutes the Queen appeared wearing an ivory white silk coat and brown breton, waved, and waited for something to happen. The band, mesmerized, were sworn at by protocol officials 'Toque, toque, play play', which they eventually did – the British national anthem sounding like the last dirge of a naval quintet sinking below the waves. Next, introductions to ministers, church leaders, ambassadors, military men, mayors, police chiefs, protocol men, air base commandant, and assorted officials. Fifty-two altogether. And their wives. To each one, a gracious nod, a smile, an outstretched hand. Then, to the sound of 'Colonel Bogey', which follows the Queen almost as much as the national anthem precedes her, she drove to one of the seventeen presidential suites of the Hotel Nacional, where the royal bathroom had been completely re-fitted to include a sunken tub set in a marble floor; and a staff of two house-keepers, nine maids, three valets, two head-waiters, six waiters, and twelve busboys awaited the royal couple's pleasure.

She was only just thirteen when it happened, on the morning of 22 July, 1939, a sheltered, privately educated, gauche, shy, not particularly intelligent girl, far less self-assured and aware than a thirteen-year-old today.

King George VI was going to Dartmouth with Queen Elizabeth and their two children, Elizabeth and Margaret. Lord Mountbatten was asked if he would like to go along to see his nephew, Philip, who was eighteen at the time. He accepted the offer.

They arrived rather late on Saturday evening in the royal yacht, Victoria and Albert. There was an epidemic of chicken pox and mumps at the school, so the doctor advised against the two Princesses attending church on Sunday. Lord Mountbatten thought this would be a good opportunity to meet Philip, so he asked to be excused as well . . . . .

Elizabeth inherited from her father a strong sense of her own dignity, and visibly dislikes any situation that seems to mock it. Sometimes this is admirable, at others it has the unfortunate effect of allowing her to make a fool of herself, such as delivering a speech of appalling banality in terms of reverential plumminess, and giving listeners the schizophrenic conundrum of applauding something their senses tell them is awful. Philip is the opposite. He knows when he is making a bad speech and tends to falter over words. But he is excellent

35

in a potentially undignified situation and has the politician's ability to turn it to advantage. So it was with the ritual present swapping at the Palacio da Alvorada, Palace of the Dawn, the Brazilian President's official residence which overlooks the artificial Lake Paranoa. This was Christmas-time with a vengeance, the ultimate in bread and circuses play acting.

The Palacio was flanked by magnificently dressed guardsmen, their uniforms reverberating in the shallow ponds in front of the building, and reflecting in the mirrored walls at the entrance.

The Queen and Prince Philip were delicately conducted up the stairs by the President and Doña Yolanda. 'Are you the commanding officer of the Lake?' the Duke asked a monumentally decorated Admiral.

Doña Yolanda said to Philip: 'Is that what you were given last time you were here?' pointing to the star on the left breast of his white Air Marshal's uniform.

'Yes, I've been polishing it ever since.' Visiting Brazil in 1962 Philip had been given the Grand Cross of the National Order of the Southern Cross. Today he was going to be presented with the Grand Cross of the Order of Rio Branco.

Medals, medals, mere lumps of iron with decreasingly respected symbolic value. The Queen had just invested the President as a Knight Grand Cross of the Most Honourable Order of the Bath, to which he had responded by presenting her with the light blue ribboned Great Collar of the Cruzeiro, created in 1822 as an Imperial Order by the first Emperor of Brazil Don Pedro I.

Lord Mountbatten and the two Princesses went into the cabin of the Captain, Admiral Sir Frederick Hew George Dalrymple-Hamilton, K.C.B. They waited a few minutes, chatting. Then suddenly the door opened. In walked a six-foot, blue-eyed, fair-haired boy. He was self-confident and cheeky. Elizabeth stood absolutely still. The colour drained from her face. Then it re-diffused and went red. But she still stared at him, and for the rest of the day she followed him everywhere, glancing towards him with undiluted admiration.

When it was time to leave, the boats of the college came out as an escort for the Victoria and Albert. Philip was in one, rowing. The King saw he was going too far out to sea, where it was rough, and he shouted: "Get back, get back." Elizabeth had been watching all the time. Margaret, enjoying the excitement, turned to her sister to comment. She was amazed at what she saw.

"Look, mother," she said. "Lilibet's crying."

From that day on, Elizabeth never looked at another man.

They moved into the drawing-room of the Palace for the formal handing over of presents. Already there were two sets of London swans, delivered by the Ministry of Public Building and Works, floating on the lake. Two onças, a female of eight years old, and a male of a mere seven months, who would have to be kept apart at London zoo for some time in case the female tried to molest her partner, were being transported to Britain with instructions that their diet was four pounds of raw meat, one raw egg a day each, and a freshly killed chicken (uncooked, with blood) each week. In addition, there were the more personal gifts: a gold balanganda to the Queen and an oil painting of birds by Grauben Lima to Prince Philip from the President. An eighteen-inch silver centrepiece with acanthus leaf decoration, caryatid handles, pedestal fluted foot and engraved inscription to the President, and an eighteen carat gold bracelet set with the royal cipher to Doña Yolanda from the Queen. Plus, of course, the reciprocal signed photographs in silver frames. Members of the royal family do not pay duty on official presents. A list is made of everything they are given (Appendix), duty assessed, and an application made to the customs for release of duty. It is always granted.

This harmless charade has to be witnessed by the world,

and in England it is recorded by perhaps one or two photographers on a 'rota' basis. As she went into the lounge, the Queen was expecting possibly three, maybe four outsiders. But, roped off a few feet from the desk were nine rows of photographers, television cameramen, radio reporters, a nightmare of communicators, each shoving the other in order better to relay this 'informal' moment in the tour. The perpetual spectacle. The everlasting wedding photograph.

Philip, on the other hand, rather enjoyed teasing Elizabeth. He thought she was sweet, especially as she knitted socks for him during the war, but there were others. In particular, in 1943 he fell for an extremely beautiful Canadian girl. She had money, a good family, and was devoted to him. Relatives thought it was certain he would propose. When he didn't, they realized he must be serious about Elizabeth. "He was very concerned about the restrictions on his liberty" says one. "There was no question of his pressing her, or of Lord Mountbatten being the wicked uncle who threw them together and organized a successful marriage. Above all, it's a great love story. Very important to remember that."

At first, the Queen's parents ignored the relationship that was developing, and George VI found it difficult to believe his daughter had fallen in love with the first man she met.[2] He took her to South Africa, making the excuse the family should stay together, but in fact to test his daughter's love. He liked Philip, a naval Lieutenant earning £11 a week, who had become naturalized in order to join the British Navy, but had declined the title of His Royal Highness. Marriage to his elder daughter, though, who had been so sheltered . . .

The ceremony took place on November 20, 1947, and they would be celebrating their twenty-first anniversary the day after returning from South America.

The Queen was displeased and embarrassed by the scuffle of photographers. Prince Philip moved the President to one side as he was blocking the view needed for a 'family' picture.

[2] *King George VI*, by John Wheeler-Bennett (Macmillan, 1958) p. 751.

The Queen, standing in the middle of the room, wearing her new Order, glanced at him, a blank miserable expression. He smiled, touched her arm, and she relaxed, smiled nervously back, a tender look of tragic implications. Theirs was a relationship deepened with arguments, made lonely by his travels, scrutinized everywhere, derided by cynics, devalued by schmaltz. A relationship made more poignant because she had only ever loved once, only could love once. Like other women who have had deep affection for their father, this had all been transferred and heaped exclusively on one other man and, whatever her position, whatever her obligations, even if she had lived in a semi-detached in Pinner, it would have been no different. She knew his faults, his reputation, his frustrations. She had heard rumours about the women who played doormat to his vanity, and his absences hurt. But, imbued with the British middle-class respect for cool, she did not often show her feeling in her face, not like Queen Fabiola who had an outgoing personality and would pick up children, and kiss them. At times like this it was unfair to say the Queen was grim. She was a timid woman doing a job that provides more than the usual amount of idiocies. At times like this, more than any other, it seemed unfair to submit such a woman to the ordeal. The ritual sacrifice of a human personality, accompanied by mass media hyperbole, is one of the least attractive sights of the twentieth century.

'Very important to remember that. It's a great love story.'

The Queen smiled, a non-public smile, and the photographers took more pictures. 'Look this way, Elizabeth.'

The three-speech day had hardly begun.

The first two speeches, introduced by the obligatory sets of national anthems, were written in ambassadorial sedative style by Sir John Russell with a few remarks designed to compliment the Brazilians on their genuinely multi-racial society and one or two tongue-in-cheek platitudes.

'My husband and I,' a perfectly reasonable phrase that is mimicked with exaggerated hoity-toitiness by anyone wanting to send up the Queen, appeared in the first sentences of practically every speech she read, a pity because in private she always refers to him as 'Philip' or 'Prince Philip', even to strangers.

She doesn't enjoy making speeches and knows she isn't very good but, unlike Margaret, it is a chore she can't avoid (Appendix). Every introductory variation, even 'I and my husband' and 'Me and my husband' has been tried, but they all sound uneasy except 'We'. Philip, anyway, prefers her to say 'My husband and I' (Appendix).

She also invoked God, frequently. At the Supreme Court: 'I pray for the success of your endeavours.' And a few yards away, speaking to a special Joint Session of Congress: 'May God bless your deliberations and grant success to your labours.' The Congressional building stands at the front of the square of the three powers – executive, legislative, and judiciary buildings heaped conveniently together. It is two oblong structures, separated by a corridor, like an H with blank concrete walls down the thin edge; and behind are two cupolas inversely constructed so that they look like saucers, one upside-down, the other the right way up. It is the tallest building in the city, to symbolize the power of the people, but neither they, nor God, had much effect because on 13 December, three weeks after the Queen left South America, President Costa e Silva sent warships into Guanabara Bay, declared an 'institutional' act, prorogued Congress indefinitely, and stripped more than two hundred public figures of their political rights for ten years.

Perhaps this wouldn't have surprised or worried Prince Philip too much. He startled one Government official by saying there wasn't much wrong with representational government, a system in which only certain people are allowed to vote, because there was no guarantee the majority were always correct. Perhaps he was right about Brazil.

40

'The politicians have backbones like bananas,' said an American Embassy political expert.

But in the fantasy world of public speeches and international make-believe it was important to maintain good taste, even if it was at the expense of reality. 'The essence of the Parliamentary system,' said the Queen, 'is that it should be dynamic and vary according to the requirements of the age and circumstances. Parliament is the means by which ordinary citizens can influence the way in which they and their country are governed, and therefore any Parliament must undergo a process of continuous readjustment and rebirth. In Brazil, the Legislature has to meet special and unique requirements. Not only is Brazil vast, but within her frontiers are wide and regional differences: geographic, ethnic and economic.

'Your legislature is therefore faced with problems of a complexity and size which few nations have been called upon to meet. And upon you lies the heavy task of creating unity from this diversity. Yet, Mr President, one of the things which impressed me most is the patriotism and unity of the Brazilian people. In this, you have a deep source of strength.'

Meanwhile, politicians were knifing each other with a marked lack of dignity even for that specialized activity, students were rioting, half the nation was illiterate, many starving, generals were hatching shabby plots, and political prisoners were being tortured to give information. Admittedly, it is difficult for the Queen to give a 'political' speech, but the ham-fisted niceties trilling from her mouth do not flatter the bureaucratic minds for whom they are composed, nor the institution she represents. Sometimes, it isn't really her fault. Perhaps the worst speech she has given for years was at the centenary banquet of the Trades Union Congress[3] where she recited a drab, schoolgirlish account of trades union history in a voice made more nervous by the fact that she thought George Woodcock the T.U.C. general secretary,

[3] 5 June, 1968.

was dozing off in front of her. He was, in fact, buried in preparation for his own speech. Whatever the excuses though, a man – Prince Charles – could never succeed if he delivered such disinfected ideas, and it is a delicate aspect of Monarchy's role that needs re-thinking. The fact that the Queen can give a good speech, and does involve herself in politics, was to be shown effectively a few days later.

For the present, though, she was off to meet the press. On every State visit, one of her first duties is to invite all accredited reporters for a drink at her hotel. Nothing significant is ever said, but the occasion is an easy and efficient way of ensuring sympathetic treatment during the hot-house unreality of the next few days when everyone will become annoyed and the ladies of the British Press, if that is not a contradiction in terms, will start to confuse themselves with their subjects. The major newspapers tend to send women on royal tours, because Monarchy is a basically feminine pre-occupation. They are the 'puppet masters'[4] as one of them graciously explained. Sometimes, shame to say, they are treated disdainfully by the puppets. 'Shove off,' said Prince Philip in the naval vernacular, to one photographer running alongside the royal car in a motorcade. A newspaper reporter, claiming some skill at lip-reading, saw the incident and asked a passenger in the car to confirm the remark.

'I'd never heard the word before. I think it was French,' said the passenger diplomatically.

Reading about the incident in the papers the next day, the Queen asked, smiling. 'Philip doesn't speak French, does he?'

One of the worst clashes with the Press was during the Caribbean tour in 1966 when Prince Philip had an unfortunate conversation with the matron of a hospital he was visiting. 'We have a lot of trouble with mosquitoes,' said the matron.

'I know what you mean,' replied Prince Philip. 'You have mosquitoes. I have the Press.'

[4]*Daily Mirror*, August 1969.

The sensitive souls of the reporters were deeply shocked by such a remark, an apology was demanded, and received, from the Prince. He knew the value of good public relations. His life sometimes seemed geared to its successful exploitation – in spite of occasional lapses.

Now the Press stood drinking the Queen's whisky, and being seduced by the small talk of weather, horses, and magnificence of the country. In small groups like this the Queen is impressive – if only because she actually takes the trouble to appear interested – and her effort is always repaid. In Brazil there were eight hundred Press accredited throughout the six-day tour. Five hundred and eighty of them came from Rio alone where the papers printed 426 photographs, and 38,715 square inches of news coverage between 2 and and 13 November. This is equivalent to 129 whole pages, and at the then advertising rate of £700 a page was worth about £90,300 – slightly less than three times the amount taxpayers paid for the RAF planes. The Queen asked for English *résumés* of all the stories to be sent to her by 7.30 every morning. In addition the BBC's 3 a.m. news bulletin was collected from Bush House, in the Strand, by a uniformed Admiralty official, coded, flashed to the yacht, de-coded, typed and included with the newspaper *résumé*.

From the apparent search for truth and reality of a Press conference back to the hotel bedroom to change into an aquamarine and silver dress for the accepted deception of a State banquet – the first of four formal occasions in five days. It took place at the Palacio Itamaraty, perhaps Niemeyer's most spectacular building, shallow moated and graceful, with courtyards and fountains. Tactfully, the Queen wore a £50,000 aquamarine and diamond necklace given to her as a Coronation present by the people of Brazil. She had to more than sing for her supper.

'It is with the greatest happiness that my husband and I find ourselves your guests tonight in this splendid and unique city of Brasilia: visionary in concept, pure in its lines, and

43

an inspiration to the nation: and a city, may I add, Mr President, with which it is so happens that I share a birthday . . . '

The President, mellow in the euphoria of a magnificent banquet, overwhelmed by the visit's initial success, slowly rose from his chair, glass in hand, bristling with mellifluous congratulations, prepared to give a toast, surprised perhaps that no one had briefed him. He felt a tug at his tails. It's not the Queen's birthday. She was referring to the inauguration of Brasilia on 21 April 1960. 21 April is her birthday.

Ah . . .

'At some crucial moments in history we have been closely associated. It was a Squadron of the British Navy which escorted King John VI from Portugal to Brazil in 1808. More recently, Brazil and the Commonwealth stood side by side in two world wars to defend those principles to which we are equally dedicated.'

She didn't know that the Ambassador to succeed Sir John Russell would be Sir David Hunt, who had written a book and mentioned about his experience as Intelligence Officer in Italy: 'Next to arrive was the Brazilian Expeditionary Force commanded by General Mascarenhas de Moraes, the Brazilian dictator of that date, General Dutra assumed command of the force for twenty-four hours in August. His critics said that this was in order to qualify for a campaign ribbon. This was the first, indeed the only, South American Army force to take the field in either of the two wars.'[5]

Nor could she know that Philip was to ask a military man later in the evening where he got his medals.

'In the war.'

'I didn't know Brazil was in the war that long.'

'At least, sir, I didn't get them from marrying my wife.' There are many stories like this about Philip. Maybe some are apocryphal, but they exist with commendable certainty in the minds of witnesses.

The Queen continued her speech, talking about the trade

[5] *A Don at War*, by David Hunt (William Kimber, 1966), p. 267,

in ideas. 'In this traffic of intangibles Brazil and Britain have, I believe, much to offer each other – in science, the arts and the humanities. True and lasting understanding between peoples and nations can only develop when we begin to appreciate and admire each others' ideas and talents.

'Our two peoples, Mr President, are both devoted to the basic concepts of justice, liberty, and tolerance. We both believe in the essential equality and dignity of man. Few countries illustrate that fundamental concept better than Brazil.'

The President replied with a barrage of piety about the role of the two countries 'on the stage of world affairs', recollections of trade, and that old emotional standby, the war. 'Your Majesty will find in our country a people determined to spare no effort to achieve development through democratic and peaceful means, a people willing to do its share for the improvement of international relations. In those ties that bind us together we see, beyond the satisfaction of mutual interests, a means to foster a stronger and closer relationship between Europe and America.'

And still the day continued. A reception for the *cercle diplomatique*, in which she shook about a hundred hands, followed at eleven by a reception, also at the Palacio Itamaraty, for leading politicians, industrialists, members of the popular 'jeito'[6] profession, and other luminaries of Brazilian social life. 'Same people, in different clothes,' remarked Prince Philip.

In the toilet, the mayor of Brasilia, Wadjo Gomide was talking to the President of the Senate, Gilberto Marinho, about the Costa e Silva *faux pas* at the banquet. What a ridiculous thing to do. Opposite them but behind a partition, was the Brazilian President himself. Anyone who makes anything but a grunt in public lavatories deserves to lose his job. Marinho was made redundant.

The girls were beautiful, the women elegantly coated

[6]A Portuguese word encompassing various aspects of 'fixing'.

with precious jewellery, the men white-tied and important-looking. They meandered, be-medalled and occasionally be-fuddled around the fountains and pillars, chatting, eating, drinking, staring over Brasilia, noticing who was invited, remarking on who wasn't. Georgiana Russell, her blonde hair swept Grecian style, posed for cameramen.

The Queen, pressed from all sides, glazed with tiredness, made her way through the curious crush to the exit. She knew that most of the guests probably didn't think she was elegant[7] and she nodded now and again, in a dream-like way. Her movements seemed automated and jerky, like a robot, and her smile was politely fixed, a bit like her mother. It was 12.30 a.m. A day of fresh problems had already begun.

São Paulo, a perpetual traffic jam of one million cars, provided the usual formalities. Introductions cut down to twenty-six, with wives, at the airport, wreath laying at the Independence Monument, presentation of a gold key to the city by the Prefect, and a visit to the largest reinforced concrete structure in the world – after which Prince Philip's car, a 1930 Buick refused to start and had to be pushed, with him standing up and waving to some of the million crowd and 10,000 security men. The car that was pushing burnt out its clutch. 'They weren't designed to be driven slowly through crowds on very hot days,' said Philip. 'People started throwing rice in the car and we were all getting rather anxious the Queen wouldn't end up as a rice pudding.'

The Queen rested while Philip set off for the British Consulate, where he was to give a Press Conference, and the Sergeant Footman, Frank Holland, tried to organize the distribution of luggage amongst three residences where the

[7]An opinion poll published in *Journal do Brasil*, on 4 November, 1968, stated that in the higher social classes, 44 per cent thought the Queen was not elegant compared with 39 per cent who thought she was. In all classes, 83 per cent considered her 'simpatica', and 66 per cent thought she was elegant. Nearly two-thirds said that monarchy had no place in the modern world.

Household party were staying. Neither was entirely successful.

Frank Holland, a bundle of tact and efficiency who had to co-ordinate the Army, Air Force, police, airlines and local officials all of whom at various times thought they had the exclusive honour of handling the Queen's luggage, at last found himself outmanœuvred by the indigenous chaos of Brazil. Luggage was sent to the wrong places, and that evening Sir Martin Charteris had to attend the dinner and reception wearing blue trousers instead of the proper Household evening dress.

Prince Philip, meanwhile, was being led in the wrong direction by his motor-cycle escort. 'I don't think they've got a clue what they're doing,' he said, as he arrived half an hour late at the British Consulate, a pleasant house with swimming pool on the outskirts of the city. His style was more impressive than his words, and he appeared confused over the more important but less dramatic aspects of trade. A persistent question about actual as opposed to apparent, export figures was treated first with puzzlement, then casual derision, then annoyance.

More important, though, the performance greatly impressed the Brazilians and was an expert mixture of flattery, drum-beating, conventional common sense, and gentle self-mockery. He had to be reminded by the Ambassador that one of the tangible results of the trip was the signing of a reciprocal scholarship agreement (which had been discussed for a long time previously). He boasted about Britain selling Hovercrafts to the United States for use in Vietnam, and happily illustrated the myopic quality of State visits, by his answer to a question about increased technical aid to Brazil. 'Anyone who sees Brasilia, and has seen São Paulo, would think that technical aid here was not necessary compared to the Indian sub-continent or parts of Africa', which is as curious as spending six nights in the presidential suite of the New Stanley Hotel in Nairobi and asserting that, compared with Ireland, Kenya has an excellent plumbing system.

Then hurriedly back to the Palacio dos Bandeirantes, the Governor's mansion, where he and the Queen had been provided with a suite of four bedrooms and private bathrooms, two living-rooms, a dining-room, a library, study, and two small gardens decorated with treasures provided by some of the oldest families in Brazil.

These families, and their cousins, and their friends, and the Governor's political cronies, and the enemies he couldn't afford to ignore, and the usual dignitaries, and the State visit camp followers, and all their friends and every second cousin were dressing themselves uncomfortably in the stifling heat and were about to demonstrate that there is no correlation between 'class' and 'taste', correct dress and good behaviour.

Two thousand had been invited to the reception, but about five thousand crammed into the Palacio, wedged tight as a rush-hour underground, and not much more distinguished, kicking, shoving, sweating, elegant *alta sociedade,* swearing, stampeding, free-loading *alta sociedade,* pompous, pretentious nouveau riche *alta sociedade,* in a reverie of vicious rubbernecking, stuffing themselves with turkey, chicken in aspic and champagne.

The Queen came out on to the balcony overlooking the reception room – pink gowned, diamond tiara'd – and walked down a staircase to the accompaniment of delirious applause and a string band playing *The Yeomen of England.* She was supposed to make her way, 'informally', through the crowd to a throne where she would sit to receive the extra special *alta sociedade.* The more rumbustious, and clearly less privileged *alta sociedade* made this impossible by their enthusiasm, so the Queen retreated to the balcony, gave a wave, and went sensibly to bed.

'I was told many things about São Paulo. I now realize what I heard was an understatement,' she said next day as she inaugurated the new museum of modern art, which had been founded twenty-one years earlier by a former Ambassador to London, Assis Chateaubriand. Chateaubriand, a press lord who owned magazines, newspapers, television and radio stations, had died the previous year after collecting the money by indiscriminate praise of donors and equally indiscriminate condemnation of those who refused. He called one industrialist a 'bandit, pachyderm, hippopotamus, filibuster, Barbary pirate', and his posthumous reward for such originality in fund-raising was this visit by the Queen.

From there to one of the perennial royal visit chores – the Commonwealth community reception. These can illustrate – and did later in the year, in Austria – exactly how and why Britain is a decaying power. They are a microcosm of a 1930's world, a lost heritage re-vamped in alien lands, a search for a cause d'être that is conveniently supplied by the Queen and her retinue. At times, as in São Paulo, it is performed with skill and enthusiasm that excuses nostalgia. On a manicured green field of St Paul's School, perhaps £3,000 had been spent preparing stands with crenelated blue and brown canvas awnings decorated with orchids, poinsettia, and tropical foliage, and laid with a new red carpet. About 3,000 guests lined up in orderly profusion, with a smattering of elderly Boy Scouts in reassuringly long grey trousers, schoolgirls evenly spaced to wave their Union Jacks. 'Now, look this way, Lucia, and when SHE comes WAVE YOUR FLAG,' ordered a schoolmistress. It looked as if an Agincourt film set had been taken over for speech day at a minor British public school. Brazilian photographers threatened not to take pictures if they were forced to remain on a roped-off stand at the side of the field, a matter hurriedly decided in their favour as one São Paulo newspaper alone had devoted eight pages to the visit the previous day. Security men stood on buildings overlooking the scene, and police in uniform saluted as the Queen arrived. An elderly couple were propped

49

up and gently sat down again when the Queen had passed. The national anthems were sung delicately by sweet, children's voices. The garden party strut, of which more later, was danced to the tinkling accompaniment of the admirable Guarda Civil police brass band, and four months planning was swallowed in an hour's remembrance of an England that lay down forever on 3 September, 1939. And can never be resurrected.

An hour and a quarter's flight in the Comet to the reality of horses at Campinas and, after visits to an agricultural institute and experimental farm, collection of presents (gold plaque in a leather case, and white and gold coffee service respectively), she went for a rest at the Estancia Eudoxia described as a 'small farmhouse' sixty-eight miles from São Paulo, owned by Sergio Pinho Mellao, a banker brother-in-law of the State governor. It has six bedrooms, four bathrooms, aircraft landing strip and radio transmitter, a half-mile drive lined with orange trees, and is decorated inside by dozens of rare Mexican, Brazilian and Peruvian ornaments. Sir John Russell had made a special trip to the ranch to check that the horses for the Queen and Prince Philip were suitable and not too frisky.

'We went for a ride on a horse – one horse each that is – and here in this humble bush was all this coffee. I thought, now I'm in Brazil. The roads are the same, the hotels are the same. But riding through the coffee bushes you realize you're in Brazil,' said Prince Philip.

'My main impressions of the country were the size of the place, and the gentleness of character of the Brazilians.' He and the Queen rode with friends for an hour and a half around the estate, and over to a farmhouse where other members of the entourage were staying until, at mid-day they left the Estancia to visit the Jockey Club stud farm and then flew from Virascopos airport to Rio. The Queen travelled in the Andover because it could land at Santos Dumont airport, near the centre of Rio. Thus saving fifty minutes by

Comet, which was lighter than expected because Lady Russell and Georgiana were not allowed on board – Lady Russell because she insisted on taking a harp with her, and Georgiana because she wanted the more tangible company of her Brazilian boy friend. They were told by the RAF they would have to make other arrangements. Sir John Russell himself was to have problems later in the day.

There were steel-helmeted guards with sub-machine-guns surrounding the airport at six-foot intervals and Brazilian Air Force fighter planes cruising overhead as the Queen arrived at Santos Dumont. Four fire engines with six outriders accompanied the plane from the moment of touchdown. Security arrangements were so tense, and the division of responsibility so delicate (Federal police were responsible for the Queen's safety when she was out of her car; State police when she was in it) that the strain was to drive some of the Queen's protectors to an over-indulgent use of the hospitality provided, and others to virtual punch-ups with rival groups of security men. The Queen looking incongruously placed for such shenanigans, went by barge to *Britannia*, which she thought was incorrectly positioned. There would be trouble.

Rio is not the sort of city where one expects anything but contented chaos, a city too beautiful to take itself seriously, parenthesized by sex and religion, the Sugar Loaf mountain on one side and the Corcovado Statue of Christ the Redeemer on the other, daubed with girls sunning themselves seductive brown along the pellucid and provocative Atlantic from Flamengo, Copacabana, Ipanema to Leblon, where the surfing is also good but undercurrents can drown the most experienced swimmers including a Russian ambassador and his secretary. Rio, with a style of its own that is youthful, gentle, tolerant, corrupt, sophisticated, the city dramatizing the collective inefficiency that is the salvation of people living under military dictatorship, breathing a casualness that, with the exception of the telephone system, stops tantalizingly this side of anarchy. What interest would this city take in an ancient symbol? A lot.

The Queen thought her yacht was swaying too much. No, it wasn't because she had spent a long time in the air recently and had forgotten the comparative restlessness of ocean life. It was definitely rolling, and her dinner aboard that evening for fifty-four important guests could easily be ruined.

'Get it moved,' Prince Philip muttered angrily to Sir John Russell as he and the Queen came ashore at the Yacht Club that evening for the Commonwealth Ambassadors' meeting and yet another Commonwealth Community reception. The Queen wore the expression of grim displeasure that, surprisingly, sends brave men, much older than her, quaking to the nearest scotch. The trouble was that the Port Commander refused to allow the yacht to be moved because it would then be in line with Santos Dumont airport and, while he had every confidence in Brazilian Air Force pilots, he couldn't possibly let *Britannia* anchor near the end of their runway. The Queen insisted, and eventually the yacht was moved four hundred yards into the shelter of the bay. 'Royal displeasure ruined that evening,' said a Foreign Office man.

The Queen disembarked from a royal barge at Rio Yacht Club, which had been dredged and re-surfaced for this, and the other ten occasions she would use it, at a cost of £10,000. Non-Household members of the party and the yacht's crew landed half a mile away. After the initial embarrassment over the yacht's position there was panic in case an ocean swell made the jetty unusable. It was a five hundred to one chance, but it happened – two weekends after the Queen had left.

Under the shelter of palm trees, in the shadow of the Sugar Loaf, round a pool, with an immaculate brass band playing light musical comedy numbers, whisky was served, hats were worn, gloves were clutched, excitement was generated, and a few lucky souls were nervously prodded into the front line of spectators. Some of them would be introduced to the Queen by Neville French, Head of Chancery at the British Embassy, 'How long have you been here? Where do you come from? How interesting.' Well what else could she say, patricularly when she was seething about the yacht and worried about the evening.

As it happened, the banquet wasn't very good. Only fifty-four people could be invited to sit down on the Hepple-white chairs (fourteen reproduction, the rest from the former royal yacht *Victoria and Albert*) at the horse-shoe table because of the limited accommodation on board. The meal of Dover sole, and saddle of lamb, the Queen's favourite, was slightly unimaginative. Temporary praise that charac-terizes all such gatherings set in, though, and everyone said they enjoyed themselves. Four weeks later, when unction was sieved through reality, the impression was different. 'Food was bad, and the company dull,' said a senior Brazilian diplomat. But British hospitality was to be jerked flamboy-antly the following night.

Saturday was originally to have been a free day, but en-gagements crept in gradually, particularly unveiling a plaque on the site of the Rio-Niteroi bridge being financed largely by a £25 million British loan.

The morning was overcast, so a planned trip to Corcovada was cancelled and a shorter tour of Rio substituted. First to the Dona Marta Belvedere below Corcovado where buzzards and butterflies circled in the humid air, and she could look down on Guanabara Bay, the turquoise Atlantic lolling on to the thin semi-circular strip of white sand, the breast-like humps of Rio's hills haloed in the morning mist, the sky-scrapers haphazardly strutting in puny competition to the natural scenery, and the *favelas* creeping, seeping, stenching down the hill even into the back garden of the Ambassador's residence, an imposing white elephant built by the Labour government in 1950 to prove that Britain had recovered from the war.

'What,' said the Queen, 'a very remarkable view.' She does not emote on such occasions, does not flirt with tourist gestures; a depressing experience for officials trying to wheedle some reaction, watching, thinking she must be bored, or ill, or tired. She is, of course, satiated with picture postcard views.

Then, in an open vintage Rolls Royce as part of a twenty-four car cavalcade, she proceeded along the two mile Avenida Atlantica peered at by curious crowds perhaps two or three deep, blowing bubble gum, thrusting her picture towards her on broom handles, clapping . . . faces, faces, faces, blurred colours, and gawping eyes, while many more continued playing volley ball on the beach, sceptical of such parades. She stopped at the chapel of Our Lady of Glory, eighteenth-century Brazilian baroque used by twentieth-century Brazilian high society as a magic box for God's indulgence when they marry, or die, or are born, and surprised a few old ladies, dressed in black, who were actually there to pray. The bells played *The Girl from Ipanema,* mingling with police sirens as she left, back to the yacht, and the conventional prize giving of medals, cuff links, and powder compacts to British Embassy staff. (Appendix.)

Lunch was provided by the Governor of the State of Guanabara agreed upon after much indecision and rivalry between the State Government and Foreign Office officials. Originally it was going to be at the golf club, but that was considered too far away. Understandably, the Rio authorities, who had vehemently denied the two-day visit cost much and who were going to say the figures were impossible to gauge, as with all accounting on royal visits, but who had in fact spent £23,000 (55,000 dollars), and had sent their head of protocol, Lael Barbosa Soares, to the airport twenty times to check arrangements, wanted to produce a public function worthy of the private effort.

54

They made special dress uniforms, dating back to the imperial past of 1815, to be worn by one hundred military police forming a guard of honour through which the Queen would walk to her lunch of *pâté de foie gras, délice de sole nuebourg, suprême de faisan braise aux champignons,* and *mousse de fraises friandises,* washed down with champagne Pommery greno brut. They wrote a speech for the Governor, and the Embassy wrote a reply for the Queen. They hired an organist and suggested tunes he should play. They made copious plans. They decided on an exchange of presents. They insisted that Foreign Office passes would be superseded by those specially issued by the Guanabara Palace. They made, as usual, sets of arrangements for dry and wet weather. They underlined the important part of their instructions to the Press: 'In no occasion whatsoever are reporters, photographers or cameramen supposed to address Her Majesty or Prince Philip in accordance with the requirements set forth by the Protocol and the Security Service.' They invited three hundred guests, and waited with unabashed pride for the arrival of the Queen and Prince Philip. 'A few high society pigs and local political hacks,' sneered an onlooker.

'Have we got to shake hands with all those people?' said Philip, searing with one sentence the pride of Lael Barbosa Soares.

The organist began his performance. *Yesterday,* he played.

During the meal, the Queen had one of those infrequent moments of discomfort that worry most people and she asked Lady Rose Baring if it could be arranged for her to go to the toilet. Naturally, a special room had been prepared and Lael Barbosa Soares suggested the Queen should disappear during coffee on the terrace. She was talking to the Governor, who knew about the dilemma, when Lady Rose Baring came across to show her the way.

'Where are you going?' asked Philip.

The Queen told him.

55

'It's very late, and we're not going to be on time for the next appointment.'

'Let's go, then,' said the Queen.

They went off to unveil the Rio-Niteroi bridge plaque.

Captain Lewis Thomas Lambert, director of music for the Royal Marine Band (Portsmouth Group) of eighty musicians, took twenty-two with him on the *Britannia* to South America. About fourteen played during dinner aboard, and at luncheon when required. If they hadn't been needed for ceremonial occasions, he would have left four drummers behind in England.

He impressed the Brazilians by Beating the Retreat outside the Governor's palace in Recife the night before the Queen arrived, but declined to perform at the Maracanã Stadium in Rio, the world's largest football arena, because he thought they would be dwarfed and look ridiculous.

On the opulent lawn of the British residence in Rio, relaid for £150 in September, he was preparing to conduct for the resounding finale of the Queen's visit. *A Blaze of Grass, New Colonial,* and the curious Beat the Retreat mixture of hymn and chauvinistic marches – *Abide with Me, Sunset,* and *Rule Britannia* followed by the national anthems. 'It's so traditionally British that I don't think anyone takes it literally, Britain ruling the waves and all that,' says Captain Lambert.

Before this, his men sat in white tropical uniform like a Palm Court orchestra in a room of the residence serenading some of the thousand guests with light music as they gazed at portraits of royalty hanging on the walls. The residence, completed for £414,000 in 1952 (after an estimate of £150,000, and architect's fees of £25) was at last being used for its original, unspoken, purpose – as a British prestige symbol.

Brazilian security guards, who had hitherto been disguised in identical dark suits with special buttonhole badges to make them more easily identifiable to each other, were now swarming around in hired evening dress voraciously sipping pink champagne the better to pretend they were guests. Outside, their less fortunate colleagues, in blue steel helmets, lined the drive. The Royal Marine buglers, in white tropical headgear, blew a fanfare as the Queen and Prince Philip approached.

Sitting at the entrance, on a red carpet, were the Ambassador's two huge greyhounds, Zorba and Zulu, known best to Embassy staff for their dangerous and acrid wind-blowing potential but hopefully starved for the occasion, so it could look like a genuine English country garden welcome – apart from the tropical foliage, floodlit fountains, massed television lights, and assorted anticipated excitements. For weeks afterwards Embassy staff would delve amongst newspaper pictures to find a suitable one for the Ambassador's Christmas cards – a vain search finally solved by superimposing two together.

The Queen was embarrassed, patted the dogs in an obligatory way, passed her white mink stole to Perkins, and walked up the wide, spiral staircase to the main hall of the Embassy, where there was to be a show. She nodded to a few guests, spoke to others, was introduced to a few, and then sat at a green settee near the open balcony looking on to the garden, while she waited for Philip to stop talking. An equerry brought her a glass of water. She asked for champagne, which she sipped quietly, patiently, being stared at from both sides by guests who had crammed and pushed to get a better view. Lady Russell, sitting next to her, started a conversation, not too successfully, turned away to powder her nose – a feminine luxury not allowed the Queen in public.

'Have you heard the bagpipes played on the guitar before?' Sir John Russell asked the Queen, just before introducing a young mulatto guitarist and composer. She was not amused, an emotion always shown by ignoring the remark, while looking directly at its perpetrator.

And what was the guitarist called? What, in this setting

of fin de siècle splendour, could be most ironic? Churchill? Kitchener? Harold Wilson? Warmer. No, Baden Powell, of all things. He was followed by a girl who sang *Those Were The Days*. The Queen, sitting prim with her hands on her knees, perhaps conscious she looked bored, raised her silver brocade dress slightly, and tapped her feet.

And then the climax, the most spectacular event of the whole South American tour, a moment at once vulgar and exciting, unpleasant and joyful, depending on your sensibilities.

Five hundred specially chosen dancers of the Mangueira samba school gyrated through the tropical vegetation garnishing two sides of the drive, through the helmeted security guards, quickening their beat as they approached the residence, African girls in crinolines and carrying pink and green parasols, gently swaying, followed by the more vivacious, their black bare midriffs glistening with pubescent sweat under the floodlights, the indentations of their navels set in firm flesh frenziedly swivelling with year-long practice, symbolic slave chains dangling from delicate wrists and snug agile ankles, hands thrusting forward in supplication and necks jerking to the erotic, carefree, narcissistic beat, limbs caressing the sultry humidity, frivolity quickening to ecstacy as the tempo increased, bewigged men effusively costumed, exotically adorned women with tropical fruits and flowers on their grandiloquent hats, players spinning tambourines on their fingers, whining drum-like instruments, the cymbals, girls and boys acrobatically samba-ing in front of the Queen, seducing the ground with the teasing forward-back steps of dance, twitching to a peak of elegiac ululation, 'Get out of here,' said the Ambassador to a television cameraman who wanted to show the Queen, smiling, watching the black faces of the dancers, shimmering with enthusiasm, transported by the music, but their eyes, what of their eyes? as the beat was faster, faster, faster, they looked sometimes mocking, sometimes derisive, sometimes ecstatic, and none more

58

ecstatic than the King and Queen of Samba, non-hereditary titles, as they presented Queen Elizabeth with a gold medal (in a red leather case), and Prince Philip with an Order of Merit (Samba).

The dancers left, back to their *favelas*, and were replaced by the band of the Royal Marines marching with precision on the lawn and tweaking British hearts. *Abide With Me* and . . .

> Rule Britannia, Britannia rules the waves,
> Britons never, never, never shall be slaves.
>
> The Nations not so blessed as thee
> Must in their turn to tyrants fall
>
> While thou shalt flourish great and free
> The dread and envy of them all.

Guests, cloyed with goodwill, suffused with satisfaction, invaded the buffet of large prawns, turkey, beef, trout, salmon, fresh strawberries, soufflés, dozens of different coloured ice creams, replenished their champagne, and ate. What the hell are the British staking in the world? Was this in its parade of Africans masquerading as slaves a mockery of our past? Or was it just good fun, everyone enjoying themselves on Foreign Office pink champagne salmon, and strawberries? Time enough tomorrow to think about the problems of the world.

Sunday, the last full day of the visit, provided an opportunity to witness the twin specialities of Brazilian myth: *favelas* and football. First, as it was Remembrance Sunday, there was the laying of a wreath on the monument to the unknown warrior, a duty performed by two soldiers while the Queen watched and was smothered in rose petals strewn from above. Then the Anglican Church service, and finally a trip to a part of the *favela* in the grounds of the British Embassy, developed by Lady Russell as a nursery school. A special path had recently been laid to the school, and a wall blocking the *favela* was whitewashed for the occasion. The Queen was introduced to half a dozen be-hatted and stout committee women, three representatives of the *favela*, and three children. Other children stood behind a fence at the top, and the Queen gave them a half-hearted wave as she left, having been presented with a stone reproduction figure of a saint by the sisters of the crèche. Sir John Russell had tussled to include the visit, against the wishes of the Brazilians. Perhaps if more dramatic acknowledgement that Brazil wasn't just sunshine, samba, and fresh strawberries, had been planned nothing would have happened. As it was, the Brazilians practically ignored the recognition of their problem.

One of Rio's senior security police was not being treated with the sort of respect his position deserved. At the Cenotaph on Sunday morning, he and his men were barred because the Army said they were in control, and he had been given the sort of brush-off reserved for bank clerks trying to pay by cheque at a restaurant owned by a man who had that morning been refused an increased overdraft. The police chief's discomfort was caused by a similar vicarious vendetta. A few years previously, when influential in the Copacabana police force, he tried unsuccessfully to arrest a General's under-age daughter who was illegally enjoying herself in a night club.

Now, as he arrived at Maracanã with two hundred hand-picked men in regulation dark grey suits, he found his entrance temporarily barred once more. He shouted, he swore, he pleaded, he was allowed in, and saw that the security was so good he wouldn't be needed. He left with his men, in a huff.

For him, the royal tour was over.

Only the game now had to be played. Originally it was going to be between Brazil and the World. But the British Embassy vetoed this as it was possible a British player, George Best, would be in the World team. Next suggestion was

Brazil against Chile, but this was thought unwise as whichever lost would feel demeaned.

Then Brazil and Peru, but a revolution was imminent in Peru. A week before the game, the teams hadn't been officially decided, until someone suggested Rio against São Paulo. A good idea. But supposing it was a draw? A disaster. Impossible. There was a three-hour meeting to decide what should happen in such an unlikely event, and a compromise reached: the Queen would present the cup to the President of the Brazilian football association to give to the winners of a replay.

One hundred and twelve thousand fans, forty thousand less than capacity, filled the stadium, the largest in the world, built for the World Cup in 1950, made with enough steel to go one and a half times round the equator and enough concrete to build a ten-storey wall along thirty-three blocks both sides of Park Avenue. They saw a very bad match, both teams unwilling to stretch themselves for a 'friendly' game. Pelé predictably scored a goal, his nine-hundredth, and was presented with a cup by the Queen as his team, São Paulo, won 3–2.

'Bicha, bicha,' jeered the crowd at one player.

'What are they shouting?' the Queen asked her interpreter.

He said it was a word of abuse, but declined to enlarge.

'What *does* it mean?' she asked Sir John Russell.

'It means "queer",' he said.

In the evening there was a private dinner aboard *Britannia,* and next morning, after saying good-bye at the airport to fifty people (and wives) she left in the VC10 for the 1,980-mile journey to Santiago, Chile.

'People ask why we're only going to two countries, but look at the distances,' she said. 'Philip's been to a lot of the others.'

The VC10 headed west blowing the top off a hangar, but hurting no-one. Britain had more selling to do in another of the twenty Sovereign States of South America. This time there would be a tangible result.

The Road Show – III

'Which might be better for encouraging trade with other countries: Monarchy – 53 %; Republic – 28 %; Don't know – 19 %.' *Long to Reign Over Us?* Leonard M. Harris (William Kimber, 1966) p. 32.

'Wherever she goes, that spot is momentarily the centre of the Commonwealth, and the soldier on parade, the artisan at his bench, the nurse by the bedside and the patient under her care, are enabled to feel themselves exalted by the recognition of their place in a world-wide family and a vast design.' *The Work of the Queen*, Dermot Morrah (William Kimber, 1958) p. 43.

POLITICAL AND TRADE IMPLICATIONS of the Queen going anywhere outside England are immense. Because of arguments about the three 'Fs' (rival claims of the Falkland Islands, international football disputes, and the foot and mouth epidemic supposed to have been imported to England in cans of corned beef) she could not visit the Argentine. And she was unable to sail to the Falkland Islands, one of those strange outposts of the British Empire populated by a lot of sheep and two thousand people, because such snook-cocking could harm trade.

Eventually, and in subtle ways, the Falklands were to be returned to Argentina, according to British diplomats involved, but for the moment a performance of righteous indignation was necessary to prove to the public that a bunch of darkies couldn't destroy Our Way of Life, however remote from tedious reality. Most of the British wondered if the

Falklands were north of Scotland, and gave a yawn – until the Queen became involved in the political imbroglio. Would she go? Wouldn't she? Thankfully, for her, the Government didn't allow the trip.

In Buenos Aires, there were murmurs about being snubbed, and a COI film of the South American tour was tactfully distributed in every country but Argentina.

In this case, the Queen was involved in a political situation, but sometimes she can't even watch horses without being described as a pawn. Lord Porchester, a personal friend who became her racing manager during 1969, spent months arranging an informal visit to the Normandy château of the Duc d'Audiffret-Pasquier in May 1967. There was endless speculation about it being connected with Common Market negotiations, particularly when President de Gaulle sent her red roses, and English swans were placed on the lake. To support their theory of the royal family's involvement in politics, people recalled how Princess Margaret had cancelled an evening at a Paris film première in 1963 because of a de Gaulle rebuff.

Since she came to the throne, the Queen has made twenty state visits lasting between one and ten days. (Appendix.) The formula is always the same. Fundamentals don't seem to have changed since the summer of 1520 when Henry VIII initiated royal exchange systems by meeting King Francis I of France to satisfy the terms of a tenuous treaty made by Cardinal Wolsey. Both kings were vain, arrogant men who had been curious about each other for years. Henry insisted they met on English soil, which they did, in the ground between Guines and Ardres. He took 4,500 men – plus his Queen of the time, Katharine of Aragon, who had 1,300 men to prevent her feeling lonely. Fountains in the courtyard of the English pavilion sprayed white and red wine.

At first, the two kings rode out alone, waited, stared, embraced on horseback, dismounted, and embraced on foot. They liked each other. From then on there were the usual festivities. 'These sovereigns hate each other very cordially,' reported an Italian, who was watching, as Italians usually are.

Good will is still created, of course, but the age of influence by serenity, smiles, and show is over. After four hundred and fifty years, old attitudes about protocol, and etiquette, and precedent need blasting from the petrified imaginations of bureaucrats who plot the itineraries.

The dilemma of state visits is that of many other activities pursued by British Monarchy: trappings essential to the system are being squeezed into unnecessarily outdated formulae by timid organizers. For instance, the Queen's visit to Australia in Spring 1970 (technically not a state visit because she is Queen of Australia) was originally based on her 1963 visit, which in turn had tried unsuccessfully to recreate the enthusiasm of the 1954 tour. Largely to inhibit rivalry between the offices of Prime Minister and the Cabinet in Canberra, a retired general was wrenched from the serenity of his farm in Victoria to organize the programme.

Understandably, one of his main considerations was to offend as few people as possible. He wanted a quiet life. When he brought the draft schedule to Buckingham Palace for the Queen and Prince Philip to approve in summer of 1969, he was sent away to try and arrange for them to meet more of Australia's 'horny handed men of toil' and not the bevy of ersatz Ascot matrons that give so many royal occasions the aspect of a superior bingo hall in Ashtead.

In Commonwealth countries, the visits reach their peak of bastardized concoction, an unhappy combination of reality and never-never land. This is largely because of the strange situation. It is incredible that the Queen should call herself Queen of Australia, and only visit the country for six weeks every seven years. Why not spend a week or two there, and in Canada, every year? Or actually live in the country for six months? There are two avid supporters of this in the Household – Bill Heseltine and Master of the Household

Geoffrey Hardy-Roberts. Politicians have tried to suggest it, notably Selwyn Lloyd when he was Foreign Secretary between 1955 and 1960. 'I think it should be arranged for the Queen to spend a month in Australia each year,' he says, 'perhaps a fortnight in Canberra and a week in two of the States by rotation. I should like her also to have a week in New Zealand and to commute to Canada perhaps three or four times a year. Of course, her engagements in the United Kingdom would have to be substantially curtailed to enable her to do this.'

There has been no success, and won't be without strong public pressure. The Queen likes her routine and intends to keep to it. Prince Philip enjoys his, and feels the Commonwealth must be satisfied with an absentee Monarchy if it wants one, which it probably doesn't any more, and a heritage based on an offshore island as much as 12,000 miles away.

He is happy to upset them now and again in a way that can only hasten the inevitable end of remaining Commonwealth ties. On an eleven-city tour of Canada in October 1969 he annoyed people nearly everywhere and told an audience in Ottawa; 'The answer to this question of the Monarchy is very simple – if the people don't want it, they should change it. But let us end it on amicable terms and not have a row.

'The Monarchy exists not for its own benefit, but for that of the country. We don't come here for our health. We can think of better ways of enjoying ourselves.'

He may have to. A few weeks later, the Canadian government ordered the Queen's portrait to be removed from some banknotes and replaced by pictures of former Canadian premiers. Prime Minister Pierre Trudeau hinted at the future: 'I think there will be a great deal of change in the 1970s. Institutions of government and society will have to adapt a great deal. The values of the new generation and tremendous technological changes may lead Canada to give up its connections with the royal family in the coming decade.'[1]

[1] 23 December, 1969.

Australians, wondering about the benefit of Monarchy, have also been nettled by Philip on a number of occasions. In May 1968, replying to a speech by Chief Justice Sir Garfield Barwick, he said: 'I think national pride must have gone away with him for a while. I got the feeling, having listened to Sir Garfield, that you may get the impression that in Australia nothing has ever gone wrong.

'When he was on the subject of being wedded to democracy, I had to laugh at that. They had a referendum recently on the subject of increasing the numbers of Members of Parliament in Canberra which was completely defeated.

'Sir Garfield also mentioned that there were few religious divisions, but it is a strange coincidence that of the two main political parties one is predominantly Roman Catholic and the other is predominantly Protestant, and there is, in fact, a racial minority (the Aborigines) here in Australia.'

After that, the *Melbourne Herald* suggested: 'Someone back home, preferably the Queen, should tell the Prince it's time he grew up. Royalty, and the representatives of royalty, long ago lost the right to make this sort of silly intrusion into local politics.'

In New Zealand, he was attacked by a newspaper, *Truth*, as The Prince of Arrogance. 'The Duke's visit, highlighted by his arrogant disregard for the public, was a waste of time, effort and money.'

The Monarchy's most popular justification is the way it is supposed to keep the Commonwealth together.[2] For those

[2]An Opinion Research Centre poll, published in the *Sunday Times*, 29 June, 1969, asked the importance of various reasons for the monarchy. The percentages are those who answered 'very important'.

Helps keep the Commonwealth united	69%
Adds colour to people's lives	66%
Makes violent revolution less likely	64%
Sets standards of morality	61%
Prevents political parties becoming too powerful	58%
Sets standards of manners and dress	52%

66

who believe this, royal visits are a badly missed opportunity that can never be overcome.

The hopeful catechism of various Government departments, that royal tours are good for trade, may have been slightly true thirteen years ago, when in April, there was excitement because live television pictures could be transmitted from Paris to London, and the Queen's visit could be called 'a triumph for television transmission'!

Now, the television spectacular is a bit of a bore, and businessmen are usually more interested in delivery dates, and prices, than the casual fairy-land image of a country represented by a Queen, or her relatives, travelling in a carriage with a vast retinue to satisfy the fertile whims of protocol ministers.

'It was always thought that if you didn't take a large staff, people would say it was done on the cheap,' a member of the royal family told me. 'Junior, fringe royals should use local people. When we went to Canada the result was a terrible balls-up because the organization was so out of date. I don't see why we shouldn't use the RAF to travel to a number of places for short periods. Let tomato juice be spilled down the necks of the ladies-in-waiting by inexperienced stewards. It doesn't matter. And we could meet different types. All we see at the moment are mayors and civic dignitaries.'

Maybe it is the fault of exporters, but royal visits have no impact on trade figures – and indeed they can deteriorate after such a performance of gaudy flag waving. (Appendix.) In Brazil, exports fell and imports increased in the months following the royal visit (Appendix), a fact airily dismissed by the Board of Trade as 'seasonal'.

Sad though it may be, interest in Britain is provoked increasingly by trends antipathetic to Monarchy: pop singers, clothes, and a bit of easy sex.

Even an admitted hard sell campaign such as Prince Philip's ten-day tour of the United States in March 1966 – which he disliked and said he would not repeat – may be excellent for the sponsoring organization (this one raised more than a million dollars for Variety Club charities), but has no effect on national trade. In 1967, British exports to the United States fell by £28,000,000 ($75,000,000).

Perhaps Britain could learn from Canada. A week before the Queen arrived in Chile, their Foreign Secretary, four ministers, and thirty officials descended on Santiago as part of a nine country Latin American sales tour. The British Board of Trade, with a strategy based on Brazil, Argentina, Mexico and Venezuela, had never considered Chile very important. It is a country of under ten million people stretched along a three thousand mile strip of thin, unprofitable land, cut off from the rest of South America by the Andes and the Pacific. It has a balance of payments problem that worries exporters and makes Britain's financial policy appear as stable as a Mother Superior's virginity. It is a country of quaint charm, both decoratively (octagonal red and black pillar boxes, refugees from some Victorian junk heap), and intellectually – 'I'm all for freedom of speech, so long as no-one is offended. At least those who have always had power know how to use it,' says Chavella Edwards, dowager hostess of Santiago's social élite.

A country, then, that appeared tacked on to the South American trip in lieu of Argentina, a make-weight after politically and economically important Brazil. This was not so. It was decided to visit Chile long before Brazil, and the Queen and British Ambassador, Frederick Mason, had known the date for at least two years. Hints had been made to Embassy officials in September 1966, so they could prepare themselves and their wives, who would need hats and gloves. Curtsies had to be practised, myths exploded – such as you can't wear black in front of the Queen, you have to wear gloves, and you must wait until you are spoken to. A communications system had to be arranged between the Embassy and London and there was the logistic problem of how a

68

three-car Embassy could transport a thirty-strong household. For ten months, seven officials spent fifty per cent of their time on arrangements, increasing during the last six months to about ninety per cent. 'We feel very isolated here in Chile, particularly,' said Dick Neilson, the Information Officer.

Officially, the visit was to return President Eduardo Frei Montalva's five days in Britain in July 1965. Unofficially, the British Government wanted to encourage a stable, democratic form of Latin American government; and the Chilean Ambassador, who sometimes met the Queen at week-end house parties, had been a persistent lobbyist. A charming, cultivated man, Victor Santa Cruz is proud of his English social contacts, eats regularly at White's, and is derided by many of his countrymen, including the President, as being a mock Englishman.

Protocol demanded the correct procedure, so on 18 January, 1968, President Frei wrote to the Queen, 'Good and big friend' inviting her to stay. The Queen accepted 3 February, on dramatic, unbending gold-rimmed cardboard about 10 inches by 6, somewhat less effulgently, starting 'Mr President' and ending, 'Your good friend, Elizabeth R'. The announcement was made at 1300 hours on 24 April.

'I think it's the only real secret that has ever been kept in this office. It's one of the most secret secrets we ever had,' boasted Mariano Fontecilla, head of protocol and a veteran of twenty state visits.

For four months before the Queen arrived, he and six helpers met British Embassy people every Monday at 2 p.m. Ambassador Mason was worried the visit would be dull after the razzmatazz of Brazil, but Fontecilla co-operated with a strenuously practical attention to detail. He arranged for a gun salute to be fired at mid-day when the Queen was doing the ritual tree planting, so that the Minister of Agriculture, a man notorious for long speeches, would be unable to indulge himself with more than the allotted few sentences. He hired ceremonial carriages and horses for a full day, even though they would only be needed for an hour or so in the morning – as he proudly re-assured Sir Martin Charteris during the planning stages.

The Cousiño Palace guest house, where the royal party were to stay, was re-decorated and exotically furnished. Then, a few weeks before the visit, it burnt down. No panic, the Queen could stay at the Carrera Hilton Hotel, in the centre of town. Four floors, including the roof-top swimming pool, were taken over, and the Queen's suite, number 1422 (subsequently re-named 'Royal'), of bedroom, dressing-room and sitting-room, was re-painted off-white, furnished with light blue couches, and fitted with two new bathrooms. Prince Philip had a bedroom and private bathroom. New doors were made, with a hand-beaten copper shield of Great Britain on the Queen's, and a lion rampant on Prince Philip's. Decorating cost the hotel £5,000 ($12,000), and the head painter, who worked ninety-six hours non-stop, was rewarded with the Royal Victorian Medal (bronze).

Arrangements were made for twelve security guards with walkie-talkies to patrol the hotel twenty-four hours a day. A special room was set aside for the 'investigation bureau' with a high-powered radio transmitter and receiver.

The airport arrival and departure was discussed for two months before satisfaction was achieved, and the Queen could be awaited with trepidation, and no little enthusiasm.

In the VC10 flying between Rio and Santiago, Lord Chalfont read the chintzy rhetoric prepared by the British Embassy for the Queen to read at a joint session of Chilean Congress. It was an anodyne, Foreign Office drudge of a speech, full of clichés about 'harmony', 'goodwill', and 'friendship' which both he and Prince Philip thought was 'bromidic'. Together, they wrote something that would at least cause some excitement.

Lord Chalfont, as Minister in Attendance, was the senior person on the tour after the royal couple. He had to offer

political advice whenever needed, a task he considered somewhat superfluous before he started. Now he realized there
were times when he was useful. The Foreign Secretary himself used to travel on royal tours, but Michael Stewart thought
he had more important functions. He went for a few days
at the beginning and end of significant visits, like the one to
Germany in 1965, but that was all. 'Don't you like travel?'
Prince Philip asked him.

Selwyn Lloyd always accompanied them. 'Sweden, Denmark, Portugal, France, the Netherlands, and the United
States. I thought it was my duty to go, and there was always
a very good chance of useful talks with political leaders. In
Portugal I saw Salazar four or five times. He was a very
difficult man to meet otherwise. Nothing tangible may come
out, but such a visit gives the opportunity for talks in an
informal way.'

The Queen landed in Santiago after lunch on Monday,
preceded by six Hawker Hunter jets recently bought by the
Chilean government. She was wearing a fuchsia-coloured
dress, in consideration of the flower that originated in the
country, listened politely to the Chilean national anthem
which is in three movements and lasts two and a half minutes
and, serenaded by *Land of Hope and Glory*, drove into the
centre of town to be made an 'illustrious citizen' by the
mayor.

'Your words of welcome this afternoon have already made
me feel at home,' she said. 'So does the name of your city,
which corresponds to St James in English, the name of my
Court in London.'

Twenty-five thousand people clapped, cheered, and waved
her back to the Carrera where women in hats, gloves and
their best dresses would wait patiently to cheer again when
she returned at half-past midnight from the State banquet –
one of the cheapest ever given in Santiago because no outside
help was needed in the preparation.

She was already a success. One magazine greeted her in English. 'Politically, she is considered the most important woman in the world, and just arrived in our modest country, she was able to shew herself plenty of pomp and ostentation. Anyhaw her appareance simple, her good manners, her treatment to de Duc of Edinburg as "my husband" and not as "Your Highness", very quickly conquered the devotion of our people.

'Very much obliged, Your Gracious Majesty, for your kindly visit.' (sic)[3].

Next day, with the temperature in the eighties, she sat in the hired, open landau with a grey rug over her knees, and escorted by Prussian-uniformed soldiers, went to deliver her best speech of the year. First, though, she laid a wreath on the monument to an illegitimate son of a Chilean woman and an Irish immigrant from Sligo, a hero whose name reverberates with dual nationality – Bernardo O'Higgins – the first Supreme Director of the country, who liberated it from the Spanish in 1817.

The procession made a strange picture. The Gentlemen of the Household and the Gentlemen of the Chilean Government – for Gentlemen they must be called, such was the grandness of the occasion – were in morning dress with black silk top hats which they mostly carried, sweating, from place to place. Strange how formality is always in inverse proportion to importance. Mariano Fontecilla was shocked when it was suggested black top hats was pushing ceremony a bit far. 'It would have looked ridiculous without them. I mean, you can't go in a carriage in a cardigan, can you?'

The incongruity of their dress was even more ironic at the National Congress where a speech of welcome was being given by sixty-year-old Dr Salvador Allende, pro-Castro leader of the Frente de Accion Popular and President of the Senate, a man who had already annoyed Prince Philip

[3] *Topaze,* 15 November, 1968.

72

at the previous evening's white-tie State banquet by arriving dressed in a lounge suit.

'Why are you dressed like that?'

'Because my party is poor, and they advised me not to hire evening dress.'

'If they told you to wear a bathing costume, I suppose you'd come dressed in one?'

'Oh, no, Sir, our Party is a serious one.'

Dr Allende could, of course, have compromised like Signor Pietro Nenni, Italian Foreign Minister and leader of the Socialist Party, later in the year at the State banquet given in Windsor Castle on 23 April, 1969. He was appalled when told it would be white-tie because he feels his somewhat squat figure thus clad isn't shown to its best advantage. Moreover, what would his supporters say? Capitalist turncoat, and so on. He asked the Queen if she would mind if he didn't dress up. Not at all, she said. Come how you like. Signor Nenni puzzled about this, and eventually decided on a solution. He would wear a white tie – but withdraw to another room when the pictures were taken. So, image overcame reality once more, a small principle was apparently satisfied, ridicule was prevented and dignity remained intact – a masterpiece of political manœuvrability.

There was no such compromise for Dr Allende, either at the banquet, or the joint session of Congress. Members of the Household guessed as much. Sir Michael Adeane stood impassively behind the Queen clutching a copy of her rewritten speech. He declined to give it to the interpreter until the last minute, causing her to stumble over the translation and complain afterwards. Dr Allende began, limiting the niceties.

'In our country's attitude towards you, there is a basic aspect of great significance. You will no doubt have been aware, and will have been able personally to corroborate during your present visit, that there are in our country a variety of factors which have engendered political stability.

What, however, of our social reality? With scant shades of difference, this is the same as that prevailing among the 1,400 millions of people (representing forty-seven per cent of the world's population) who make up the Third World and who, their lives a sad masquerade, inhabit Asia, Africa, and Latin America.

'The effort of the people throughout 150 years of emancipation from colonial rule have not enabled them to escape from the great collective risks of unemployment, misery, ignorance, and sickness.

'Such a system results only in work, sweat, and tears. You well know the meaning of these words. Between your experience and ours, however, there is an abyss; at the close of the dark period of history through which England lived, she could envisage the emergence of a comforting dawn. At the close of ours, we see only more and more darkness.

'A system so arbitrary cannot last for ever. In Latin America, and also in Africa and Asia, new generations are emerging which show no inclination to renounce their expectations, nor compromise the interests of their countries. A strong and increasing torrent of social tension is noticeable and should not be ignored.

'I have addressed myself to you in these terms because I know you to be the sovereign of a great community of nations and because I am certain that you yourself believe in that biblical phrase which one of your illustrious ancestors caused to be engraved on the monument erected to the Minister who contributed most to the greatness of his Empire: "Kings love him that speaketh right".'

The Queen stood to reply. It wasn't particularly earth shattering, nor original, but it was so different from most of her speeches, in that it actually said something, and was not delivered in half-bored, sing-song lullaby tones.

'In the seven hundred years of its history, the British Parliament has gone through many changes, but above all it has learnt the virtue of tolerance – tolerance of differing views, and tolerance of minority opinion. Real freedom is the freedom to make choices and Parliament has learnt that this is only possible when people exercise self control and where the law is only needed to reinforce self discipline. It has learnt to encourage every citizen to feel a sense of responsibility for the welfare and security of his country.

'Every generation is inclined to be critical of the apparent weaknesses and shortcomings of their own democratic systems. This is inevitable because it is hard enough to define and understand the principle of democracy, it is even harder to achieve a practical and workable system of democratic government. All systems are capable of improvement and each one needs to be modified as conditions change, but we need to be very careful that criticism and dissatisfaction succeed in producing a better system and do not simply weaken and undermine confidence in the one that we have.'

She then walked to the Supreme Court, same routine as in Brasilia, off to lunch with Foreign Secretary, Gabriel Valdes, followed by the Cuadro Verde equestrian demonstration team of Chilean Carabineros, a mediocre horse-show with an enlarged reputation, and the inevitable playing of *Colonel Bogey* and *Lady of Spain*.

At the British Embassy residence, a building less imposing than that in Rio, the evening's banquet was being prepared. A tent had been placed over the lawn, leading from french windows in the lounge. In the kitchen Ernest Bennett, the Queen's page, and three footmen were supervising dinner for forty-four people. 'A lot of us thought we weren't given enough to do,' said an Embassy wife, as Bennett, a rotund, Pickwickian figure with a high-pitched voice and two sons, fussed around.

Bennett, formerly with the Duke of Connaught and Princess Alice, has developed the exquisite conditioning of his calling after a life-time of royal service: an avid concern

75

for propriety combined with a sceptical sense of humour. At one State banquet in Dominica, a politician decided to demonstrate how much of a waste of taxpayers' money he thought such gatherings were – not enough to stay away, but even politicians need a free meal sometimes. He entered the dining-room smoking, remained smoking throughout the meal sitting at a table directly below the Queen. Bennett, overcome, glared ceaselessly to no effect. The Queen ignored the situation. Afterwards, Bennett took to his bed for a rest. One of the royal party mentioned his sorrow at Bennett's discomfiture.

'Don't worry, sir,' said the page stoically, 'he must have been a Communist.'

There were no such problems in Santiago, where the only thing that worried Ambassador Mason was whether he'd offended, by not inviting, too many friends he made twenty years ago when he was first secretary. He only had room for three hundred of Chile's most worthy citizens at the reception in his house after dinner.

Behind the delicacy of the state visit, the final act of a ruthless and devious two-year business battle between the French and English was reaching a climax. President de Gaulle, just before retirement, was to be up-staged by the Queen.

A British firm, Fairey Engineering of Stockport, Lancashire, had been approached by Chile at the end of 1966 to build a nuclear reactor near Santiago – an extremely important contract, not necessarily for its size, but because of future business. There was only one similar power reactor in South America, bought by Argentina from Siemens of West Germany. Both the French and British needed to compete in a potentially vast market.

In October 1967, Fairey's commercial director, Mr Peter Bray, D.F.C., was in Chicago when he heard the Chilean Foreign Ministry had accepted a French reactor because it was combined with a long-term loan at low interest – three and a half per cent over twenty years. President de Gaulle promised such generosity because France was prevented from using the Sahara as an atomic test centre, and wanted to transfer to the South Pacific. The British Government could not compete.

Later that year, however, Bray met the executive director of Chile's Nuclear Commission, and put in a bid. By the middle of 1968, it was obvious the finance would be difficult so he wrote to banker Eddie Rothschild, and the then chairman of the British Nuclear Forum, Kenneth McKillop.

'We thought it would be very good if Philip could say what a splendid thing British nuclear policy was. I felt the Chamber of Commerce lunch in Santiago would be the best time to do it, and the Chairman of the Forum wrote to Philip. He got a letter back from Major Andrew Duncan, Philip's then equerry, agreeing.'

On 13 November, at his speech to the Chamber of Commerce, Prince Philip did not specifically mention nuclear policy because talks between Lord Chalfont and Señor Gabriel Valdes were at a critical stage.

'Co-operation and collaboration between Chileans and British works, and works well. This is the best possible basis for the further development and expansion of trading and commercial activities of all kinds. I am certain this is possible and indeed desirable for both countries.

'The pattern (of trade) has changed dramatically in the last twenty years alone. The Chilean economy is totally different and vastly more developed. Equally, British industry has become immensely more sophisticated technologically and scientifically.

'And that is not all. Trade is no longer a simple matter of exporting and importing, or straightforward financing and investing. Many other factors have entered into the business, and today credit terms, co-operative enterprises and all sorts of subtle variations have to be devised to keep

77

the wheels of trade turning smoothly to the mutual benefit of both partners.

'As far as British exports to Chile are concerned, there can be no doubt whatever that British industry has a very great deal to offer Chile. Every kind of advanced technological equipment is available, but someone has to make it his business to convince potential customers in the teeth of efficient and ruthless competition.'

During the following week-end at Antumalal, Lord Chalfont badgered Señor Valdes about the deal. He was surprised that Peter Bray was not in Chile to increase pressure on the government. Bray, in Washington for a meeting, operated on the subtle presumption that seduction should be diffident rather than dramatic. Nothing ever killed love so easily as anxiety. Besides the French were wed to the Chilean Nuclear Commission with, apparently, a signed agreement.

President Frei, though, realized life was more than scraps of paper. A former schoolmaster and manager of a publishing firm, he retained at times a donnish indifference to the hurly-burly of politics, was fond of quoting esoteric French literature, and thought that Chileans were too dour, too pessimistic, too English really. Fifty-seven years old, with six children, a kindly, avuncular man, overwhelmed by the Queen's charm and the effect she was having on Chile, he insisted that the British firm should supply the reactor.

Early in December, Peter Bray flew to Santiago, and the agreement – worth at least £635,000 initially – was signed on the 19th. 'We couldn't have unseated the French without the royal visit,' said Bray. 'They were in.'

It would be a mistake to become too euphoric about misty-eyed Presidents, and business by enchantment. In the same month, Chile was asking Washington for a $150 million loan – and President Frei was not so overcome by the Queen that he neglected domestic politics, which were being quietly re-arranged while the visit attracted all the publicity. He accepted the 'resignation' of Jacques Chonchol, 42-year-old left winger, and principal figure in Chile's most important policy: agrarian reform. Chonchol angrily announced that his job had been made impossible – a statement greeted with as much interest as the Queen's food at the state banquet.

The Queen did not visit a co-operative farm, evidence of Chile's most controversial attempt to break from a feudal past, but she did go to plenty of schools. On the day that Philip visited a copper mine and addressed the Chamber of Commerce, she was at the Escuela Ingleterra, which had adopted the name England in 1951. 'Thrilled by the recent spectacle of Her Majesty's Coronation, and full of admiration of Her Majesty as a person, it was natural that the teachers should vote to name the school England,' said the head-mistress, when the building was inaugurated by a British Council representative. Now the Queen came, dressed in drab green, and was met by excited children in cardboard bearskins and home-made Household Cavalry uniforms doing the Highland Fling to a loud gramophone.

She was in a grumpy mood, in earlier days one would have called it 'queenly', but as so often when she meets children *en masse* she seems ill-at-ease. Perhaps she was think-ing about the next appointment – the traditional tree-planting performed by every celebrity who visits Chile in order to encourage aforestation. With a gold spade, she took three shovels of earth from a baize-covered table and gently deposited them around a manio shrub, watered it with a gold-plated watering can, signed a commemorative parchment with a flourish (chiding the Mayor for his squiggle, 'Is that a signature'), and left to see a few of the ten thousand Anglo-Chilean community at the Chilean-British Institute.

After lunch, another school, followed by the Prince of Wales Club, visited as were so many other places by the Duke of Windsor when he toured Chile in 1925. Originally, all club members were English. Now they represented only fifteen per cent. Two thousand were expected. Five thousand arrived.

In the evening, a football match which had, inevitably, caused trouble. Who should play? The teams were changed three times in two weeks, until it was decided that the two universities in Santiago should compete against each other. Naturally, the President of the Football Association couldn't get a seat, because his block had been taken over by the Senate. And neither could Ambassador Mason until the last hour.

The following day was not very fortunate for Mason either. He stood at the foot of an Andover to wave the Queen goodbye to Valparaiso. As it took off he realized, with one of those dismal feelings of inadequacy, that he should have been aboard. The next plane, a DC3, didn't leave for half an hour. He tried to hire a helicopter, with no success.

At least he missed a near riot.

Valparaiso, which used to be the most important Pacific port until the San Francisco gold rush, has a number of statues to Chilean heroes of British ancestry, so it had to be visited. The juddering, jumping crowd, overwhelmed by the honour, broke through police cordons along Avenida Brasil, as the Queen was walking from one monument to another, and mobbed her like a film star. It was the worst moment Perkins had known in seventeen years. For several minutes the Queen was surrounded, bewildered, startled, wiping dust from her eyes. Philip clutched her left arm. Perkins pushed in front, clearing a way. Philip's detective, John Thorning, moved people from the other side, Chilean police, after looking apprehensive and out of control, drew their truncheons in a half-hearted way. A small boy was knocked over by one of the ceremonial cars, which continued without stopping.

The Queen, regained composure as if she had been for a quiet stroll, unperturbed by the commotion engulfing the rest of her Household, and prepared herself to watch a parade of goose-stepping soldiers.

Marching, marching, marching, national anthems and more national anthems. Nothing of importance. And in the evening, a small dinner party for eighteen where there were no servants to pour drinks beforehand, just equerries Andrew Duncan and John Slater. The state visit was almost over.

Next day was holiday time, and she flew south to the Antumalal Hotel, Pucon,[4] a frontier village in Southern Chile, four hundred and ninety miles from Valparaiso where, for two days, she could rest from the strain and a cold that was becoming worse, and Philip could fish for salmon. He caught three tiddlers.

It wasn't all so rustic. The ten strong force of carabiñeros was increased to 150, and there was an obligatory photo-call that the Queen abruptly curtailed when someone seemed more intent on photographing her legs than her face.

Saturday, picnic day. Not a bottle of wine, a few sandwiches, mosquitoes, and dirty knives. 'I remember going for a picnic on one of the tours,' recalls a former British Foreign Secretary. 'I thought it would be groundsheets and that sort of thing. But no, it was in a monastery, and there was gold plate, and a footman behind every person.' This picnic, a lamb barbecue, wasn't quite like that, and it did have its share of surprises. Ambassador Mason lost his way, the Queen lent her knife to a guest, noticed someone else didn't have a glass ...

Back to Santiago on Sunday where she was photographed with the aeroplane crews, had lunch at the Club Hipico racecourse (also visited by the Duke of Windsor) with furniture provided by Maples, binocular-clad women more interested in her than the horses, and presented a gold cup for the Isabel II stakes. Prince Philip played polo, and they both met

[4]Antumalal, an Araucanian word meaning Land of Sun; the hotel is one of the most expensive in Chile, at the foot of a smouldering volcano and at the edge of a lake. It is a copy of a similar hotel in Prague.

for an Anglo-Chilean society reception before attending an investiture for members of the British Embassy by the Carrera pool. Frederick Mason received his 'K', and a travel agency had to hurriedly change all his holiday air tickets to 'Sir Frederick Mason', such are the hazards of the British honours system.

A private dinner that she chose herself: vichysoisse, turkey, cauliflower, meringue and ice cream. And at 11.45 p.m. Sir Martin Charteris asked the manager if hotel staff could see her at 9.45 a.m., just before she left. She gave small presents – brooches, powder compacts or silver pocket combs for the women; pencils, wallets or cuff links for the men. As with medals, there is a hierarchy about presents:

Powder box (A)	Square silver box with raised royal cypher in centre in a stamped, red leather box – from Cartier.
Powder box (C)	Small, round, silver, with cypher engraved in centre. Unstamped box.
Cuff links (A)	Gold, with cypher on both links. Red stamped box.
Cuff links (B)	Gold, oval, with cypher. Red stamped box.
Cuff links (C)	Gold, with cut corners. Cypher in blue enamel, flush. Royal blue box, stamped.
Wallet (A)	Pigskin, embossed with cypher. Unstamped box.
Wallet (B)	Brown, pin seal, fitted with gold corners. Cypher in top right-hand corner. Unstamped box.
	(Both wallets come from Jarrolds.)
Picture frame (A)	Blue leather with roll top, stamped with cypher.
Picture frame (B)	Blue leather with flat top. Unstamped.
Picture frame (C)	Brown leather with flat top. Unstamped.

| Cigarette lighter | Engine-turned silver, with cypher engraved in front centre. Stamped red box. |

Through the night, a silent crowd waited outside the hotel, gloved and hatted in respect, waiting to see the Queen. President Frei, at his summer house in Viña del Mar, pondered on the success of the visit, and decided to hell with protocol between heads of state. He would go to the airport to wave the Queen good-bye.

Unfortunately, the following morning was foggy, and his helicopter couldn't take off, so he had to drive to where the mist had cleared and the helicopter could land on a road. The Queens' escort, travelling at normal speed to the airport, were told to slow down, which they did, almost to a crawl, while the President was on his way. He had to be there first. Protocol insisted.

At the airport, folksingers dressed as cowboys and standing on the stairs were preparing an esquinazo – surprise – and as the Queen arrived, half an hour late, they sang, *'Will Ye No' Come Back Again'*. She looked pleased, happy, thanked the singers, and posed with her motor-cycle escort before walking to the VC10, ringed with police holding their batons to make a full circle. The national anthems played. She turned to wave to the crowd.

'Of course it's a fairy tale. People like fairy tales,' said Augustin Edwards, editor of *El Mercurio,* Chile's most prestigious newspaper. 'But I wouldn't write that in the paper, because it would be rude.'

The VC10 ambled to the runway, guarded by six fire engines. One more backward glance, a band still playing, the President watching, crowds waving, police sighing with relief. It took off, into the strong sun, and was gone. The anti-climax came immediately. The carriage was turning into a pumpkin.

Lord Chalfont gave a press conference. 'We regard the

visit as having been a very memorable and moving experience, as well as having practical results.' So far there was an exchange scheme for one post-graduate a year, a cultural agreement, and a £4 million loan – small by international standards.[5]

Any questions?

Two trivialities about the Queen's visit. The rest on the Falkland Islands, where Lord Chalfont was travelling in a few days. Beggars returned to the vicinity of the Carrera Hotel. Schoolteachers in the interior went on strike because they hadn't been paid for three months. The Government wondered about the bill, estimated at between £75,000 and £100,000. Food and board at the Carrera alone was £2,700 ($6,500). It began to drizzle, the first rain for a year.

The Queen, having convinced British Ambassadors in both countries that she enjoyed her visit with them most, spent the night on *Britannia* anchored off Recife. On board, in spite of gallant efforts by Rear Admiral Patrick Morgan, flag officer Royal Yachts and the only Admiral in the Navy who is also a ship's captain, a sloth had been deposited by an admirer and was living on deck in a box. Hazards of royal travel. In Gambia[6] the Queen had been presented with a crocodile in a pierced silver biscuit box, which had been passed down the queue of dignitaries until it reached Sir Martin Charteris. It had to stay in his bath for the rest of the trip.

Next day, back via Dakar, to London, where there was a financial crisis, talk of a coalition Government, and the Foreign Secretary to meet her at the Palace. 'Mercifully, nowadays we don't have to go to the airport,' says Michael Stewart.

'It seems odd,' says the Queen, 'to be welcomed into one's own house.'

[5]Early in 1970, though, a £30 million contract for warships was signed between Britain and Chile.

[6]1961.

'This isn't ours,' says Philip. 'It's a tied cottage.'

Quite so. And the Queen's houses have become so expensive, that the Government have found ways of giving her slightly more money without actually increasing her allowance and thus risking political uproar.

The story of the Queen's cash is one of the more intricate and intriguing aspects of Monarchy.

Interlude - 1

ON 6 DECEMBER, 1968, between seeing Sir John Henniker-Major, director-general of the British Council, and His Excellency the Panamanian Ambassador, Señor Don Eusebio Morales, the Queen was given the not altogether surprising news that she was descended from a prophet. The Queen of England's meticulously charted pedigree can prove anything – encouraged by the elastic imaginations of Heralds and genealogists. Sir Anthony Wagner, Garter King of Arms, the most authoritative explorer in the ancestral burial ground, who answers the telephone 'Garter here', discovered the Queen's American heritage. 'I've had the disease from early childhood,' he explains. 'There's nothing you can do about it. You recognize it immediately in others. I traced the Queen Mother's ancestry, and noticed that in one part there was a link with Virginia. That was very strange, I thought. I delved. And, lo and behold, it came to George Washington. It was really extraordinary.'

But the prophet Mohammed was not his responsibility. This hereditary bauble was dangled before the Queen during an infrequent skirmish with the world of poetry. She was informed of it by a co-descendant: Robert Graves. Neither Graves nor the Queen actually descended from heaven on a pink cloud, in spite of occasional evidence to the contrary. Graves was born in Wimbledon in 1895, a part of suburban, commuterized Britain that he left for his adoptive Majorcan village of Deja thirty-three years later, and whose nymphs, and muses, and myriad classical ghosts he had temporarily deserted in order to travel to Buckingham Palace by taxi to collect personally the Queen's Medal for Poetry. This was a rare honour, as the medal had previously been sent by post, poetry not being one of the more noticeable royal enthusiasms, although the Queen Mother is adored by some of the more respectable poets since she told one of them she sits in bed eating chocolates and reading poems with true eighteenth-century gusto.

Graves had spent the previous evening with Poet Laureate Cecil Day-Lewis. 'He told me about Mohammed over dinner, and he told me again in the taxi, and by God, didn't he tell it again to the courtiers who met us at the door,' recalls Day-Lewis. 'I told him to save it for the Queen.'

The two poets, one lean, ascetic, with scarlet socks. The other large, white-tangled hair spilling from his head like unravelled cotton wool, bubbling with supercharged enthusiasm, were conducted into the presence where they said a few conventional lines of greeting for the benefit of television cameras. Then the proper Audience began. As with all others, it was about twenty minutes and no written record was kept.

'I don't know if you realize, ma'am, but you and I are descended from the prophet Mohammed.'

'Oh, really?'

'Yes.'

'How interesting.'

'I think you should mention it in your Christmas message, because a lot of your subjects are Mohammedans.'

The Queen remained cool. 'In so far as she can gibber, she gibbered,' recalls Day-Lewis. 'She couldn't say, "What absolute rubbish." In fact, she could hardly get a word in. Poets either dry up, or they don't stop talking. Graves has a very considerable brain, but his mixture is too rich. He's mad as a hatter, but brilliant.'

'Of course,' continued Graves to the Queen, 'I would never accept this medal from a politician.'

Thrilled, he exclaimed later, in a reference to the mystical nature of the Coronation service: 'The holy oil has taken for that girl. It worked with her all right.'

'It's very good for the Queen to meet a quite different sort of person now and again,' said Day-Lewis who succeeded John Masefield as Poet Laureate in Ordinary – 'God knows what that means, I've never dared ask.'

His job ranks immediately above the Bargemaster but below Keeper of the Jewel House in Royal Household hierarchy, and is one of the oddities that makes the English Monarchy such a remarkable institution. Cecil Day-Lewis, appointed in 1968 on the recommendation of Prime Minister Harold Wilson who once wanted the job himself, used to be a committed member of the Communist party and sold the *Daily Worker* on street corners – unusual qualifications for a job initiated by Queen Elizabeth I as a sort of Court Copywriter, obliged to compose lyrical jingles in praise of the Sovereign at least once a year and a few stanzas at regal crisis points such as deaths, marriages, births or illness.

With the mass media swooning delightedly at most royal events, the post is largely superfluous, and Day-Lewis told the Queen as much. 'I had lunch at the Palace, one of those with the riff-raff they have. She asked how I was getting on with the job. I said there's really no job. We had a jolly conversation about Ireland. She's not allowed to go there.'

Pay has remained the same for 300 years – £70 a year plus £27 in lieu of 126 gallons of sack and a cask of Canary wine, with the additional perk of being allowed burial in Westminster Abbey. The money is paid out of the Queen's salary by the Privy Purse office and taxed at source. Worried no doubt about the effect of spiralling costs on royal finance, John Masefield sent his poems to the Palace accompanied by a stamped, addressed envelope in anticipation of rejection. The present Laureate increases the meagre pay

88

by writing thrillers under the pseudonym Nicholas Blake.

His only obligation is to chair a committee that awards the Queen's Medal for Poetry. 'Old Masefield had the idea that the medal should be given to someone distinguished one year, and someone not well known the next. Well, they made some terrible mistakes, giving it to people who were never heard of again. The first thing I did was ask Tryon,[1] "Do you mind if I sack the committee?" I wrote them polite letters. The new committee meets once a year, instead of doing it by postal vote.

'Of course I never thought I'd get the job. Robert Graves was my bet because I thought it should go to the best British poet. I enjoy it. It's a feather in the cap, dammit, and I like trailing the coat, accepting a job people think I should refuse. To hell with what people like Christopher Logue think.

'I'm still very left wing, neither Monarchist, nor anti-Monarchist. One always felt the Monarchy was antiquated, but not an anachronism. There should be a word – not quite hypocrisy – for what it does or doesn't do. A lot of people aren't keen on it – particularly the young. Look at all the dressing up. Look at the judges in their dreadful clothes. I wouldn't stir an inch for the fancy dress stuff, but I can't stand people who automatically sneer. I don't think I've taken the bribe and sold out, gone from being wild red to died-in-the-blue Tory. If you live long enough, and have success in your profession, you find yourself sucked into the Establishment, whatever you do. It happens to anyone who lives to a decent age. Maybe my poetry's got much worse. I can't tell. All that one ever hopes for is that a few poems will survive a few years.'

His first few lines as Laureate, *Then and Now,* extolling a naïve British fit of patriotism called Backing Britain, is best forgotten, but it illustrates the saleability of anything that can be stamped 'Royal'.

[1]Brigadier Lord Tryon, Keeper of the Privy Purse.

THEN AND NOW
by the Poet Laureate C. Day-Lewis

Do you remember those mornings after the blitzes
When the living picked themselves up and went on living –
Living, not on the past, but with an exhilaration
Of purpose, a new neighbourliness of danger?

Such days are here again, Not the bansheeing
Of sirens and the beat of terrible wings
Approaching under a glassy moon. Your enemies
Are nearer home yet, nibbling at Britain's nerve.

Be as you were then, tough and gentle islanders –
Steel in the fibre, charity in the veins –
When few stood on their dignity or lines of demarcation,
And few sat back in the padded cells of profit.

Boiler-room, board-room, backroom boys, we all
Joined hearts to make a life-line through the storm.
No haggling about overtime when the heavy-rescue squads
Dug for dear life under the smouldering ruins.

The young cannot remember this. But they
Are graced with that old selflessness. They see
What's needed; they strip off dismay and dickering
Eager to rescue our dear life's buried promise.

To work then, islanders, as men and women
Members one of another, looking beyond
Mean rules and rivalries towards the dream you could
Make real, of glory, common wealth, and home.[2]

'An absolute stinker. The telephone kept going all the time
I was writing it. I often wonder, "Was that the last nail in
the coffin of the Backing Britain campaign?"'

The first, and only 'official' poem he wrote during the year
was for the Investiture, a ceremony that didn't inspire him

[2]Published in *Daily Mail*, 5 January, 1968.

too much, and to which he wasn't invited – not that he would have gone because he suffers from claustrophobia and hates crowds. He felt deep sympathy for Charles having to wear ridiculous garb and an abiding admiration for his intellect. 'Anyone who learns that bloody awful language, Welsh, well enough to make a speech, deserves our respect. I wrote the poem in longhand on parchment, and bunged it along in a taxi to Buckingham Palace with one of the packers from the publishers, and a note asking if the Queen would accept it for her library. He had to wait outside the gate because they were changing Guard when he arrived. He was very thrilled. One never knows if the Queen or Prince Charles read it. Afterwards, I was asked to write a poem for an American newspaper about the moon shot, but I couldn't feel it. I'd much rather knock something up about the Investiture, however idiotic. I told them to leave the moon for someone younger.

'I don't know if the job's a good thing, but it's easy to think of reasons why one should exist. Poetry is after all, a great English art. We are a philistine nation, so we produce good poets, because of the friction between them and society. I'm interested in what the job can do for poetry.

'I'm using it to write poems of occasional interest. Ordinary people should see that poetry is for them, not for other poets, which is a bore. I sold my National Library Week poem to the *Daily Mirror*[3] – not *The Times*. You get paid a darned sight better, for one thing. Anyway, the *Times Literary Supplement* wrote something nasty about me, so I thought, "Bugger *The Times*".

[3] 10 March, 1969.

GEORGE V
(b. 1865. 1910–1936)
m. QUEEN MARY

1.
Edward,
Duke of Windsor
EDWARD VIII
(abdicated 1936)
(1894–)
m. Mrs Wallis
Warfield Simpson
(1896–)

3.
Mary,
Princess Royal
(1897–1965)
m. 6th Earl of
Harewood
(1882–1947)

4.
Henry,
Duke of Gloucester
(1900–)
m. Lady Alice
Montagu-Douglas-
Scott
(1901–)

5.
George,
Duke of Kent
(1902–1942)
m. Princess
Marina of Greece
(1906–1968)

6.
John
(1905–1919)

7.
(Albert)
GEORGE VI
(b. 1895. 1936–1952)
m. Lady Elizabeth
Bowes-Lyon.
Queen Elizabeth
(1900–)

George,
Earl of Harewood
m. 1: Marion Stein
1949
(3 sons)
m. 2: Patricia
Tuckwell
(1929–)
(1 son)

Gerald
Lascelles
(1924–)
m. Angela
Dowding
(1919–)
(1 son)

William
(1941–)

Richard
(1944–)

Edward,
Duke of Kent
(1935–)
m. Katharine
Worsley 1961

Alexandra
(1936–)
m. Angus Ogilvy
1963

Michael
(1942–)

George
(1962–)

Helen
(1964–)

James
(1964–)

Marina
(1966–)

1.
ELIZABETH II
(b. 1926. 1952–)
m. Philip

2.
Margaret
(1930–)
m. Antony Armstrong-Jones,
1st Earl of Snowdon

Charles,
Prince of Wales
(1948–)

Anne
(1950–)

Andrew
(1960–)

Edward
(1964–)

David
Viscount Linley
(1961–)

Sarah
(1964–)

Royal Family Inc. - I

'As a nation, we have forsaken God for Elizabeth II, with Prince Philip as a latter-day John the Baptist,' *The Monarchy and its Future*, essay by William Hamilton, M.P. (Allen and Unwin, 1969), p. 66.

'The example of a united family life set by the Queen and her consort is a real contribution to the nation's morality.' Norman St. John Stevas, M.P. *Spectator*, 1968.

'My father was frightened of his mother; I was frightened of my mother; and I'm damned well going to see to it that my children are frightened of me.' George V.

'The long running show, *The Royal Family*, which has for the last thousand years been one of the most popular hits with the British public, has been "axed" it was revealed today. The show centres around the person of the Queen, a demure, upper-class housewife living mainly in London with her family.' *Private Eye*, 1969.

THE BRITISH MIDDLE CLASS have formed the royal family in their own image, and the family have been happy to comply. Solid, honest, suspicious of intellect, supporting the accepted and apparently correct virtues of duty, family and God. Ordinary enough not to offend, startling enough on occasions not to be dull, they nevertheless had a cardboard image at the beginning of the year. The fictions about their private life provided comforting titillation in Britain, and imaginative scandal throughout the rest of the world, demonstrating the endless appeal of the trivial.

93

Perhaps it is unfair to probe deeply behind the enormously successful façade that was being cleverly erected, to examine the reality behind the shifts in emphasis that were being encouraged – from elegant dowdiness to aggressive trendiness, from arrogance to humility; from the Queen to Princess Anne, from Prince Philip to Prince Charles. They didn't ask to be placed on the pedestal available because of genetic accident, nor do they enjoy the sometimes embarrassing adulation that accompanies them, and the interest they provoke. 'In her heart of hearts, the Queen probably wishes you weren't writing this book. None of our family likes publicity. I suppose I've been brutalized in a way,' said one relative, who also thought the Queen was an adequate substitute for God in a largely un-christian country.

In order to understand the institution, to assess its value and the pressures, it is necessary to know the attitudes of those involved. It is no longer acceptable to say simply: 'It works, therefore it's good.' Any institution that lapses into a period of largely apathetic acceptance, such as the British Monarchy, is in danger of being abused. On the day that an end to Nigeria's thirty-month war was announced,[1] and the newspapers were crammed with horrific pictures of emaciated children, what news came from the Queen? She had given a royal warrant to a Dutch ditch digger and, in the evening, played a merry joke on the King's Lynn fire brigade by initiating an alarm hoax that sent seventy men and ten fire engines rushing to Sandringham to spray the lawns. It was, of course, all good practice, and the royal children were delighted by the spectacle.

The minefield of bad taste between gossip and fact, the relevant and irrelevant, has to be trod hopefully, if reluctantly at times, when describing the reality of an institution that by its nature insists on massive injections of unreality.

How relevant, for example, are Prince Philip's finances as he swans round the world delivering homilies that are

[1] 12 January, 1970

given instant profundity by his position? Is it important to know the Queen's attitude to her Government's atavistic colonial twitches, such as sending London policemen to invade Anguilla? Should one describe the daily ritual of dog feeding, and other astonishing luxuries of Monarchy in the 1970s? Is Princess Margaret's attitude to motor-cycle escorts important? Snowdon's domestic set-up? Anne's toughness? Charles's ethereal softness? Should family feuds remain private, when they could affect a nation? Is it pitching it too high to say that the Greek and Roman empires collapsed when they became self-indulgent mockeries of their past, and we are giggling and bamboozling ourselves into the same situation? Daylight was let in upon the magic[2] during the year, but the spotlight was carefully directed. Numerous aspects of the Monarchy still remain hidden – or an illusion.

'I know as well, if not better than anyone here, that life in Britain is not wholly rational,' says Prince Philip.[3] In an age of package tour abortions, Biafra, and Vietnam, and when the whole basis of family life is being questioned, it is delightful to have as an object for national aspiration an uncomplicated husband and wife team with a nubile daughter, a serious son, two attractive reserves for the teeny bopper market, an obtuse uncle, and a wacky sister performing in a never-never land of flunkeys, equerries, and processions.

But the Queen is not simply a useful adjunct to the tourist trade.

During the years there were a number of important political decisions on which she advised the Prime Minister. She was not in favour of invading Anguilla, and reminded Harold Wilson there were two British frigates patrolling in the

[2]'Above all this our royalty is to be reverenced, and if you begin to poke about it you cannot reverence it. When there is a select committee on the Queen, the charm of royalty will be gone. In its mystery is its life. We must not let daylight in upon magic' – Walter Bagehot.
[3]Minerva Dinner, 26 November, 1968.

Caribbean which could easily prevent trouble.[4] But Wilson embarked upon 'Operation Sheepskin' and sent forty hand-picked London policemen and a force of Red Devil paratroopers to quell the 6,000 inhabitants of a thirty-four square mile island – to the amusement of the rest of the world. This was all done, of course, in the Queen's name.

The issues raised are of fundamental importance. It is not impossible in a few years time for the Queen to have a Prime Minister young enough to be her son. Her experience could be extremely helpful. It could be a hindrance. Either way it will be an important influence.

[4]Anguilla, colonized in 1650 had been 'federated' in 1967 by the British with the more wealthy islands of Nevis and St. Kitts. They resented the St. Kittian Prime Minister, Robert Bradshaw, and in May 1967 seceded from the Federation. In January 1969, they declared themselves independent of Britain. On 19 March, they were invaded.

Royal Family Inc. - II

'For the first few years of her reign, she was the subject of an adulation unparalleled since the days of Louis XIV, and calculated to turn much older heads than hers.' *The Modern British Monarchy* by Sir Charles Petrie, Eyre and Spottiswoode, 1961, p. 26.

'There can be no rational explanation for this sudden attack of reginaphilia, a disease that has become increasingly rare in Fleet Street, and is now almost entirely confined to the giddier pops.' *New Statesman*, 16 August, 1968, p. 200. 'Next week, profile of the Queen. Paul Johnson.' *New Statesman*, 16 August, 1968, p. 190.

FOR FIFTEEN MINUTES every morning, while the Queen breakfasts, at any of her homes, Pipe Major Andrew Pitkeathly of the Argyll and Sutherland Highlanders marches outside the dining-room window playing his bagpipes. It is a sound that inspires no apathy. Just delight or disgust. Prince Philip wanted to curtail the tradition, begun by Queen Victoria, but it is one of the few domestic differences he has lost.

The Queen, after reading *Sporting Life* and other newspapers, goes to her study on the first floor of Buckingham Palace, often taking the *Daily Telegraph* in order to finish the crossword puzzle, of which she is an avid fan – so much so that she was engrossed in it minutes before she opened Canada's Parliament one year. She works at a cluttered desk formerly used by her mother, Queen Elizabeth, and grandmother, the late Queen Mary.

As the country's top Civil Servant, for that, stripped of

97

chi-chi, is an important aspect of her job, the Queen has innumerable papers to sign. Her private secretary, Sir Michael Adeane, bows his head as he enters with a trayful, and explains the background to some of them. Many will be from the Home Secretary, the Queen's constitutional link with the public, advising her on the Royal Prerogative of mercy, orders of precedence, ecclesiastical matters, appointments such as Inspectors of Fire Services, and decrees appointing Councillors of State. The Queen signs at the top. He counter-signs at the bottom, in order to give effect to the command. 'I suppose each week the Queen and I between us sign twenty of these orders,' says James Callaghan.[1] 'They're written in olde English, but I don't think that makes any difference.' Possibly the whole bureaucratic parchment writing industry would crumble if the language was made intelligible.

Constitutional theories confuse the reality. The Queen, sixty-third British Monarch in a line going back one thousand years, inheritor of thirteen thrones, head of a Common-wealth comprising nearly a quarter of the world's popula-tion, forty-second Monarch since William the Conqueror (Appendix), finds herself in an advisory and symbolic capa-city. When a crisis affects the country, her name is invoked, and during a financial panic of December 1968, some city dealers became so distraught as to believe rumours that she had abdicated.

In a small way, this is indicative of the impression the Queen has made on the country. Previous Monarchs have tried to leave some indelible print on the nation, and have made the job suit their personality. The Queen, more than anything else, has allowed the job to shape her and, therefore, the Elizabethan Age, so stirringly trumpeted when she ascen-ded the throne in 1952[2] has not been fulfilled. It was, anyway, dewy-eyed wishful thinking, and the cause of Monarchy was best served by a reserved woman. 'God's tooth, what a

[1]Appointed Home Secretary, November 1967.
[2]George VI died on 6 February, 1952.

narrow squeak Margaret wasn't the elder daughter. That would have been a catastrophe. I have no particular regard for her at all. How long would it have lasted if Snowdon had been consort? Dreadful, dreadful,' said a member of the royal family.

Suppose, too, a man had ascended the throne. If he was intelligent, he could not have contorted himself into the incredible poses demanded of a British Monarch in the seventies. Edward VIII couldn't do it in the thirties, but the Monarchy survived, eclectic, astute, and so aware of public opinion that George VI changed his name from Albert to encourage feelings of continuity with his father. 'A stroke of genius,' said one of the family.

The Queen and Prince Philip have been an admirable duo, popularizing the Monarchy, changing its appearance, exquisitely justifying their nicknames, Brenda and Keith.

But to pretend that the Queen is a 'normal' woman, or even wants to be, is absurd, in spite of the headscarf and tweed upper-middle-class image represented by Badminton and her frenetic Windsor, Ascot, Balmoral ambiance; in spite of the fact that she can be referred to publicly as 'a middle-aged housewife with a *pied-à-terre* in town and a castle in the suburbs';[3] in spite of her seamed stockings, 'sensible' clothes, and ability to let down the children's clothes, rather than buy new ones.

Basically, she enjoys the private life of the privileged Victorian upper class, leavened with a dry sense of humour ignored by her critics. She is particularly good at mimicking the more outrageous colonial administrator, and she has an attractive self-mockery. A young man, obviously an avid reader of Court Circulars, used to position himself outside the gates at Buckingham Palace on every occasion the Queen was due to leave for a public engagement. One of the ladies-in-waiting made a slightly derogatory comment.

[3]Oxford Union debate, on 8 May, 1969, during a discussion on, 'the monarchy should be sacked, Buckingham Palace given to the homeless, and the corgies put to productive work.'

'You are talking,' said the Queen, 'about my only loyal subject.'

Her private life is protected, as it should be, by a discretion that shames any other aspect of British public life. It is possible to sit for hours talking to one of her friends who will suddenly lean over conspiratorially as if to divulge the most intimate scandal or, at very least, a soupçon of criticism that will reveal a glimpse of her true character. You wait, giddy with anticipation. 'Don't quote me.' The suspense is unbearable. No, no, go on. 'Please don't quote me. She is' – the words come slowly, pedantically – 'an expert horsewoman, you know. And she's very interested in the breeding side. Racing is her only hobby, other than labradors.'

Surprise, surprise.

Can the Queen really be so dull that all she inspires is flabby praise, and negative enthusiasm? 'It's a hell of a job, but she does it superbly.' The answer is a guarded No.

There are two distinct sides to her character: the one seen on public occasions, and controlled on television films (see 'Image and Reality', page 199). And the other, which is sure of its place in the world, yet has little interest in the subtleties of power or the cynicism of high office; a family woman, yet retaining a lingering dislike of her uncle because she feels her father died prematurely as a result of unexpected strain; a strong enough aura to terrify experienced politicians, yet lonely enough to choose as confidante a woman from a totally different background (see page 153); a cosmopolitan woman with simple tastes, unsophisticated enough to appoint a homeopath,[4] Dr Grace Blackie, as Court physician.

She is perhaps the last Monarch in Western civilization

[4]Homeopathy, sometimes considered a 'cult' or fringe branch of medicine is based on the theory of an eighteenth-century German physician, Dr Samuel Hahnemann, that disease should be treated by small quantities of drugs that produce, rather than relieve, the symptoms: nettles to treat burns, spider venom for angina, mistletoe for cancer. It has been popular with the royal family since Queen Victoria.

to hold a residual belief in the inviolability of her position. She was complaining once about the rudeness of her grandfather, George V. A listener said he admired people who spoke their mind. 'It's refreshing, and you can always be rude back.'

'Not to the King. You can't be rude to the King.'

'There is,' says one of her close former staff, 'an automatic reflex. She is terribly vulnerable. She is top of the ant heap. I was amazed how people gravitate around it. The English are an astonishing race. How can they ever compete in the world, when they love living in the past so much?'

The Queen has inherited from her mother the impervious public façade, although she doesn't feel it necessary to smile graciously so often, or retain quite the same quality of etiolated sanctity. Visiting a factory, the Queen Mother was shown the spot where nineteen workmen had been killed by a bomb. 'Poor things,' she said, and walked on.

The Queen herself finds the spontaneous gesture less easy than Margaret, who tends to whoop when pleasantly surprised. 'She looks a bit miserable at times because she's been trained to resist emotion of any kind, like a Grenadier Guardsman,' says a close friend. 'She throws all her affection into her dogs, but she can't do it with human beings because of her upbringing. She's terribly proud of the necessary, but slightly unfeminine, abilities she's mastered. She's the only woman I know who can salute properly, for instance.'

But it is in the domestic details that the Queen differs so much from her subjects, and yet appears to be the same. Everyone likes to see their young children before they go to bed. Not everyone has to ask the Prime Minister to come round half an hour later, at 6.30 p.m., for his weekly audience, so she can do so.

Not everyone needs to take a staff of fourteen when spending the week-end at their country home, in this case Windsor

Castle. Not everyone has a uniformed police sergeant sitting outside her bedroom all night, or has monogrammed butter pats for breakfast.

Most people feed their dogs. Not everyone feeds corgis (Appendix) with elegant ritual. Each evening, at about five o'clock, a footman brings to her sitting-room a tray of three dishes and several bowls. The dishes contain, separately, cooked meat, dog biscuit, and gravy. A white plastic sheet is placed on the carpet. With a silver fork and spoon, the Queen dishes out portions of the food and gives it to the dogs. 'Those bloody animals,' says a friend, with whom the Queen stays. 'I hate them.'

She doesn't need a dog licence, as she wasn't mentioned in the Act. Neither does she need to pass a driving test,[5] and she is not named in the Traffic Act 1960, or in the Motor Vehicle Driving Licence Regulations 1956. She cannot be sued in court, nor can she give evidence – because it is her court.

Not every woman is technically a man in various parts of the country. The Queen is. In Lancashire, she is the Duke of Lancaster because Queen Victoria considered it proper for the holder to be called a Duke, whether man or woman. In the Isle of Man she should be toasted 'The Queen, Lord of Man'. In the Channel Islands, she should be known as the Duke of Normandy.

Not everyone can gamble freely in their own home. The Queen can:

An Act for the more effectual preventing of excessive and deceitful Gaming:

'Nothing in this Act shall extend to prevent or hinder any person from gaming or playing at any of the games in this or any of the said former Acts mentioned, within any of His Majesty's royal palaces when His Majesty, his heirs, or successors shall there reside.'[6]

[5]Halsbury's *Laws of England*, third edition, volume VIII, para, 536.
[6]Act 12, George II, Chapter 28, Statutes Revised, Volume I, p. 571.

She does not take advantage of this privilege. Her tastes are simple and safe: Handel's 'Water Music', biography, Agatha Christie, and historical novels. She speaks fluent French, but no other language. Her favourite hobby, fortuitously, is acting, and house guests indulge in The Game, a sort of charades race. Two teams sit at opposite ends of the room. In the middle is a man with a list of novel titles, play names, or makeshift phrases. Players take turns to be told a title, the subject of which they have to perform until one of their team, sitting in a circle, guesses the name. Winner is the first team to finish the list. 'I looked forward to it with total horror,' recalls one friend. 'Imagine making a fool of yourself in front of the Queen and Prince Philip. In the event, it was one of the most enjoyable evenings I have spent.'

When she and Prince Philip stay with friends, they take a staff of three – detective, valet, and 'Bobo' MacDonald. Every afternoon a red box is brought from the Palace, and the Queen works on State papers for about an hour and a half, usually from six until seven-thirty.

'When the telephone rings over the week-end, it is often bad news of the death of some important person or distant relative,' says Lord Porchester, who is frequently host to the Queen at his beautiful William Kent bungalow in Hampshire. 'If it is State business, the private secretary can speak to the Queen in her room on a scrambled line.'

He and his American wife, Jean, are friendly, lively, and unpompous. Apart from extensive farming interests, forty-six-year-old Lord Porchester has been involved in local government for most of his life. He arranged for Prince Philip to sit in on a regular planning committee meeting of Hampshire County Council, and then spent a day travelling round the countryside showing him the reality of previous decisions that had been taken.

'The Queen is a wonderful person who enjoys her brief visits with friends, away from State problems when she can see her studs and look at her race horses,' he says.

103

'But there is far more than that. I have heard her give such a breathtaking dissertation on how she sees the future of the Commonwealth. I only wish people could hear her speak on such important issues more often, and in an unrehearsed way.'

The Queen does not like change. Neither does Prince Charles. This is understandable, but the limitations imposed upon them paradoxically mock the institution. The Queen is not a bird in a gilded cage, more a symbolic offering to suburban fantasy. She is always belle of the ball, always cheered, always over-praised. The virtually uncritical acceptance from all those she meets is perhaps one of the most potent forms of human degradation.

So what does she do when she is alone, and Prince Philip is on one of his frequent safaris abroad? She watches television a lot, likes *Dad's Army* and Dudley Moore.

'I mean, can you imagine her? She's often alone in that house, that huge house, Buckingham Palace, with no one to talk to, and she has a meal on a tray in front of the television,' says a friend.

'It's a very lonely life.'

Royal Family Inc. - III

'One of the outstanding monarchical triumphs since the Second World War has been achieved in Greece, and that is not the least of the reasons why Great Britain has cause to rejoice that the Queen's consort is a Greek Prince.' Sir Charles Petrie, *The Modern British Monarchy*, Eyre and Spottiswoode, 1961, p. 218.

King Constantine and his family fled in a private plane from Greece and arrived at Rome airport at five o'clock in the morning of 14 December, 1967. They have been in exile ever since.

NO MEMBER OF THE BRITISH, or any other, royal family appears in so many guises throughout the year as Prince Philip, Monarchy's answer to the modern world. Wild life expert, big game hunter, businessman manqué, sportsman, youth leader, sailor, pilot, solicitous escort to the extraordinary lacklustre regiment of Presidents' wives, Admiral, Air Marshal, Colonel in Chief. He has the charisma of a Prince: tough-looking face, hard mouth, penetrating eyes, a voice pitched between arrogance and a certain peevish querulousness, heart-throb to the provinces, wise-cracking his way round the globe, peddling bright hopes and salutary advice. A man attractive to women, envied by men, a bit vicious on the polo field, autocratic, something of a ham actor – and in the red. He lives a good life, but he has to pay for it, and he has never been rich.

Far from having nearly all his annual £40,000 allowance from the Government written off as tax-free expenses,

Prince Philip is only allowed between fifty and sixty per cent by the Inland Revenue. The rest is taxed, and he has to pay his own staff: chief policy adviser and his treasurer for ten years, Rear Admiral Sir Christopher Bonham Carter, aged sixty-two; private secretary James Orr, a fifty-two-year-old bachelor educated at Harrow, Gordonstoun and Sandhurst, a veteran of thirteen tough years that could have shattered a less stolid man; six officials, clerks and secretaries, and two pages. An equerry is supplied by the Army, and a detective by Scotland Yard. Assuming he keeps £7,500 from the taxed £20,000 his net income would be £27,500 – puny by some business standards, and certainly not excessive for his work and responsibility. He shares his wife's perks, though (see 'The Cost').

All his helpers are adept at smoothing troubles. A detective recalls calming an irate Dutch chauffeur who had listened to Philip's wry comments on the drive from Amsterdam airport. 'What a po-faced lot these Dutch are. Look at them.' On more important occasions, the Queen is particularly good at compensating with her charm for his public moods.

It is difficult for any man to pursue his wife's inherited mystique through life, particularly when they are related (Appendix), and more and more Prince Philip seems irritable with the strain. He has done an immense amount for the Monarchy, popularizing it in much the same way as Prince Albert, but the tension of repeatedly meeting sycophantic dead-heads is beginning to tell. The flippant comments are less funny. The hectoring is less excusable. Outbursts against reporters are drearily repetitive, and his flair for self-humiliation – such as becoming involved in a public row over the quality of Tom Jones's singing – is undiminished but less endearing with age. At forty-eight, with Prince Charles now becoming the more important male member of the family, he is surely not doomed to an increasingly restless repetition of the last few years, the ubiquitous chanting of interestingly wrapped truisms, and royal circus parades. It is a sad prospect, whose reality can be glimpsed briefly at the perennial Garter ceremony, a noble pantomime performed each June[1] for the benefit of tourists – mainly from Australia and Germany – whose double-decker coaches clog the streets outside Windsor Castle.

This, 'the most noble and amiable company of St George named the Garter' is the oldest order of Christian chivalry in Britain, dating from 23 April, 1349, when Joan, Countess of Salisbury, was dancing with King Edward III and seductively allowed her blue garter to slip from her thigh to the floor. Edward, gallantly no doubt, picked it up and, noticing his grinning courtiers, said: 'Honi soit qui mal y pense – Shame on him who thinks evil of it.'

The British, with an innate grasp of sanctified show-business, have turned this casual flirtation into a ceremony that combines historical relic with contemporary patriotism, and draws a crowd of unflinching rectitude. They stand, some in morning dress, while the Household Cavalry, dismounted and with drawn swords, line the route to St George's Chapel.

First, though, before lunch, there is a private ceremony of praying and oath-taking in the Throne Room of Windsor Castle where the Queen invests the knights elect by buckling the blue and gold garter on their left leg.

'To the honour of God Omnipotent, and in Memorial of the Blessed Martyr, Saint George, tie about thy leg, for thy Renown, this Most Noble Garter,' says the Prelate, the Bishop of Winchester. 'Wear it as the symbol of the Most Illustrious Order never to be forgotten or laid aside, that hereby thou mayest be admonished to be courageous, and having undertaken a just war, into which thou shalt be engaged, thou mayest stand firm, valiantly fight, courageously and successfully conquer.'

Then, with more oath-taking and admonitions, the Queen

[1]The one referred to here is 16 June, 1969.

puts the riband and star on the knight elect, and places the mantle and collar over his shoulders. The newly-invested knight then takes his oath:

'You being chosen to be of the Honourable Company of the Most Noble Order of the Garter, shall promise and swear, by the Holy Evangelists, by you here touched, that wittingly or willingly you shall not break any Statutes of the Said Order, or any Article in them contained (except in such from which you have received a Dispensation from The Sovereign), the same being agreeable, and not repugnant to the Laws of Almighty God, and the Laws of this Realm, as farforth as to you belongeth and appertaineth, so God help you, and His Holy Word.'

Originally, there were twenty-five knights, including the King, but in 1831 this was expanded to allow the Prince of Wales and other members of the British and foreign royal families to join in.

After lunch, dressed in blue velvet and plumed hats, with the large blue Garter insignia on their left breast, they process forward, preceded by the Military Knights of Windsor (looking solemn as befits their original duty, which was to pray by proxy for the knights) and various heralds in motley tabards. Prince Charles, standing on the right of his ever-beaming grandmother, looks sheepish, pink-cheeked with embarrassment. It is a dreadful imposition for an adequately intelligent twenty-year-old. Lord Mountbatten gives a confident wave to the crowd, who return his salutation by whispered reverences. 'That's him, did you see him on the telly the other evening?' Lord Avon smiles. The Duke of Norfolk looks straight ahead except for a few seconds when his eyes turn slowly to look at the audience. Then another clutch of elderly gentlemen, made important and signifi-cant by their clothes, with expressions of steadfast sincerity in no way dampened by the drizzle. And now, here come the Queen and Prince Philip – the latter smiling in a resigned way. It is a hell of a bore for him but, he thinks, the tourists enjoy it, and life would be terribly dull without a bit of a show. It only lasts about half an hour anyway.

'On these occasions,' said a former equerry. 'I actually found myself thinking, 'Maybe I should stand on my head because everyone would think it's part of the act. A lot of them say they don't believe in it, that it's just fun and part of the heritage. But you have to believe in the ceremony for its own sake, otherwise you couldn't do it.'

Prince Philip's escape has been studying wild life, bird watching, shooting. Occasionally, with Prince Charles, he travels to Wood Farm, former home of a local G.P., on the 20,000 acre Sandringham estate for a peaceful week-end. A woman in the next cottage 'does' for them, and they massacre the birds with enthusiasm and expertise. In ten years, about 72,000 pheasant have been shot (8,000 in the 1968–9 season, a mere 6,500 during 1969–70), and are astutely marketed by Prince Philip for 36s. 6d. a brace. Cruel?

'Pesticides, insecticides, poison and pollution have destroyed more life than man has ever taken, and by affecting the capacity to breed and by destructive interference in the food chain, whole populations of species are being exterminated.

'What man as a hunter has failed to do in millions of years, man as a businessman and scientist is achieving in a couple of generations, and with every general approval. We seem to exist with a rather strange morality in this country. Everything which is pleasant must of necessity be sinful, and everything that is done for money – that is professionally – cannot possibly be enjoyable,'[2] says Philip.

He makes films for the World Wildlife Fund, of which he is an international trustee, and some of his trips abroad are at their expense. His American television debut sponsored by Quaker Oats, took place in January 1969 in a film about the Galapagos Islands, *The Enchanted Isles*.[3] The *New*

[2]Wildfowlers' Association, diamond jubilee dinner, 9 July, 1968.
[3]Made by Anglia Television and shown in Britain in December 1967.

York Times said his interest in science was 'scant justification for such a dull and tawdry undertaking'.

Indeed, the more Prince Philip experiences the real world, as opposed to lecturing about it, the more he seems disgruntled about his position. Can it be true, as he said himself[4] that his only tangible contribution to British life has been to improve the rear lights on lorries? At times, maybe, he wishes he had stayed in the Navy, and a fifth of the 382 organizations he patronizes are connected with the sea. There would, at least, have been far fewer controls.

'Over everything you try to do there is a control or sanction. I know that in Scotland, we had to get planning permission to block up a fireplace in a cottage . . . Really, it's unbelievable.

'There are controls saying you can't build a woodshed nearer than twenty-five feet to the back door of a cottage. If you ran a ship on the book of rules the whole time, with penalties and God knows what, you'd soon come unstuck.

'Now everybody is a yes-man. They say, "We'd better not blot our copy books because we won't get promoted, and what will the wife say? . . ." This is ridiculous. But this is the situation which occurs in industry.'[5]

When asked to take part in the debate on the Monarchy at Oxford University, he declined, but wrote: 'One of the peculiarities of this home of democracy and free speech is that there is a convention that members of the royal family are expected to refrain from practising free speech on matters loosely termed political. The most assiduous guardians of this conversation are members of the House of Commons. I presume this is in case any of us could be quite so profoundly stupid as to say something with which members might disagree.'

He dislikes the world of pre-packed safety and easy conformity, yet what he says has no real effect because everyone knows his position allows little control even over his own

[4]*Face The Press*, Tyne-Tees Television, 20 March, 1968.
[5]Interviewed in *The Director*, March 1969.

destiny. Not even his children bear his adoptive surname and, in spite of discreet pressure by members of his family, he will have to wait for great grandsons before they are allowed to be half-way his heirs: Mountbatten-Windsor.[6] Willing to learn, to advise, to warn, to watch, enthusiastic, he is like a eunuch, prevented totally from trying to prove what he thinks he knows. 'I exercise no power,' he says, when compared to Machiavelli's Prince, who could be both loved and respected.[7]

Talking to a hostile audience, he is at his best – and worst. At worst, he is unnecessarily rude. He left a lunch table rather than prolong a conversation with a businessman (later to become a distant relative, by marriage) about the niggardliness of his firm's charity donations. At least it had an effect, though. The firm contributed more in future.

During the year, there were several occasions when he was at his best, mostly with students. At Edinburgh University,[8] of which he is Chancellor, he was constantly heckled during a question and answer session.

'This generation is the first to have no knowledge of what life was like before the mechanical age. All the institutions we have were developed in the pre-mechanical age . . .'

'Like the Monarchy,' yelled one student.

Someone asked a convoluted question on procedure.

'Shut up, and grow up,' said Philip angrily. He thought they were a bunch of bores, but didn't dare say so for fear of being called a 'Blimp'. Their main worry was the discussion might be controlled.

'Do you think I would come to this meeting assuming you would not be free to discuss things?' said Philip. 'We

[6]On 9 April, 1952, by an Order in Council, the Queen announced that her descendants, other than female descendants who marry, would be called Windsor – not Mountbatten. In 1960, she said that certain of her descendants would bear the name Mountbatten-Windsor.

[7]Anglo-Chilean lunch, 24 July, 1968.

[8]23 May, 1969.

III

may be incompetent, but we're not dishonest. I know about freedom of speech because I get kicked in the teeth often enough for saying things. I am told I damned well ought not to say them. So why should I tell you what to say? But freedom is not licence. You can destroy freedom as much by misusing it, and making a mockery of it, as you can by repression.'

He is always willing to reply to critics, sometimes seems to seek them out where they don't exist, and a lot of the time his real personality is protected by officials anxious to cocoon him in gift-wrapped platitudes. It is the exasperation this inspires that is responsible for his more outrageous statements, and also provokes him into unnecessary argument. The most unlikely moments provide his protectors with palpitations.

During a cocktail party at Lancaster House in aid of a Human Rights Year campaign,[9] he was waylaid by a student who complained that such functions didn't help anyone. The organizer tried to move Philip along, but he turned to speak.

'You don't like the system because you're not part of it, yet.'

'And I never will be.'

'That's being a dropout.' Philip wagged his finger, and walked on, smiling. He often seems curiously at a loss to understand the most simple arguments, either because he is temperamental and doesn't want to understand, or because he genuinely doesn't. 'You've got to remember, the fundamental thing about Philip is that he's a philistine at heart,' says someone with whom he has spoken on many occasions.

Indeed his vision of the future is not that of an imaginative man. Talking about the American moon shots, before the event, he said: 'It seems to me that it's the best way of wasting money that I know of. I don't think investments on the moon pay a very high dividend.'[10]

He is not too good at protecting himself from the sudden low blow – but again this is hidden, and the reality appears

[9] 18 December, 1968.
[10] São Paulo Press Conference, 6 November, 1968.

smooth. During an interview for Tyne-Tees Television,[11] the general line had been agreed but not specific questions. One interviewer asked his reaction if one of the children wanted to marry a coloured person. He hummed, hawed, said it was a difficult thing to answer and rambled at some length. After the broadcast the master copy was locked in a safe, employees sworn to secrecy, and the question and answer cut from the actual transmission.

He is himself an immigrant, as he often says. Although he considers himself a European, he doesn't think there will be a united Europe in his lifetime. He is too aware of the sophisticated bitchiness between nations. Discussing Queen Frederika, mother of King Constantine, and a cousin of Philip's, someone commenting on her ability to be strong minded, added, 'but of course, she is German.'

'Prussian,' said Philip. That was the end of the conversation.

His restlessness stems from his upbringing, and his stubbornness from his mother, Princess Andrew, who died in December 1969 at Buckingham Palace where she had stayed – bedridden for most of the time – since the Greek royal family was exiled at the end of 1967. She got on well with the Queen. Princess Andrew, eldest sister of Lord Mountbatten, had very definite ideas of her own. In 1949, she founded a monastic order, the Christian Sisterhood of Martha and Mary, became its life president, and went everywhere in a grey nun's habit. She overcame deafness by formidable self-instruction in lip reading, and Philip has inherited her powerful character. 'Very much the mother of the son,' says a friend.

She married Prince Andrew of Greece, Philip's father, when she was eighteen. He was twenty. A year after Philip was born at Corfu on 10 June, 1921, the Greek Monarchy was overthrown, as it was frequently, and the family was exiled. Prince Andrew was saved from being executed with three ex-premiers, two former ministers, and the

[11] *Face The Press*, 20 March, 1968.

commander-in-chief of the Army by direct intervention of King George V.[12] He went to live in Paris where he died, virtually stateless and with very little money, on 3 December, 1944, aged sixty-two. His wife ran an embroidery and jewellery boutique for some time.

Philip's parents decided they didn't want their only son (there were four daughters) brought up in the maelstrom of coups and double-cross endemic to Greek politics, so he was sent to Cheam prep school for four years. Various relatives looked after him, but mainly the second Marquess of Milford Haven. When he died in 1938 the younger brother, Lord Mountbatten, assumed responsibility and has always had an influence on the royal family – although not, perhaps, so much as he would like to think.

After Cheam, Philip went to Salem, in Germany, for three terms in 1934, where, being a foreigner, he was not forced to give the Nazi salute. When the school's founder, Kurt Hahn, moved to Gordonstoun, Morayshire, Philip followed. Hahn wrote: 'Prince Philip is a born leader, but will need the exacting demands of a great service to do justice to himself. His best is outstanding – his second best is not good enough. Prince Philip will make his mark in any profession where he will have to prove himself in a full trial of strength. His gifts would run to waste if he was soon condemned to lead a life where neither superior officers, nor the routine of the day forced him to tap his hidden resources.'

Increasingly, and ironically, this prophecy is being fulfilled. He cannot win his battles against routine – the obligatory conversations with dreary local dignitaries – as he learnt early in his career when Lord Derby was showing him round the Liverpool docks. They were leaving to return to Lord Derby's house. 'Well, that's it. That's the finish, is it?' said Prince Philip.

Could he stop one minute at the dock gates to meet the mayors of Bootle and Crosby?

[12]*King George VI*, by John Wheeler-Bennett, Macmillan 1958, p. 747.

'I haven't come here to see your bloody mayors. I came to meet the dockers.'

He was persuaded that this was part of the system, and later Lord Derby explained: 'I must tell you that one of your bloody mayors was a docker, and the other works on the railways. The people here would have been very upset if you hadn't met them.'

Because he is not allowed to involve himself in politics, he is sometimes forced into ludicrous and humiliating situations. What can you ask a man who is forbidden by protocol to discuss specific issues of importance? 'Are you still wearing your polka-dot underwear?' said a reporter at Dallas airport during his Variety Club fund-raising tour.

'I'll wear almost anything, providing it fits.'

His speeches, practised on a tape recorder in his study, are becoming less stimulating, hardly surprising as during the year he made fifty (Appendix). Even that was well below the previous year's total of seventy-six. Often, they begin in the same mock-humble way: 'Mr Chairman, I appreciate that it is customary for the chairman on occasions like this to make some kind remarks about the chief guest and to give him a welcome, but today you have gone well beyond the call of duty' – to the British Chilean Chamber of Commerce on 13 November, 1968. Thirteen days later, in London at the Minerva Dinner, he was saying: 'Mr President, I realize, of course, that chairmen of dinners such as this are expected to say something nice about the chief guest, but, Mr Chairman, I hope you will forgive me if I say that on this occasion you have applied the gilding a bit too lavishly.'

Often, too, he discusses his *bête noire* University education: 'University is not a mystical and exclusive fraternity which automatically confers some form of privileges on its members. Perhaps the most important point is that for the people who go there, it is a beginning and not an end in itself.'[13]

[13]Westward Television, October 1968.

And: 'One of the major difficulties produced by an obsession with "paper qualifications" is that they have tended to create a sort of academic hierarchy within professions and vocations. While the qualifications may be valuable in terms of scholarship, they qualify for very little else.'[14]

He is proud of his bluff approach to life, suspicious of intellect, and often sounds like a scoutmaster out of his depth, a bit 'wizard prang' diced with the easy excesses of suburban prejudice. 'I'm one of those stupid bums who never went to university, and a fat lot of harm it's done me.'

Not every naval cadet marries a future Queen.

'I am not quite the right person to be addressing the British Trade Council in Austria. I don't know anything about trade at first hand and I know even less about Austria from personal experience. The trouble about trade is that it has become involved in economics.'[15]

Perhaps trade, like Monarchy, should operate on the old pals' network?

Philip is, of course, at his best in the jock-strap-scented atmosphere of boys' clubs, enmeshed in a sort of Gordonstoun rejuvenescence. Each year, he spends a night visiting London boys' clubs – he has visited sixty altogether – informally and with great enthusiasm, joining the 'in' jokes about organizers, listening to long, amusing speeches by loquacious local characters, and then getting up to reply, simply: 'Thank you for inviting me to this revivalist meeting. I did have a proper speech, but I don't think I can add anything. I mean, I'm all for having a party.'

His interest in youth (he is godfather to twenty-five children aged from twenty-eight to fifteen years old) has a tangible outlet in the Duke of Edinburgh's Award scheme,[16] an attempt to encourage leisure activities amongst young

[14]Royal Society meeting, London, 15 May, 1969.
[15]Speech to British Trade Council, Vienna, 7 May, 1969.
[16]Started in 1956. 130,000 people a year take part, and 20,000 reached 'gold' standard in the first thirteen years.

people that seems slightly square in spite of attempts to enliven it. Inevitably, as anything connected with royalty, it is accused of being a 'social bandwagon', and the National Association of Youth Clubs have introduced their own similar venture.

Prince Philip's interest is not merely confined to the clean living, essentially extrovert award winners. During the year, he visited a Borstal in Scotland and a drug addiction centre in Chelsea[17] – a more hazardous outing than might have been expected. As he was leaving a charlady rushed up and kissed him. 'Ooooh,' said Mrs Eileen Barton. 'It's not many women who actually get to kiss the Duke.'

The film star image pursues him remorselessly: American fashion writers vote him best-dressed man of the year – ahead of dress designers, public relations men, couturiers, photographers and other stalwarts of the trendy scene. He wins the Greyhound Derby with an anonymously donated greyhound[18] gives the 'V' sign to reporters from the turret of a Chieftain tank[19] and, perhaps in desperation, suggests marching on Downing Street.[20]

What else can he do?

'I'm self-employed,' he says. 'I try and react to what I suppose people expect. In addition, I feel that I may have a position. Whatever influence I have I want to use for the benefit of the country. Needless to say, there are some ways that I'm invited not to.'[21]

Public opinion polls have shown him to be the country's most popular candidate for President,[22] or Dictator, ahead

[17] July 1969.
[18] 22 June, 1968.
[19] March 1969.
[20] 28 November, 1968. To Salford University students he said: 'If anyone would like to perhaps we could go in academic dress to Downing Street which might liven things up a bit.'
[21] *Face The Press*, Tyne-Tees Television, 20 March, 1968.
[22] Gallup Poll published in the *Observer*, March 1968, gave him between 13 and 16 per cent of the votes – more than any other candidate.

of Enoch Powell, Harold Wilson, and the Queen.[23] An over-ambitious suggestion, perhaps. But there is no reason why he should not have executive responsibility in a nationalized industry. Embarrassing if he failed, but it would be far more satisfactory than many of the engagements he was to fulfil during the year. They could hardly 'tap his hidden resources'.

[23]A Gallup Poll survey published in the *Daily Telegraph* Magazine on 26 September, 1969, asked people who would be a good dictator and who would be the best. Results:

	A Good Dictator	The Best Dictator
The Duke of Edinburgh	32%	21%
Enoch Powell	29	16
Harold Wilson	14	7
David Frost	12	5
Barbara Castle	11	4
Frank Cousins	10	3
Edward Heath	9	4
The Queen	8	4

Royal Family Inc. - IV

'For sixteen years the Crown has been worn by one who has not an undivided right to it. Our Princess Margaret has been unjustly deprived of her rights. Let her now ascend the throne and reign in sororal amity with our present Sovereign.' *Eton College Chronicle*, October 1968.

'Princess Margaret? ★★★★★ !!!!!! – and don't for heaven's sake quote me.' One of the royal family, 1969.

LIKE ANY OTHER GROUP, the royal family suffers from competing vanities. These unite temporarily when discussing Princess Margaret and her husband, Lord Snowdon. They are, by general consent, the black sheep, although it can be said they have interested a fringe intellectual and artistic circle in the Monarchy. Alternatively, they have been conned by the jaded hipsterism of London pseudo-life. Margaret – kaftanesque, talking French to Brigitte Bardot, attending a Save The Rave charity concert, being offered a job by Count Basie after watching him perform at the Aldeburgh Festival, or hearing a poem recited by comedian Spike Milligan to Peter Sellers with whom she was visiting a Soho jazz club: 'Wherever you are, wherever you be, please take your hand off the Princess's knee.' Snowdon – fast becoming an adjective on his own. Both forty during 1970, but looking younger, occasionally.

They are the most interesting royals because some sort of reality slinks out about them now and again. Her faults are paraded publicly, exaggerated privately, and fuelled by an unfortunate ability to hire the wrong people. Her footmen change sex,[1] her butlers turn spiteful. 'I was mortified by the strange standards imposed upon me,' twittered Thomas Cronin after leaving.[2] 'For the sake of the royal family, I must speak.' Even a biographer changes sex and marries a Negro butler.[3] Endless rumours circulate about Tony and Meg, setting the cocktail party circuits of the world alive – if anyone is still interested. When is Tony going to leave? Or vice versa? Whose car was parked outside Kensington Palace, and why? Why? Where? What? How? When? God, is *that* true? I tell you, she was *seen*.

They are, in fact, a middle-aged married couple whose previous affairs have been widely and inaccurately enough publicized to give a credence to any supposition. They are no more nor less happy than many others.

All the clichés of women's magazines tumble into Margaret's make-believe character and find their truth – in what? She has an exaggerated past, far more glamorous and melancholy than the reality, which is that she fell for one of her father's few eligible staff members who was on the rebound from a difficult marriage. Peter Townsend, a man of gentle charm, who now lives in Paris as the European manager of a public relations firm, was King George VI's equerry for eight years, and the Queen's for a year before being shunted to Brussels as air attaché in 1953 at the end of his over-dramatized relationship with Princess Margaret. He probably would not have married her but the reason given for his unsuitability – his previous marriage – remains an interesting example of the part relativity plays in royal propriety. Three years before Townsend was 'exiled' to Brussels, the Queen and Princess Margaret attended a reception and lunch at

[1]David Payne, a former footman at Clarence House, underwent a series of operations in Cannes, on the French Riviera, during the summer of 1969.

[2]*The People*, September–October 1960, and May–June 1961.

[3]Gordon Langley Hall, wrote a biography of Princess Margaret in 1958. In November 1968, as Dawn Pepita Langley Hall she married her butler.

Balmoral to celebrate the marriage of Viscountess Anson and Prince Georg of Denmark. Lady Anson, a cousin of the Queen,[4] had married Viscount Anson on 28 April, 1938. She had a son and daughter by the marriage, which was dissolved in 1948 on the grounds of her husband's desertion.

The Margaret-Townsend affair was handled with a certain rigidity by the Queen's then Press secretary, Commander Sir Richard Colville.[5] He would telephone Margaret and accuse: 'Why did you do this?' instead of 'Did you do it?' She, Peter Townsend and Lord Snowdon all thought he didn't like them.

Margaret's reputation has suffered ever since, helped, to some extent, by her own actions. She draws £15,000 a year (taxed) from the Government, but doesn't really perform much for it – about one hundred engagements a year, many of which are film premières, charity shows, or gala nights at the opera. 'There are very few invitations for her to come and open things,' says a former Lord Lieutenant, 'because she is unpopular. She's relegated to opening schools, and things like that. It was often embarrassing because they used to ask if there was something that would suit her. She's done the Queen and the Monarchy no good at all.'

Indeed, Margaret does at times wield her royalty like a sledgehammer, insisting on privileges such as a two-man motor-cycle escort to help her from Kensington Palace to Waterloo Station, ordering a Queen's Flight helicopter to take her thirteen miles from London to Elstree. As she gashes bright red lipstick on to her mouth in public, she is an occasional reminder that until George V came to the throne the British royal family were more German mercenaries than British gentlemen. She may be fifth in line to the throne (Appendix), but neither she nor Tony are popular with the upper reaches of established British society.

'Jones' – the name had remained like a puddle of stagnant

[4]Daughter of the Queen Mother's brother.
[5]Retired 1968.

water in his mind. 'Jones,' sniffed the Duke of —— 'came to stay with us once. Couldn't stand the fellow. Very, very strange. And Margaret, well . . . somewhat fat. Of course, you must remember, she's a Hanoverian.'

Margaret and Tony live rent free at 1a Kensington Palace, controversially re-built inside by the British taxpayers for £85,000 (including £20,000 donated by the Queen) when they married. Tony pays rates of just over £1,000 a year, and he also rents from Princess Margaret four rooms exclusively for his benefit: a twenty by eighteen foot study, darkroom, secretary's office, and workroom. The money helps with the housekeeping.

They have one spare bedroom, and the house is not so lavish as the re-building indicates. The drawing-room is a short way down the corridor, on the right as you enter the building. It is long, large, and looks on to a garden. In the centre, at right angles to the fireplace, are two large sofas, one with a children's comic in the middle. A low stool holds neatly stacked magazines and large books, including Snowdon's *Private View*. Behind the sofa is a drinks' trolley and, opposite, a desk jumbled with papers. Underneath the desk is a shopping basket and handbag. Small trinkets, *objets d'art*, are cluttered around the room complimenting the Anthony Fry pictures. The focal point is the black grand piano facing you as you walk in. It is covered with photographs – of Margaret, the Queen, and the Queen Mother, Charles and Anne (the first one Lord Snowdon took of them together, standing over a globe), and the two Snowdon children Viscount Linley and Lady Sarah Armstrong-Jones. It is a comfortable, lived-in room, contrived out of a crumbling ruin and decorated in the style of the seventeen-hundreds, but with a bit of a nineteen-thirties atmosphere so you expect someone to come bounding in, "Anyone for tennis?'

'Hello, waiting for Princess Margaret? I'm sorry she's keeping you waiting.' Viscount Linley, eight years old, looking exactly like his father, helps himself to a Coke.

All royal children have a sense of presumed authority missing in most others.

The butler enters. 'Help yourself to a drink.'

This is something of an historic day. American astronauts are about to take off from the moon for the first time.[6] Princess Margaret has been up all night at Windsor, with her mother, watching the landing. They went on to the lawn to look at the moon, came back to see it on television. A curious sensation.

She enters, wearing an inexpensive orange dress, pours herself a gin and tonic, lights her cigarette in a black holder, puts on the television tucked out of the way behind the door, blows away smoke in an aggressive, resigned way. Her eyes, alternately soft and hard, beautiful blue as reflected aquamarine, gaze ahead. They have frozen many an aspiring or too familiar friend, have unnerved dolly girls making a play for Snowdon. She has a clammy chubbiness, a friendly, interested look, a regal bosom that seems too tightly corseted at times and isn't flattered by the fondness for organdies and frills apparently inherited from her mother. 'Diamond Lil,' said an unkind critic as she attended a film première, bespangled, roped in pearls, and smiling.

'Sit down,' she pats the sofa. 'Isn't this the most incredible thing? We stayed up till five o'clock watching.'

She fiddles with the television, turning down the sound. Tony comes in, wearing black and white striped pants, and no shirt.

'Turn it up a bit, ducky.'

She watches, thoughtful, intent. 'Who knows what's going to happen in the future? You can't tell the repercussions.'

It could be the first tangible step into a new awareness of the way we live, the spur that forces people to re-evaluate – even subconsciously – old institutions in the light of a new experience. What could happen to her job? What is her job?

[6] 21 July, 1969.

'In my own sort of humble way I have always tried to take some part of the burden off my sister. She can't do it all, you know. I leap at the opportunity of doing lots of different things to help.'

But functions are arranged very formally? 'Yes, sometimes. Then one tries to behave informally within that framework, such as if I see someone left out of a presentation who is obviously important, like an architect, I try to see that I meet him.'

Isn't it boring? 'No. Some of the things one does can be, but I've got a reflex against it now. I think it's very much up to one not to be bored. In my father's time, my mama, and my sister, and I had to do most of the work – and some of it was men's work really. I was so glad when Princess Alexandra grew up and could help us.'

She lights another cigarette. The Queen thinks she smokes too much. So does Tony, with his pungent Disque Bleu. Margaret's position is fascinating in the study of Monarchy because it could be paralleled by Princess Anne. The British penchant for gossipy bitchiness cannot be off-loaded on the Monarch, who is inviolate, dull, and worthy. The younger sister therefore becomes the outlet, the whipping boy for hypocrisy. Why *should* she get away with it?

'When my sister and I were growing up,' says Princess Margaret, 'she was made out to be the goody goody one. That was boring, so the Press tried to make out I was wicked as hell. It didn't always work. Whenever I got a lot of publicity, I used to get a lot of letters. Most of the nice ones came from America. They'd say, "How marvellous of you to do that", for they thought we were all terribly stuffy and Victorian. Then there were critical letters, accusing me of mis-reported things I hadn't done, mostly anonymous and mostly from England. I minded that very much.

'When I grew up it was, "No darling, I wouldn't do that. I don't think people would understand". In the last twenty years there have been enormous changes. Now I could do pretty well anything, apart from tearing one's clothes off and jumping into the fountains at Trafalgar Square – which I don't want to do. Of course, in those days, one never gave interviews. One just never did. I used to get appallingly upset, with no way of hitting back. I was an absolute wreck after some of the publicity but, luckily, that's all over.'

Or is it? During the year, the hell-raising image was boosted when she went to a noisy party at the Kensington home of Prince Rupert of Loewenstein-Wertheim. Guests included Mick Jagger, Lord Harlech, Cecil Beaton, Peter Sellers. Entertainment was provided by three pop groups and a mobile discothèque. One hundred people complained to the police, and one person was told that not much could be done because Princess Margaret was a guest. Another example of the royal family being harmed by those who seek to over-protect. She didn't even enjoy the party. Arriving with a group of friends, she saw a lot of people she'd been trying to avoid for years. Most of the men seemed queer to her, and wouldn't dance, so she left as soon as possible.

Back at Kensington Palace, she pours another gin and tonic, and continues: 'I've been lucky with Tony because I've had fairly good contact with newspaper people lately.

'Anne's much more positive than I was, so I think she'll be all right. She's much tougher, too, and has been brought up in a different atmosphere, and went to school.'

Tougher? Princess Margaret has a reputation for imperious behaviour, for ignoring people who don't call her 'Ma'am', for being rude to public officials.

'I have never been imperious to officials. It's part of my job not to be.'

And friends?

'Well, I think everybody has the right to stick up for themselves. My friends used to tease me and call it looking acid drop. They'd say I'd got my acid drop expression. That doesn't happen a lot now, though. I'm much nicer in my old age.'

Regrets?

'I'd like to travel more. Having been brought up during the war I wasn't able to. I went abroad for the first time when I was seventeen. When I married Tony I thought I would travel, but that didn't work out. And, anyway, what can one do with the £50 limit?[7] No, I don't have much of a sense of frustration.'

The Queen? Her point, and her role, and her influence.

'I think she's got an aura, a twentieth-century aura. I get enormously impressed when she walks into a room. It's a kind of magic. At the moment, she's a pretty, young woman. I feel that the longer she is sovereign the more her experience will affect decisions by Prime Ministers, and she will have influence. She will be the great hope of the country in the future.'

The Monarchy?

'As long as the family can produce nicely brought up young people, it will be all right. Queen Victoria got wildly out of date by retiring from public life. King George V and Queen Mary were out of date in the twenties, but they were a stabilizing influence in those days of change. Their four sons were very up to date – including my father who took over that difficult job and led us so magnificently through the war. He brought the Monarchy nearer to life as it was lived then.

'Perhaps it is lucky that we've always been a little bit flexible because we have no written constitution. We can fit in with life as it is lived in our country at any given moment in time.'

Lord Snowdon's study, adjacent, is fitted with an oblong glass peephole which comes out into a china cabinet in the drawing-room. His room is an intricate adventure land, a pot-pourri of gadgets, pictures, magazines, photographic

[7]As part of currency restrictions, British tourists were only allowed to take £50 abroad, between 20 July, 1966 and 1 January, 1970.

equipment, and recording-stereo apparatus that can be switched to any part of the house. He sits with his back to the window at a large, clean desk he designed and built himself. He is dressed, this day, in sneakers, trousers, and a blue denim jacket decorated with a formidable array of zips. Although it isn't sunny, he wears gold-rimmed sun glasses. He had been placed fifth in the Birmingham Ophthalmic Council's annual awards for 'tasteful' spectacles – sandwiched between a comedian and a dancer.[8] 'I've often wondered whether I should have accepted a peerage,' muses the former Antony Armstrong-Jones. 'What do you think?' He fusses a bit about his wife, calls her Princess Margaret which although perfectly correct, sounds somehow odd, a bit too Establishment, coming from him.

It was an important year: designer and co-choreographer, with the Duke of Norfolk, for his nephew Charles's Investiture as Prince of Wales, a surprisingly harmonious combination of competing talents. The crusted Duke in his bowler and the new-fangled Earl in his . . . well, did you hear about the other night?

A preview at the Imperial War Museum[9] of Lord Mountbatten's television series about his life. The building is floodlit for the occasion and in the draughty foyer, a shivering group of dinner-jacketed executives who made the films are awaiting nearly every member of the royal family.

'Just look at all those elegant jury men,' says Princess Alexandra as she is led to the presentation line.

'Hi, Dickie. Hello,' announces Princess Margaret, alluringly plump in yellow, arms outstretched, pounding in for the ritualistic royal cheek kiss. Lord Mountbatten, suffused with the elegance of the evening, the importance of it, doesn't wince. He responds with urbanity, and then catches sight of Tony. What the hell is he wearing? Dear God. *And* he's

[8] July 1969.
[9] 19 December, 1968.

quiffed his hair forward in a gentle blond curl over his forehead. He might look divine at a camp Kensington soirée but this, dammit, is the Imperial War Museum, Lambeth Road, London, S.E.1.

Perhaps there would have been even more dismay had it been known the suit was won in a fashion show raffle a few weeks previously.

Designed by Valentino, Mrs Jacqueline Onassis's favourite Italian designer, it was made of black velvet. The jacket, hanging to mid-thigh, had watered silk lapels in midnight blue with a moiré waistcoat of the same colour. Accessories included black suède shoes. He did look a bit like a 1950's Teddy boy. But wait.

'An individual variation on the way evening dress is going,' said John Taylor, editor of the *Tailor and Cutter*. 'The dinner jacket is becoming the most formal thing in evening wear and a lot of tailors are trying to break away from the uniformity of it. They're now being called after-eight suits. Lord Snowdon is in a kind of limbo in that the people who take notice of him are not likely to be influenced by his ideas, and the young people who might like his fashions regard all royalty as square.'

At a party after the screening, a mêlée of royalty converged for a celebration in several rooms. The Queen was relaxed and animated amongst a group of friends, eyes shining, hands gesticulating. She has a loud, high voice – not shrill, but somewhat imperious. A blonde girl, who had come to the party with one of the world's richest men, prissily tried to join the conversation, fluttering her eyes and being neglected. She moved to Philip's circle, and he also ignored her, except for a cursory up and down glance. The rich man, knowing that patronage but not friendship could be bought from the British royal family, stalked out of the room, furious, lost his car, stumped indignantly along the Lambeth Road, and disappeared into the delights of the South Bank clapped by a crowd of about twenty party-goers wearing paper hats and carrying balloons who had stopped by to see the Queen. She left shortly afterwards, so delighted by the film that she was to watch every instalment, changing the time of dinner at the Palace to do so. Margaret and Snowdon stayed to talk.

'I'm not a great one for dressing up to see the première of a television series,' explains Lord Snowdon, sitting back in his chair. 'Television programmes should be seen in the living-room on a proper set, not in the theatre.

'What is a black tie anyway? They are all Victorian. The ignorance of people who only go back one hundred years. They wore velvet coats in the eighteenth century. Of course, it's different when it becomes rude to be badly dressed. If you accept to go to a function, you go under their terms.' Whenever Lord Snowdon acts in an official capacity, his clothes are restrained.

He and Princess Margaret are more popular abroad than in England. In Tokyo, when they opened British Week at the end of September 1969, they drew the largest crowds of any visiting foreign royalty, and Lord Snowdon's pictures of old people and mental patients helped bring some reality to the irrelevant beefeater image of England so cosily perpetuated throughout the world. His skill as a photographer is one of his difficulties. It puts him on the same level as every other wage earner, and makes his private life, absorbing as a member of the royal family, seem fair game.

'Obviously it would be much more acceptable if I worked in the city. If I was in a cocoon, I wouldn't be criticized. When I married, I said it was essential one should hang on to one's own job.

'I don't mind fair criticism and always listen when it's about my work. I think it's terribly important that one is criticized. If you can't pigeon-hole someone it's more easy, but I'm not prepared to alter my life to fit in with gossip writers or critics who are not concerned with my work. They would criticize me, whatever I did.

'If I go to official engagements with Princess Margaret, it's purely as a background figure, to help her. I hope this works. I can't alter my personality, and I'm not a great County person. In the day-time there are certain voluntary things I do, mostly concerned with the arts. I never take part in anything to do with the Services. I don't think it's my job, as I wasn't in them.

'What I hope I've done, is sort things out, live two or three lives: one, to back up Princess Margaret; two, to have a job and make money; three, to have my own voluntary work. A man cannot not make money, and naturally I don't get an allowance from the State, thank God. I will not take pictures, or work on stories, where it could be said I had an unfair advantage. I hope it's totally accepted by Fleet Street that I haven't tried to scoop other photographers. Editors have accepted this, and kindly leave me alone when I'm working – which is essential.'

It is written into his contract with the *Sunday Times* that he is never specified as photographer when an assignment is being arranged. One left-wing magazine editor, telephoned to ask if he would be profiled in the *Sunday Times*, is reported to have said Yes – and the photographer could lunch in the pub. When he saw it was Tony, he immediately changed his mind and rearranged the table to include another place. A whole profession can be upgraded by being entwined in the mystique of royalty.

Often there are tangible results. A photo-feature Snowdon did on the Middlesex Hospital for *Look* magazine resulted in a large and much-needed donation to the hospital. 'I haven't set out to do good. These things interest me as subjects,' he says.

He refuses to accept enlarged fees simply because of his name, and insisted on the same £2,100 payment as colleague Derek Hart for an award-winning television documentary about old people, *Don't Count The Candles*. A follow-up about the British attitude to animals, *Love of A Kind*, provided one of those eccentric rows with which Britain frequently swings. A sixty-year-old housewife, Mrs Ella Petry, was seen apparently hatching an egg between her breasts. Eleven years previously Mrs Petry had in fact performed this remarkable maternal feat, but in the film she merely provided a reconstruction.

'I only had the egg in my cleavage for a matter of minutes,' she admitted later. 'I was given a number of eggs at various stages of incubation at a hatchery. I was there for three or four hours, and they were filming all the time. Lord Snowdon insisted that I wore a nylon nightie and went to bed to hatch the egg. God knows why. The whole idea shook me rigid. Lord Snowdon seemed very amused by the whole thing, but he did not say an awful lot to me. It was a deception. There is no other way to describe what happened.'

Perhaps Lord Snowdon's most satisfying pastime is the unpaid work he does for the Council of Industrial Design. 'I love the whole job. It's super. I go on working factory visits with Paul Reilly (Sir Paul Reilly, director of the Council of Industrial Design). I've been to Czechoslovakia twice and various parts of England. It wakes up some of the more out of date manufacturers who have no design policy.'

He has criticized most souvenirs sold in Britain as 'a load of old rubbish'. On a practical level, he has designed a number of things, from a motorized platform for wheel chairs called the Snowdon Chair Trolley, to a birdcage at London Zoo.

'The cage was sent up rotten at the time. Whizz kid, Snowy, they said. Now the architectural Press write very nice things, and six million people have passed through it.'

Not that he doesn't enjoy the privileges of royalty now and again. Often he travels in his Aston Martin to a small cottage he owns in Sussex. Once a police patrol car stopped him for speeding, recognized him, apologized, and let him continue. He followed them for approximately ten miles, then overtook, and told them they had been speeding at various points.

'I like Tony very much. He has a lot of charm. But I wouldn't really trust him. He's a good-time Charlie,' says a close friend who has known him and the family all his life – and has no reason to be unduly malicious. Of course, Tony is tough. How else could he withstand the pressures and the rumours, the discomfort of being the easiest target in the royal coconut shy?

Every year, a few blows hit. In November 1965, he and Princess Margaret went to the United States, costing the Foreign Office £30,000, as part of a British Week tour. Many English newspapers inferred they spent most of their time at parties, and were really in the United States as a promotional stunt for Snowdon's *Private View*.

'Because of the time differences, and newspaper deadlines, all the parties got coverage and none of the serious functions which don't make such good reading. We had two or three days off in two weeks. Anyway, the book was sold to an American magazine group before I left. It sold 45,000 copies, which isn't bad for exports and the promotion of British artists.'

In 1967, he went to Japan for the *Sunday Times,* grew a beard, and arrived in New York on the way home to discover there were rumours about his marriage breaking up. He telephoned Margaret and, assuming his phone was tapped, joked: 'Let's meet in Reno.' Next morning, there were more than a hundred reporters besieging the friend's house where he was staying.

During 1969 he was to be criticized, as usual, but perhaps nothing hurt so much as an anonymous profile, 'Uncle Taffy', in the *New Statesman*. It was vicious, frequently inaccurate, and read like peevish Crawfie,[10] the only satisfaction being that it was the responsibility of the *New Statesman's* editor, Paul Johnson, a man with an enduring reputation as

[10]Marion Crawford, governess to Queen Elizabeth and Princess Margaret, a trendsetter in unctuous royal story telling, published her 'inside story' in the fifties.

an intellectual and social snob: 'Tony's origins are slightly ambiguous, in the sense that he comes from an uneasy mixture of the professional, Forsytian upper-middle-class, and the minor aristocracy. His paternal grandfather was a doctor specializing in mental diseases, who may have numbered among his patients Jack the Ripper. Tony's father was a wealthy barrister. But the ambience of Tony's childhood owed more to his mother's background . . . a smart prep school, and Eton. His parents' wedding was a Forsyte affair . . . There was a certain note of social uneasiness about it all. Though Grandfather Jones had been knighted, the hyphenation of the family name had only been arranged by deed poll as recently as 1913 . . . indeed the marriage was aptly described as an "apple pudding set in a soufflé". It broke up in 1935, the wife moving upwards into the aristocracy, the husband opting for the theatre in the shape of actress Carol Coombe . . .

'His (Tony's) next big break came with the death of Baron, which left a gap in the ranks of royal photographers. Tony boldly wrote to the Duke of Kent, and got a commission.

'Meanwhile, socially, he was slowly but steadily moving upwards from the third eleven of the smart set. He still seemed to know people rather better than they knew him . . .

'As a mark of her approval, when the engagement was made formal, but still secret, at Balmoral, the Monarch changed the evening film programme and put on *Bridal Path*. Against all odds, Tony had done it; in this case, the truth undoubtedly is, to paraphrase J. M. Barrie: "There is nothing quite so impressive as a Welshman on the make."

'Needless to say, he designed his wife's engagement ring, though the Queen officiously insisted on providing the wedding ring herself.'[11]

Lord Snowdon took the article from a cabinet next to his desk, and looked at it again. 'I minded that piece. Obviously, you mind. Unlike the anonymous author, I'm not worried

[11] *New Statesman*, 27 June, 1969.

about class. I'm proud of what people do, and what job they have. I'm very proud of my family. My father was a barrister, one great grandfather was a doctor, and another was a political cartoonist. I don't think that's tremendously ambiguous.'

There were slip-shod mistakes. 'He didn't even spell my name correctly, got my salary wrong, didn't translate the motto correctly. They may have shown *Bridal Path* at Balmoral when we got engaged. I don't know, because we were at Sandringham. I bought the engagement ring from a commercial jeweller. I didn't write to the Duke of Kent. He wrote to me after seeing the pictures I took of Prince Charles and Princess Anne.'

Misinterpretation, which the royal family have been slow to correct when it is in their favour (see 'The Cost'), is one of the hazards of the Monarchy game, part of the continuing struggle between appearance and reality. To deny something authoritatively often means you have to reveal so much that the denial rebounds. Members of the royal family have to play footsy with the truth, enough to tease and stimulate, not enough to encourage the tedium of further exploration and possible dissatisfaction at the end.

Tony's facility at the game is admirably illustrated during Ascot week. He stays with Princess Margaret at Windsor, gets up at seven every morning, drives in black leathers to London on his Norton 500 c.c. motor-bike, works either at Kensington Palace or the *Sunday Times* office, leaves at 12.30 for Windsor, changes into morning dress, rides smiling along the course in the royal procession, and leaves after the first race to go water ski-ing. It is an arrangement that provides every ingredient for a successful system: hard work, circus spectacular, and pleasure.

Whenever it seems a little silly to Lord Snowdon, he starts on some new work – designing or photographing – often at the country cottage. 'That's very private, very important to me.'

Interlude - 2

'I used to think the Investitures were one of the best contacts the Queen had with all sorts of people, particularly the smaller people, the OBEs and MBEs,' the late Lord Scarbrough.

'I'm really rather ashamed of having accepted the C.B.E. It is proof to myself of the attraction of the Establishment for me.' Vanessa Redgrave, interviewed on *The World this Weekend*, March 1969.

'We thought being offered the M.B.E. was as funny as everybody else thought it was. Why? What for? We didn't believe it. It was a part we didn't want. We all met and agreed it was daft.' John Lennon, quoted in *The Beatles*, by Hunter Davies (Heinemann, 1968) p. 219.

ON ABOUT FOURTEEN OCCASIONS EACH YEAR, the Queen holds an Investiture, a personal prize-giving for those who have been recognized in the honours lists announced on New Year's Day and her official birthday in June. It is one of the more Ruritanian aspects of Monarchy, seething with charming antiquity, which at least allows the Queen to overrule her Prime Minister in some small ways. To understand, this, though, it is necessary to appreciate the pride with which accolades are generally accepted. The honours system may have degenerated into a self-congratulatory romp for the professional middle-class, a substitute pay rise for elderly swingers of the Civil Service, and the recipients (with one or two miscalculated lapses) may provide a dismal indication of how bureaucratic Britain rules the waves, but presenting medals is an essential part of the Queen's work.

'The throne is the fount of honour,' said Lord Palmerston, adding a warning that seems to have been ignored, 'not a pump.' The fact that the Queen bestows honours gives the system a respectability that would otherwise be missing, sanctifies the pecking order, and simulates a romantic past that has been a bit battered by the reality of historical disclosure and pre-empted by computerized moon-shots.

None of this is discussed as recipients and their guests arrive at Buckingham Palace shortly after ten o'clock in the morning, drive through the arch, and park their cars in the courtyard. They walk through the red-carpeted Grand Entrance, turn left up the stairs flanked by cuirassed Household Cavalry, and are ushered into the Ball Room. Built for Queen Victoria in 1855, it is the largest of the state apartments – one hundred and twenty-three feet long and sixty feet wide. At one end are two thrones set on a red-carpeted dais and recessed under a canopy. Six immense chandeliers, looking slightly dirty since the room was redecorated, provide an atmosphere of relatively impecunious refinement, heightened to some extent by the band of the Royal Marines playing *If I Were A Rich Man* from the musicians' gallery at the opposite end of the room.

Relatives and friends of recipients sit quietly on delicate white chairs with red satin covers. Most of the men are in morning dress, their women in fox furs and pearls. The ceremony appeals to their sense of vicarious masochism. 'What a terrible job she must have.' 'Fancy having to do this sort of thing. I don't envy her a bit.' 'I suppose she'd be at a coffee morning if she wasn't here. She must be awfully tired.'

At the side of the Ball Room, recipients are being fitted with hooks on their jackets so the Queen doesn't become involved in the tricky process of pinning medals to thick material. A few minutes before eleven o'clock, when she is due to arrive, five Yeomen of the Guard march down the aisle to take their places round the throne. The music becomes more stirring, the fidgeting stops, and everyone looks towards a door at the right. The Queen, accompanied by various members of the Household, steps on to the dais. She is wearing a rather old-fashioned orange dress, and a black handbag is hung over her arm. Lord Cobbold, the Lord Chamberlain, stands facing her, and the national anthem is played.

'Ladies and gentlemen, please be seated.' The Queen scratches her nose, looks at her watch, takes the sword handed by an equerry. The band plays *I Love Paris In the Spring*. The new knights come forward, bow, kneel on the red stool in front of the Queen. If they are knights bachelor, the Home Secretary reads the names because it is technically a non-royal order. Others are called by Lord Cobbold.

Deftly, carefully, the Queen taps the recipient on his right shoulder, then with an elegant flick of the wrist, hits the other shoulder. The man stands up, shakes hands, steps back three paces, bows, and leaves.

Ideally, the ritual should be almost balletic. It is not. On the Queen's left are three men standing round a table, like waiters in an expensive restaurant. One picks a medal from a tray, hands it on to a velvet cushion held by his colleague, who passes it to the Queen. Another stands with a check list.

As one award is received, the next person is shunted forward to stand by a burly, uniformed official who, now and again, pushes a timid candidate or restrains an eager one. Little old ladies, village postmistresses, ardently loyal choirmistresses of antique disposition, who are wearing their best hats and costumes, are overawed by the protocol. They have been told: Walk to the Queen, bow, allow her to clip on the medal, answer if she speaks, if not take three steps backwards, bow again, turn right, and leave. Some stumble back, forget to bow, half turn, give a nod, shrug, look embarrassed. The Queen is particularly sympathetic to them, and more at ease. She doesn't gulp so often.

For the military awards, there is suitable accompanying

music: *Hearts of Oak*, the *Dam Busters* march, and so on. Civil Servants have the musical comedy numbers.

In exactly an hour the day's list is complete. Lord Cobbold walks to the front of the guests, faces the Queen. The national anthem is played. Everyone leaves. Some to remember the occasion for the rest of their lives. Others to grumble about the extraordinary system, and sniff cynically at its absurdity. And a few – the footballer or television personality added to the list in a vain attempt to make it appear 'modern' – to be interviewed at length about their half-minute chat with the Queen, 'It was the biggest thrill of my life.' 'She was so natural, and charming.' 'She told me she had trouble with the children as well. It made it so human.'

The British honours system, which can only be understood properly by a virtuoso of hierarchical jigsaws, is the most carefully preserved status game in the world, unchanged through hundreds of years because, unlike in other countries, it has not been damaged by revolution. So long as people actually believe a row of letters after their name means something, sets them above and apart, then it remains an extraordinarily effective form of patronage – far safer as a political 'thank you' than giving important jobs to loyal helpers. Canada abandoned the honours system thirty years ago because it was thought to be undemocratic, but in 1967 they instituted an Order of Canada, with two divisions.

The complexity of the British system adds to its lustre. An edifice with so many fine sounding and historical variations of reward must be worthwhile. Mustn't it? Forget that James I sold nine hundred and six knighthoods in four months. Forget that Lloyd George sold a knighthood for £10,000, a baronetcy for £30,000 and a peerage for £100,000. In the 1970s things are more democratic – four thousand honours a year, compared with five hundred in 1900.

There are seven types of knight: Garter, Thistle, Bath, St Michael and St George, Victorian Order, British Empire, and Bachelor. Since 1946 when King George VI persuaded the then Prime Minister, Clement Attlee, that he should be responsible for some non-political honours, the Monarchy has been responsible for the Garter and its Scottish equivalent, the Thistle. The Queen also awards the Order of Merit, and any honours of the Royal Victorian Order, begun by Queen Victoria in April 1896 because she thought politicians were allowed too much patronage. Even today, it is a useful weapon for the Queen. After the Investiture of Prince Charles at Caernarvon, Sir Michael Duff, the Lord Lieutenant, recommended the Chief Constable for a knighthood. This was turned down by the Prime Minister, on the grounds that only metropolitan police chiefs are given such an honour. The Queen then decided to give him a knighthood in the Victorian Order, considered slightly more prestigious by connoisseurs.

Below this are orders of the British Empire that do not carry the pre-fix 'Sir' – the CBE, OBE, and MBE – known when they were originated in 1917 as for 'Other Bastards' Efforts' because so many were given. Today there are about seven hundred new ones a year, but the exact amount was decided in January 1970 at the five-yearly consensus of the Committee on Honours, and Awards and Decorations which comprises the private secretaries of the Queen and Prime Minister, the head of the Civil Service, a representative from each Ministry and each of the Armed Forces, and the Central Chancery of Orders of Knighthood. The man with the most direct importance is Philip Milner-Barry, ceremonial officer of the Treasury, who has one particularly apt qualification for the job: he was British Boy Chess Champion in 1923. 'The honours system gives a great deal of harmless pleasure, particularly in the lower levels,' he says.

It is not just in the lower levels. The boardrooms of England, the green rooms of theatres, the ostensibly blasé headquarters of television executives, reek with the scrambling for honours. Politicians, naturally, adore them and Harold Macmillan, a benign distributor *par excellence*, exploited this more lavishly than any other Prime Minister. Surprisingly he declined a Garter knighthood and an Earldom for himself. He is, however, a member of the Tunisian Order of Chastity. Third class.

Since October 1966 there have been no specifically 'political' honours, although there is often a thin distinction between 'political' and 'public' service. There are still automatic rewards, such as those given by the Queen in Brazil and Chile, and knighthoods for senior civil servants. In public service, the chance of receiving an award of an MBE or above is only two to one against if you are earning more than £3,000 a year, although the odds are lengthening. In the 1970 New Year's Honours there were 159 awards for the home Civil Service – compared with 230 in 1965.

The Queen is involved with two other forms of public patronage: the presenting of royal warrants to about 1,000 firms who provide every conceivable regal necessity from chocolate noisette oysters with individually carved grooves, to creosote, crushed chalk, peat, and Rolls Royces; and, more important, the Queen's Award to Industry which, since 1966, has been awarded to about one hundred firms a year for outstanding achievement. It is always presented on the Queen's birthday, 21 April, and lasts for five years. Like other features of royal patronage, the intention cannot be faulted but the actual performance needs modernizing. Some of the smaller aspects – such as the letter to successful companies – give a pretentious gravity to real achievement:

Greeting!
We being cognizant of the industrial efficiency of the said body as manifested in the furtherance and increase of Export Trade and being desirous of showing Our Royal Favour do hereby confer upon it
THE QUEEN'S AWARD TO INDUSTRY
for a period of five years from the 21st day of April ... until the 20th day of April ... and do hereby give permission for

the authorized flag of the said Award to be flown during that time by the said body and upon its packages and goods in the manner authorized by Our Warrant of the 30th day of November 1965.

And we do further hereby authorize the said body during the five years of the currency of this Our Award further to use and display in like manner the flags and devices of any former such Awards by it received. Given at our Court at St. James's under Our Royal Sign Manual.

The lawyers' revenge on life.

All the Queen's Men

'I think the Queen, if anyone, merits a log fire.' Cecil Beaton.

'I mention the Queen because she happens to be the very apex of a pyramidal structure which went out with the ancient Egyptians. A democratic monarchy is as impossible as a pyramid balancing on its summit.'
'Then why does it exist, sir?'
'Why? Well, Private Kemp, someone once said, "It exists because no-one quite knows what to do with it".' *The Man Who Held The Queen To Ransom And Sent Parliament Packing,* by Peter van Greenaway (Weidenfeld and Nicolson, 1968), p. 17.

'Why not Buckingham Palace as a magnificent museum of art? The Palace itself is too large for contemporary monarchy.' Letter in *Evening Standard,* 24 February, 1969.

'When I go to London on holiday, the first thing I do is to go and stand outside Buckingham Palace. Royalty is something to look up to.' Rag-and-bone man quoted in *Long To Reign Over Us?* by Leonard M. Harris (William Kimber, 1966), p. 41.

THE MOST COMPLICATED semi-private household in the world requires meticulous organization and extraordinary hospitality in order to perpetuate its image and keep everyone in comfort. When guests are expected at Buckingham Palace, or any of the Queen's four other homes, a footman walks the corridors swinging a censer of smouldering lavender to freshen the air. At Windsor, visitors always find books of interest to them laid out on tables in the library. They are woken by the sound of horses' hooves as Prince Philip and the Queen take a morning ride, or the swish of brooms as a maid tidies their private sitting-room.

The unprivileged can always glimpse Buckingham Palace by asking to sign the visitors' book. It is not a particularly shattering experience, and only thirty people take advantage of it each day. You speak to the policeman at the gate, who is there, presumably, to protect the Life Guards slowly immolating themselves in bearskins and heavy uniform in honour of past glories and present tourism. Then you walk across the yard, into the Privy Purse door, on the right-hand side, where you are greeted by a uniformed footman. There is a slightly seedy stage-door atmosphere, as if you are intruding on something you can't possibly be expected to understand, that leads within a few yards into a miraculous transformation, the entrance to Alice's tunnel. In front is a wooden table, neatly piled with bowler hats, umbrellas, and dark coats, regulation uniform for executive Britain. To the left is a small room with an electric fire, a persistently unread copy of *The Times*, a mirror, a small desk, chair, a visitors' book, and four rather worn dip pens. You sign, say thank you, and leave.

The more fortunate will go to an Investiture or Garden Party (described later). The élite will be invited to a State Banquet, held in the Ball Room, which now looks far more elegant than for an Investiture. Gold plate and wine flagons are laid out on sideboards, and the Grand Service glitters on the horse-shoe table. Umbilical cord to a prosperous heritage, it was founded by the Prince Regent and includes fifty-inch-high gold candelabra made by Paul Storr in 1809. The china is Louis XV Sèvres, hand painted in apple green. Senior staff wear livery of black and gold braid with white wool breeches, stockings and black, buckled pumps.

Footmen wear gold-braided scarlet, with knee breeches and pink stockings. Members of the royal family and guests of honour, walk in procession from the music room. Just before

143

they reach the Ball Room, the Lord Chamberlain (Lord Cobbold) and the Lord Steward (Lord Cobham) turn to face the Queen, and enter backwards in front of her.

'It's one of those hangovers from the past,' said a member of the staff. 'If it was widely known I don't think it would continue very long.'

'All ceremonial is ridiculous if it isn't perfect,' says Lord Cobbold. 'The whole thing is to keep the trappings and the mystery, and not look ridiculous. People like it, and it retains some sort of dignity. As long as it doesn't get out of balance, it isn't a bad thing.'

Hidden in flowers on either side of the Queen, at the top of the table, are red and green traffic lights. They are operated by a steward standing behind the Queen, so waiters can be signalled to serve at the same time.

This combination of mediæval practice and almost vulgar modern device, is symptomatic of the Queen's Household, a closed organization whose members do not discuss their work. Until now there has never even been an accurate list of the number of people employed – an insignificant enough detail whose secrecy indicates the zealous privacy surrounding the reality of Monarchy.

Technically, the three senior members of the Household are the Lord Chamberlain, the Lord Steward, and Master of the Horse, responsible for 'above stairs', 'below stairs' and 'out of doors' duties. Until the Prince Consort began economizing (by saving candle ends and so on) and modernization in 1844, it was an institution of finicky demarcation that would have shamed even the British car industry. Cleaning inside the windows was the Lord Chamberlain's duty. Outside was the responsibility of the Commissioner of Woods and Forests. Consequently, the windows were never properly clean. The Lord Steward had to lay a fire, but the Lord Chamberlain's department had to light it. So the royal family froze in fireless elegance.

Until 1924 the three appointments were made by the

Prime Minister. Technically, they are still 'on advice' but in reality the Queen makes her own choice and the appointees agree not to vote against the Government. Three M.P.s have Household positions to ensure Parliament is properly represented and integrated into royal life: The Treasurer, Comptroller, and Vice Chamberlain. Their real importance is symbolic as much as anything.

The Court itself is significant not so much for the direct power it wields, which is negligible, as the influence extending downwards from it into all branches of British life. Anyone who has been transfixed by the schoolboy play-acting of the House of Commons on practically any afternoon, anyone who has tried to communicate with the mummified abstractions of a solicitor's mind, anyone who has seen the Foreign Office in action abroad, anyone who has experienced the uncomfortable phoniness of a 'posh' provincial wedding will understand the ease with which self-satisfaction and complacency can ultimately be defended by appeals to patriotism, 'tradition' the Queen, and the example set by her way of life. Anyone who has listened to the outpourings of royal family critics, will realize how easily 'the Court' can be ridiculed as comic relief to the death rattle of a nation.

But the British aristocracy, with an ability for self preservation unmatched by any other group in the world, with the possible exception of the ant, is eclectic and self-mocking. The former Lord Chamberlain, the late Lord Scarbrough, had a caricature of the 'Establishment' framed in his toilet. It was originally printed in a magazine as something of an insult, but he drew the attention of it to visitors and took delight in pointing out himself, beaming happily.

Since his successor, sixty-five-year-old Lord Cobbold took over seven years ago, the Household has been modernizing itself, although it is debatable whether changes have affected the reality or merely up-dated the dream. There is an in-bred caution against over-indulgence at the shrine of easy popularity when a style has been fabricated over years of trial and error. It is not the same as a chimerical political reputation founded on money, or a Hollywood spectacle based on glamour. They were willing to learn from both techniques – as was to be shown later in the year – but there were always chilling reminders, such as the Kennedys, of how self-made myth can destroy itself, by envy and over-exposure, and there are surprisingly few public lapses from a rectitude that is cruel but effective. Peter Townsend, who was Deputy Master of the Household is still telephoned by members of the royal circle when he visits England – but they do not accept his invitation to a drink.

Lord Cobbold comes from an old Suffolk brewing family, was educated at Eton and King's College, Cambridge, became a director of the Bank of England when he was only thirty-three, Deputy Governor eight years later, and was Governor for twelve years. He encouraged a better public understanding of the Bank, and to some extent this process has been continued with the Monarchy, although he has been careful to regulate the flow of information.

'It's a question of balance. The thing that interests me about the job is the pace you have to move with the times, and at the same time retain the traditional aspects. Someone in my job must not be committed politically, and it entails some experience of public life. The point is to be an outsider, not a professional courtier.'

The senior appointments he has made so far, indicate a weakening of the old Etonian stranglehold on Court life – and there is only one, Master of the Household, Brigadier Geoffrey Hardy-Roberts, amongst his first five. Russell Wood, forty-six, who became deputy treasurer at the end of 1968, is a chartered accountant who used to work for a fertilizer firm. Press secretary Bill Heseltine went to a grammar school in Australia. Assistant private secretary Philip Moore, and assistant Press secretary David Gallagher, were both chosen for ability rather than background.

'We've entirely got rid of the idea that it's huntin',

shootin', fishin' people,' says Lord Cobbold. 'When I go to the Queen I honestly don't have to worry about the background of the person. One is limited to the Monarchical countries, of course, but I would have no objection to a coloured person. I don't agree their jobs should be known in too much detail. It would be a very bad thing to have a view expressed by the Queen's private secretary – or other members of the Household. They should be allowed to get on with their job. No one likes having their servants chivvied.'

The Lord Steward's work is now carried out by the Master of the Household. Brigadier Geoffrey Hardy-Roberts, sixty-two, was for twenty-one years Secretary-Superintendent of Middlesex Hospital. He is keen on horse racing, was in the Ninth Lancers from 1926–37 which he rejoined at the outbreak of war, and farms near Worthing. His staff, like all the Palace organization, is rigidly divided between Household (those who come into contact with the Queen), officials and clerks, and Staff.

Each group has its own dining-room with varying degrees of comfort. Household members are served by pages and footmen. Footmen have a self-service canteen where drinks are provided at wholesale prices, and groceries can be bought. The social structure is closely adhered to, and there is a story of one senior telephone operator who refused to answer any internal calls except from members of the royal family. His happiest moments, apparently, were connecting the Queen with her mother. 'Your Majesty? Her Majesty, Your Majesty.'

Household members wear a special evening coat – blue velvet collar and brass buttons stamped with the royal cipher. A more dubious honour is to be invited by the Queen to wear the Windsor coat, dark blue with red cuffs, and very expensive to buy. Most of them are handed down. Prince Philip has designed his own black tie version. Correct dress is considered important. At Balmoral, for instance, the pipers wear Balmoral tartan during the day, but before two of them, led by Pipe Major Pitkeathly, play at dinner they change into the Royal Stuart.

A total of four hundred and twenty-two people work full time to keep the Monarchy functioning at Buckingham Palace, and cost the Queen at least £300,000 a year. Foreign maids (whose boyfriends have to clock in and out at the door) earn £8 10s. a week, footmen between £10 and £20. Other incomes have been up-graded in line with equivalent Civil Service ranks, and rises have to keep pace with them. Selective Employment Tax is £30,000. If cuts had not been made in ceremonial activities when she came to the throne, there would have been a Civil List of about £800,000, instead of the £475,000 at present (see 'The Cost').

The staff are:

HOUSEHOLD MEMBERS	OFFICIALS CLERKS	STAFF
PRIVATE SECRETARY'S OFFICE		
Sir Michael Adeane, private secretary		
Sir Martin Charteris, assistant		
Philip Moore, assistant		
William Heseltine, Press secretary	11	1 messenger
Anne Hawkins, assistant		
David Gallagher, assistant		
PRIVY PURSE		
Lord Tryon, Treasurer		
Russell Wood, deputy	14	9
Major J. R. Maudslay, assistant		
LORD CHAMBERLAIN'S OFFICE		
Lord Cobbold (part time), Lord Chamberlain		
Lt-Colonel Eric Penn, Comptroller		
Lt-Colonel Johnny Johnston, assistant		
Oliver Millar, Deputy Surveyor of the Queen's Pictures	13	8
Geoffrey de Bellaigue, Deputy Surveyor of the Queen's Works of Art		

LIBRARY
R. C. Mackworth-Young   5   3

MASTER OF THE HOUSEHOLD
Brigadier Geoffrey Hardy-Roberts   16   45 catering
Lord Plunket, Deputy Master   staff
                                              58 house-
                                                 maids
                                              53 pages
                                            and footmen

ROYAL MEWS
Lt-Colonel John Miller   4   11
                                            chauffeurs
                                            39 grooms,
                                            coachmen.

LADIES-IN-WAITING
One on full-time duty.

About one hundred of these people travel with the Queen
when she moves to one of her other houses for any length of
time (see 'The Cost'). In addition, at Buckingham Palace there
are nine gardeners, forty-three building staff and fifty-six
engineers who are full-time employees of the Ministry of
Public Building and Works. The builders and engineers also
work at Kensington Palace.

When the Queen travels on official engagements, she is
preceded by a squad of photographers, who receive the royal
smile, and is followed by at least four members of the Household, who tramp along in the backlash of the royal wave: a
detective, an equerry, a lady-in-waiting, and a private
secretary.

Since she came to the throne her detective has been Albert
Perkins, promoted to Commander during the year, a pipe-
smoking, rose-growing man of cherubic puffiness whose
ruddy face is occasionally adorned with half-moon spectacles.
He is reputed to be elegant, and even said to have the

nickname 'Admirable Perkins', but he nearly always wears a blue pin-striped double-breasted suit with wide bottoms, or the disguise of the day (morning dress at Ascot, the Derby, and the Garter ceremony, dinner jacket now and again). Perkins was planning to retire during the year, but his promotion gave him another couple of years' work. His deputies, Chief Superintendent John Thorning and Chief Inspector Michael Trestrail, often accompany Prince Philip – a more uncomfortable task, particularly during Ascot week when they have to wear morning dress for early afternoon and leave for polo without an opportunity to change. (A Special Branch man, in morning dress, holding a couple of polo sticks for Prince Philip, is an unforgettable sight for connoisseurs of British police folk-lore.)

In unguarded moments Perkins files his nails, but he is always watchful, walking jerkily ahead of the Queen, sitting in the front seat of her car, next to the chauffeur, fretting endlessly about photographers, carrying the Queen's fur coat, horse riding with her – an accomplishment he learnt specially. He is an expert shot, carries a gun, and is looked upon with awe by some Scotland Yard detectives, and those at Cannon Row, which is connected directly to the Palace. But he has his more mischievous side. A photographer, well known for 'intimate' pictures of the royal family, parked his car on a Scottish hillside one afternoon. Perkins saw, and recognized the car. When the photographer left, he crawled up to it, apparently to let down the tyres, only to be spotted by the photographer, who jumped from a tree and startled Perkins.

The son of a Worcestershire decorator, he went to grammar school, married the daughter of a former Baptist minister, and worked with a fishing-rod manufacturer before joining the police at the age of nineteen in 1927. He was detective to George VI for a few months before he died. 'I have an honourable and onerous task,' he says. 'I realize the responsibility of it, and dislike reading about myself. I cannot, and will not, say anything about my job. And never will.'

There are two equerries (with the accent on the second syllable), one of whom accompanies the Queen everywhere. Lord Plunket, forty-six-year-old bachelor, is the least active because he is also Deputy Master of the Household. His mother, daughter of a South African diamond mine owner and a musical comedy star, and his father were killed in a plane crash in California in 1938. They had both been friends of George VI and Queen Elizabeth, and Patrick was brought up under the strong influence of the royal family. At twenty-five, after a few years in the Irish Guards, he became equerry to the King and formed part of the younger royal circle. Inevitably, when he succeeded Peter Townsend as Deputy Master, he was rumoured as a possible husband for Princess Margaret. During 1969, the Rhodesia problem[1] concerned him because he and his two brothers grow pines and wattles on a 3,000-acre farm at Melsetter.

A tall, slim, young-looking old Etonian he is an art expert and keen gardener. He combines the traditional shooting and racing interests of the upper class with more modern aristocratic talents such as jazz playing. Like the other equerry, Lieutenant John Slater, seconded from the Navy for three years, he is adept at entertaining the Queen's foreign guests at Annabel's and other obtuberances of London's faintly chinless scene.

The ladies-in-waiting are a bit more staid – county with a social conscience and a protective sense of history to render them impervious to the occasional tedium. They are always dressed 'sensibly', with clothes and hats less noticeable than the Queen's; and they have 'sensible' faces, etched with a responsible prettiness that grows particularly well in the southern counties of England. There are eleven of them, divided into three categories.

Mistress of the Robes, the Countess of Euston, is the senior, and attends the Queen on all State occasions. Her father was

[1]Rhodesia became a republic on 2 March, 1970, after a continuing diplomatic tussle since Unilateral Declaration of Independence in November 1965.

chairman of Rolls Royce, her husband is heir to the Duke of Grafton, her brother is Conservative Member of Parliament for Westminster, three of her five children have members of the royal family as god-parents. She worked her way through the ranks, starting as a Lady of the Bedchamber in 1953, and succeeding the Duchess of Devonshire as Mistress of the Robes in 1967.

The Ladies of the Bedchamber, who are usually peeresses, attend the Queen at important events, such as a provincial tour, or a charity gala. There are two of them: Marchioness of Abergavenny, who is married to the brother of one of the Queen's closest friends, Lord Rupert Nevill, a keen hunts-woman who during the year gave up being Joint Master of the Eridge Hunt; the Countess of Leicester, older daughter of the Earl of Hardwicke, who lives near Sandringham and makes pottery (pint tankards decorated with Prince Charles's head – 10s. 6d.) although she dislikes to think it sells on 'snob appeal'; and one temporary, the Countess of Cromer.

Women of the Bedchamber do the day-to-day work, such as answering correspondence, and attend the Queen on most occasions. They work between one and three weeks rotas and have an office in the Palace. Usually, they are daughters of peers, are paid about £500 a year, plus expenses. There are four of them, with three Extra Women of the Bedchamber; Lady Rose Baring, who is connected with the banking family, and has been with the Queen since the coronation, is a pleasant sixty-year-old widow whose husband was killed in the war: Lady Margaret Hay, fifty-one, married to the Duke of Kent's treasurer, has been a lady-in-waiting to the Queen since 1947; the Honourable Mary Morrison, thirty-three, daughter of Lord Margadale who was Conservative M.P. for Salisbury for twenty-two years, grand-daughter of a Viscount, a contemporary of Princess Alexandra at Heath-field, comes from a powerful Wiltshire political and land-owning family; Lady Susan Hussey, thirty-one, is the youngest, and is virtually seconded to Princess Anne.

The ladies-in-waiting all come from the same type of conservative background. They share the Queen's interests, her hobbies, and to some extent her attitudes. Their husbands, or their fathers, or both, nearly all went to Eton or Harrow and they inhabit a world where gentility is still largely uncorrupted. It is surprising, therefore, that the woman who should influence the Queen above all others – perhaps even more than anyone except Prince Philip – is the spinster daughter of a Scottish railwayman.

Margaret MacDonald, known as 'Bobo', is rarely seen in public, although often she can be glimpsed watching with proprietorial concern and pride from the deck of *Britannia*, a room at Windsor Castle, or Buckingham Palace, as the Queen performs her duties. She is her dresser and, except for a few months as chambermaid in a Scottish hotel, she has been in royal service all her working life. Employed by the Duchess of York as nurserymaid when the Queen was four years old, she has since then fussed with no-nonsense kindness and devoted her life to the sort of vicarious maternalism for which Scottish peasant stock are particularly renowned. Her married sister, Ruby, used to work for Princess Margaret, but left when Viscount Linley was five months old.

A trim, bespectacled red-head now in her late fifties, 'Bobo' is technically a member of the Palace staff, but the Household treat her like a mini Queen. When arrangements for visits are being discussed, it is made certain that Bobo will have a pleasant room, her food at the correct time, and will be incommoded as little as possible. Her moods can ruin a whole visit, and even when she is being manifestly bloody-minded, Household members (whom she calls 'Sir') cannot win an argument. She lives in a flat directly above the Queen's apartment, with a specially carpeted bathroom, and meals brought to her rather than eating in the staff canteen. She is the ideal confidante for a Queen: discreet, dedicated, tough, and sympathetic. If she had political views, she would be even more important, but her relationship is on the basis of an adoring former nanny to a mistress who made good. Her mistress, though, has few others in whom she can safely confide – such is the nature of the job.

The political side of the Queen's life is controlled by her private secretary, Lieutenant-Colonel Sir Michael Adeane, another person who has been connected with royalty most of his life. At thirteen, when at Eton, he was page of honour to King George V, and he became assistant private secretary to King George VI in 1937 when he was twenty-six. He used to be one of the twenty best shots in the country and apart from shooting, his active hobbies are unremarkable: fishing, wild-fowling, and water-colour painting. But he has a more curious intellectual pursuit: since he took a first in history at Cambridge, he has been fascinated by Napoleon.

At fifty-nine, he looks the quintessential cardboard cut-out figure of an ideal private secretary: short (he is only five feet four inches), balding, gentle, walking with a slight stoop, a neatly-trimmed moustache. Now and again, he sidles up to someone to mutter a joke or comment in his quiet, almost conspiratorial voice, a bit like a twinkle-eyed weasel.

The job has altered in importance since his maternal grand-father Lord Stamfordham guided Queen Victoria and King George V through intricate constitutional fol-de-rols involving Asquith, Lloyd George, Bonar Law, Curzon and Baldwin. Stamfordham suggested the name 'Windsor' for the royal family during George V's reign. No surname had seemed suitable, until he discovered Edward III was called 'Edward of Windsor'. 'He (Stamfordham) was the man who taught me to be king,' commented George V.

There is little possibility of Adeane being directly involved in politics to the extent of his predecessors. The last king to dismiss a Prime Minister was William IV in 1834, who appointed Sir Robert Peel to replace Lord Melbourne. There are two instances in the last forty years when the Monarch has been instrumental in choosing a Prime Minister who was not elected leader of the party: George V and Ramsay Mac-

Donald in 1931, and George VI and Churchill in 1940. Adeane has been in the centre of devious political manœuvres only once. In 1963 when Sir Alec Douglas-Home succeeded Harold Macmillan as Prime Minister and leader of the Conservative Party in preference to R. A. Butler, it was said the Queen acted too hurriedly and on insufficient evidence. This exhaustively documented incident was as much a criticism of internal Conservative Party procedure as of Adeane's conduct, and the system of choosing a leader was subsequently changed.

During 1969 there was a more sinister indication of how Monarchy can become a potent, albeit unwilling, political tool – the more potent because self-righteous denials that the Queen could ever be 'used' do seem to have validity and can easily rebound on the accuser. Nevertheless, the fact that she is a focus for national loyalty does make the British an easily hoodwinked nation. The Second World War was probably the last occasion that the Monarchy was used as a positive focal point for high ideals, a democratic rallying point. Since then – and even more so in the future – it is in danger of becoming a plaything for politicians.

If Harold Wilson flies to Balmoral stuffed with melodramatic piety to discuss a new Governor for Rhodesia – it is, surely, coincidental that the trip takes place on the first day of the Conservative Party Conference, thus destroying their expected impact?

If the Prime Minister asks the Queen to publicly request mercy for three Africans about to be hanged in Salisbury, surely he is acting for humanitarian reasons on the best, available constitutional advice?

But:

'I was fearfully indignant about Rhodesia. It was wicked. I have the feeling that they're starting to use the Queen. But what can you do? Go to Downing Street and hit him over the head?' asked a prominent member of the royal family.

In the Spring of 1969 there was a delicate constitutional

issue when it was implied that Parliament would be dissolved if the Government was defeated on the Industrial Relations Bill. In order to dissolve Parliament, the Prime Minister has to seek the Queen's permission. Theoretically, she can refuse, and call for another Prime Minister, but in fact she doesn't. There was a feeling, rightly or wrongly, that Harold Wilson was using his power to blackmail the Cabinet and Members of Parliament into supporting his position. 'The Palace should know the Parliamentary Labour Party has the will and desire to continue in government, and any manœuvre to manipulate a dissolution would lamentably drag the Queen into the maelstrom of politics,' said Mr Leo Abse, the M.P. for Pontypool.[2]

Does the Queen automatically assent to a dissolution on the advice of her Prime Minister? Suppose he went mad? Or passed legislation increasing his term of office? Or had in fact lost the confidence of his party, and was threatening, like Samson, to bring them down with him by calling an election he knew would be lost?

Like so much in English public life, the situation would have to find its own solution depending on the circumstances, and Adeane would be of vital importance. His predecessor, Sir Alan Lascelles, writing to *The Times* under a pseudonym on 2 May, 1950, during the short period when Labour had a majority of eight and could have been defeated any day, said: 'No wise Sovereign would deny a dissolution to his Prime Minister unless he were satisfied that: (1) the existing Parliament was still vital, viable, and capable of doing its job; (2) a general election would be detrimental to the national economy; (3) he could rely on finding another Prime Minister who would carry on his government, for a reasonable period, with a working majority in the House of Commons.'

The only recent precedent comes from South Africa in 1939 when the ruling United Party was divided about its attitude to the war. A minority, led by the Prime Minister,

[2] 16 June, 1969.

General Hertzog, wanted neutrality. A majority, under Smuts, wanted to fight. Smuts won by a vote of eighty to sixty-seven in the South African Parliament, and Hertzog asked the Governor General, Sir Patrick Duncan, for a dissolution. This was refused. Hertzog resigned and Smuts formed a Government.

The conflict between the theory and reality of Monarchy will have its real battleground in Adeane's job during the seventies. The Queen has the right, and duty, to protect democracy, to be the symbolic guarantee of freedom from pressure groups – the Army, the Church, Parliament. But does she have the ability? As Britain becomes more and more an elected dictatorship, with Governments virtually able to choose the length of their administration, as the young become a more powerful political force, and as old systems are reappraised, can the Queen become anything more than a totem to the past? The extent to which she is allowed to show her opinions, and give a positive lead to Britain's future are determined more by Adeane than anyone else.

He is helped by two assistants. Lieutenant-Colonel Sir Martin Charteris, fifty-six, also an old Etonian wildfowler, and an amateur sculptor, has been a private secretary to the Queen since 1949. He is grandson of the 11th Earl of Wemyss, and married to the daughter of a former Conservative Chief Whip and War Minister, Lord Margesson. He and Adeane both have a cultivated, slightly airy attitude, as if born professional courtiers. Charteris writes most of the Queen's speeches, occasionally allowing her to joke – unsuccessfully (see 'God v. Scotland'). Philip Moore, forty-nine, has been an assistant private secretary for three years and comes from a different background. Son of an Indian Civil Servant, he won a scholarship from Cheltenham College to Oxford where he became a double blue in hockey and rugby. He was an English international in 1951, played cricket for Oxfordshire, and now spends his leisure at golf, tennis, fishing, cricket – and shooting. For four years he and his wife, Joan, invigorated the British community in Singapore, where he became Deputy High Commissioner, with such undiplomatic tastes as an enjoyment of the Rolling Stones' music.

Adeane, or one of his assistants, sees the Queen every day. They decide all major policy decisions in consultation with Lord Cobbold and the Press secretary. Every July and December they have special separate meetings with the Queen and Prince Philip to discuss arrangements for the following six months.

The Press Office, which was of particular importance during the year (see 'Image and Reality'), is also part of the private secretary's domain. Since the beginning of her reign, the Queen had been advised on Press relations by Commander Sir Richard Colville, one of her father's employees. 'Poor Richard,' she said of him on occasions and, as a former sailor, he often seemed to feel that silence was the better part of public relations. His attitude, well enough intentioned, was incompatible with modern communications. An ex-Harrovian, he seemed to think most other people, particularly the Press, were tradesmen.

When he retired, early in 1968, he was succeeded by an ambitious Australian, Bill Heseltine, a thirty-nine-year-old schoolmaster's son who was educated at a grammar school in Claremont, won a scholarship to the University of Western Australia, and graduated with first-class honours in Australian history. As an outsider he understood the absurdities of Monarchy and knew that if it was to survive the seventies at all, it had to have an amenable image. He realized, too, that in the days of McLuhan, his job was as important, if not more important, than Sir Michael Adeane's. A small, thick-set man with wavy hair, who spends unpretentious holidays in hired houses on the south coast, he compensates for sartorially undistinguished quirks such as red braces, by carrying his badge of conformity, an umbrella, with passionate pessimism, even to Victoria Station on the hottest day of the year – eighty-four degrees – to meet the President of Finland. He was former private secretary to Sir Robert Menzies, seconded to the Palace for a year in 1960. No one, least of all himself, would have anticipated his present job, but during the year he made astonishing progress. Foreign Monarchs were so impressed they sent representatives to study his methods.

The chasm between protocol and common sense usually widens at least once a year to allow the reputations of the advisers to be temporarily buried under critical rubble. In 1969 the Queen's attitude to General Eisenhower's funeral provided a landslide of grumbles – to the regret of some advisers who thought the wrong decision was made. Mrs Eisenhower sent a personal invitation to the Queen and Prince Philip, but neither attended. Lord Mountbatten, splendidly covered in gold braid and looking eminently handsome, represented them. 'The Queen never, never, never goes to a funeral except of her immediate family – with the obvious exception of Sir Winston Churchill,' explained the Palace.[3]

The Times leader said that it was 'still a cause of sorrow and unease among very many ordinary people in Britain who had a real affection for General Eisenhower'. In the *Daily Mirror*, a columnist wrote: 'Funerals are pre-eminently the sort of functions that tax-freed hereditary monarchs are good at and meant for. What else?' The *Sunday Telegraph* said: 'It is a matter of regret, widely felt throughout the nation, that neither a senior member of the Royal Family nor the Prime Minister, nor the Leader of the Opposition was able to attend General Eisenhower's funeral. The Queen's advisers have doubtless been influenced by precedent and protocol; they should have recognized that General Eisenhower's position was unique.'

Convoluted protocol priorities also caused a problem on 31 March, when Eisenhower's lying-in-state coincided with the sixty-ninth birthday of the Duke of Gloucester. Protocol demands that flags should be flown on the birthday of mem-

[3]*Sunday Times*, 6 April, 1969.

bers of the royal family – unless the Queen orders otherwise. So flags in Whitehall were at full-mast until mid-day, when the Lord Chamberlain's office decreed otherwise.

Only one small incident, by the Queen Mother, relieved the precedent-minded constipation. She and Prince Philip attended the remembrance service at St Paul's Cathedral and there is, naturally, a specially designated procedure, with written instructions, for this type of event. In the City of London, the Lord Mayor is second in precedence only to the Queen or her representative. As Prince Philip was representing his wife, he walked on the right of the Lord Mayor. Had he been representing himself, the Lord Mayor would have walked on the right. The Queen Mother should have been slightly behind. But, as they left after the service, she said: 'Let's go down together. It's so much more sensible.'

To hell with protocol. It was about time. Until then, the whole saga had illustrated a lack of imagination that was to become all too evident in the Queen's official programme throughout the year.

'We're always trying to think of new things for her to do,' said Lord Cobbold. 'But it's very difficult.'

Interlude-3

'Could they please switch these parties to Saturday, or hold them at Windsor or elsewhere in the provinces, for they are a menace in London.' *Evening Standard* leader, 11 July, 1969.

'Garden parties are the most useful thing the Queen does in her contacts with the public.' Lord Cobbold.

THERE ARE THREE TYPES of functions during the year when the Queen is host to her 'ordinary' subjects. Each provides varying degrees of intimacy but, by a universal gift for self-deception when confronted with British royalty, guests tend to cover themselves with prestige in inverse proportion to the amount of intimacy involved.

Thus, those at a small 'informal' luncheon affect a more refined casualness than those invited to a cocktail party, while a large number of the Afternoon Garden Party scrum leave Buckingham Palace suffused with a self-important glow that totally belies the fact that they probably spent two hours jumping up and down on squelchy turf, wearing uncomfortable hired clothes, trying to glimpse the Queen.

'Informality' at the Palace began really on 11 May, 1956, with the first luncheon. Since then there have been 87, plus 17 cocktail parties, and 16 dinners. Altogether a total of 1,700 guests. During the year there were four lunches (Appendix) for an oddly assorted group of people, chosen by suggestions from the Household with the aim of keeping the Queen in touch with various aspects of life in the country. Four weeks beforehand, Geoffrey Hardy-Roberts, or one of his staff, telephones prospective guests to ask if they would be available. No one therefore actually refuses the Queen's invitation which arrives a week later. Nevertheless, formal acceptance is requested. No attempt is made to match guests – on the assumption that anyone interesting enough to be invited will automatically stimulate the others.

The cocktail parties, of which there were three, are held in the 1844 room, or the white drawing-room. One was given for newspaper editors, another for senior Army officers, and the third for an assorted group of people.

But the Afternoon Garden Parties are the most fascinating occasions, particularly as an illustration of Monarchy as a spectator sport. On three Thursday afternoons in July, Lord Cobbold invites about eight thousand people to tea at the Palace. The scones, sandwiches and cake are prepared by an English firm of caterers, J. Lyons and Co., who make good Indian tea. It costs the Queen personally eleven shillings for each guest and another £1,000 ($2,400) is spent at each party on ancillary devices such as bandstands, tents, toilets and ambulance facilities. Strawberries and cream used to be served, until the expense became too high.

The garden parties were begun by Queen Victoria in order that she could meet more of the upper classes, but over the last few years there has been a conscious policy of democratization. 'The invitations is where we've made our biggest changes,' says Lord Cobbold. 'When I first went as a young man it was because I was marrying an Earl's daughter. Now it is not a snob party at all. Ninety-five per cent of the people who come are in public life. It's only reasonable they should be entertained by their Sovereign at least once in their lifetime. I put a tremendously high value on them, especially because of the amount of comments that come back to me, and the people who say "It was wonderful. Our Tom went".'

'Our Tom', though, still dresses up to see the Queen, as did the people he replaced. Lounge suits can be worn, but are considered vulgar. The reality has changed, but the image remains the same.

At about three-fifteen, the municipal black cars from West Wittering and all places north begin to arrive in the Mall, bearing windscreen stickers with a black X and passengers with tail coats, striped trousers, grey toppers – or flowery dresses and new hats. It is generally raining, as it was on 10 July, 1969, a day notorious in Afternoon Garden Party annals because it resulted in the worst traffic jam in London for seven years. Cars took two hours to move along Oxford Street, and there was a complete standstill for thirty minutes outside the Palace. Suggestions were made that the events should take place on Saturday or at Windsor or that guests should park in the suburbs and be taken to the Palace by special bus – even, beggin' your pardon, that Her Majesty would obtain a better understanding of her subjects by travelling on the top deck of a number nine.

Guests walk through the arch, queue to hand in their tickets, and on to the Bow Room, where they queue to go through the french windows on to the terrace and down to the lawn. By about half-past three, from the top windows of the Palace it resembles a human herbaceous border being squeezed out of a toothpaste tube. At the edge of the lawn, the Beefeaters stand to form a guard. Automatically, because little is demanded of them, guests begin to line up forming two rows leading from the terrace in a curve about a hundred yards long to the Queen's tea tent – for there are three separate tents on this most democratic of days. One for ordinary visitors. One for diplomats. One for the Queen and her family. Two Guards' bands are sited diagonally across the lawn and alternate in playing light melodies. *My Fair Lady*, *The Sound of Music*, Gilbert and Sullivan. Adventurous guests who want to walk among the thirty-nine acres of garden, round the lake, and past swings, tennis courts, the caravan used as a play room for the younger children, begin to swagger to the music, as if extras in a musical comedy, the men flicking out their chests, giving an extra, devilish twist to their umbrellas, standing straighter than normal and taking larger strides, strutting in hired dignity.

At four o'clock most eyes are on the garden gate at the north entrance waiting for the royal family to exit, which they do, talking to each other, ten minutes later. Stragglers are shut in the Bow Room until the national anthem is finished. First, on the terrace, the Queen and Prince Philip are introduced to tenants from the Duchies of Lancaster and Cornwall, and then they meander down the pre-formed lines. The Queen is led by Lord Cobbold and Sir Eric Penn. Other ushers, with yellow carnation buttonholes, ferret a few people from the crowd – some already warned, some not – to be received in royal conversation. Prince Philip, who goes to the right-hand formation, has a slightly less deep crush. Prince Charles is with him, Princess Anne with her mother. 'Doesn't he look young?' 'She's almost as tall as he is.' 'I love her hats.'

'Hello, General . . .'

'My dear chap, how are you.'

'Got a new uniform yesterday. We photographed it. Very hot studio. Huge camera. Took ages.'

People jump up at the back for a better view, treading on toes as they land.

The Queen Mother, Princess Margaret and Lord Snowdon are in a moving circle surrounded by ushers propping themselves on umbrellas. One of them is Charles Morris, M.P., last glimpsed waiting at the Palace during the Opening of Parliament, indulging another aspect of his intriguing life.

'Can I meet the Princess?' asks a large man, heavily encumbered with a mayoral chain, being led by his paunch with more than usual swagger.

'I've found another, Terry,' says the usher, relieved, as not too many people seem to want to meet the Princess. 'Yes, of course, Mr er . . . um, what was your name? What do you do?'

'I'm in textiles. And I sit on the Bench.'

'Oh. Interesting.'

'Er, can I get my wife?'

'Of course, but hurry, do hurry.'

The man rushes to find his wife, a demure, freshly permed matron, swathed in a lacy white dress that has taken hours to select.

'Now, sir, what was it you said you did?'

'I'm in textiles. And I sit on the Bench.'

'In where was that?'

'In a small town, up North.'

His wife preens, wipes some imagined fluff from her sleeve, blinks her eyes, pats her hair, takes a stance of nervous decorum, swallows, blinks again, coughs gently.

He stands even more erect, opens his jacket slightly further so his chain can be properly advertised.

'Now, when I introduce the Princess, Mr er, um . . .' The name is written on a piece of paper as a crib. 'When I introduce the Princess, er, what did you say you did again?'

'I'm in textiles. And I sit on the Bench. I've been on the Bench twenty years. Don't know why I was invited here. I suppose it was because of that . . .'

'Yes, now. . . .' But it is too late. Princess Margaret is upon them, waiting for an introduction, looking to her left to see how the Queen is managing, to her right to see how many people are about. She flicks her fingers to the music.

'Your Royal Highness, this is Mr——He sits on the Bench. And he's in textiles.'

'Oh.' Margaret looks at him coolly. 'Oh, you sit on the Bench in textiles. How interesting, but uncomfortable.' She walks on, and leaves Lord Snowdon to re-institute the regal image.

'Lord Snowdon has artistic interest, so he was very interested in textiles,' said the hapless man later.

'Poor devil. What a life. Want to have a peep at him through here, dear?'

Harold Wilson walks amongst the crowd to the diplomatic tea tent, scarcely acknowledged. 'I said it was you, didn't I?' He is eventually accosted by a small man with a voluminously taffeta'd wife. 'We often watch you on the telly. Harold's still there, we say. Jolly good show. Told the wife it was you.'

Wilson smiles bravely. Mrs Wilson watches sympathetically. It is a humbling experience for politicians and other public men to visit a garden party. There is only one celebrity when the Queen is on show and this, in its quiet way, does much to explain the stability of British life. Anything that inhibits the self-importance of politicians must be beneficial and, throughout the year, there were numerous examples of the Queen demonstrating her superior status.

'Let's go and have our tea first, then we can watch her having hers later.'

'Good idea.'

Collapsible wooden chairs are thoughtfully provided, several deep, in a semi-circle round the roped-off lawn leading to the Queen's tent. Expert Afternoon Garden Party-goers eat at the start and then reserve their place in the knowledge that this is where they will have the best view of the Queen.

'Quite a lot of people I meet say how they enjoyed the garden party,' says Princess Margaret. 'They're pleased they actually saw the Queen, not talked to her, just saw her.'

After sipping tea to the gallery, who are relieved to see she does it the same as everyone else, the Queen meets Colonial guests under an awning, and then makes her way back to the Palace with a few gracious nods along the way.

Meanwhile, thousands have been trying to depart, including Princess Margaret and Lord Snowdon who are due to attend the première of *Gone With The Wind*. With their detective, they are stuck in a traffic jam and they are obviously going to be late.

The detective suggests he should go ahead by underground. 'Why don't we all do that?' says Princess Margaret. She hadn't been on the underground since May 1939 when with the Queen, a governess, and lady-in-waiting they visited the Y.W.C.A. headquarters at Tottenham Court Road. So, out of the car at Knightsbridge for the four stops to Leicester Square, and 'we shot down the escalator, got a seat and everyone jammed in. Then who should come in but Mickey Renshaw, advertising manager of the *Sunday Times*, looking frightfully, frightfully grand, as he does. He didn't know whether to believe it, or not.'

'We'd better cool this tube thing,' whispered Lord Snowdon.

The Queen also had to cool her ride on the underground during the year[1] when she opened the Victoria line extension. For a start, an anonymous telephone caller said a 50 lb block of explosive had been left at one of the stations. Untrue, but the Queen was told and the station searched. Less than a week later, the same thing happened in Cambridge when she visited the Institute of Agricultural Botany. The year was more than usually littered with bomb hoaxes.

Then, of course, the Queen wasn't actually travelling as a normal passenger. She was welcomed at Green Park station by the customary committee: Sir Gerald Templer, Lieutenant of Greater London, who presented the Mayor, Chairman of the Council, Minister of Transport, Commissioner of Police, Local M.P., Leader of the City Council, and Leader of the Greater London Council. She was next introduced to eight members of the London Transport Board, and the President of the International Union of Public Transport, escorted downstairs to the ticket hall where she met a further eleven members of the British Transport Board. Now, nine minutes after arriving, she could test for herself the result of their labours.

[1] 7 March, 1969.

She was handed a sixpenny piece by John Slater, to make believe for the photographers she was paying for the trip. The sixpence went straight through the new machine and came out into the reject compartment. Oh, dear. She was handed another. The same thing happened again. Finally, a sixpence was produced that could cope with the intricate temperament of the costly machinery, and the Queen received a ticket. She went down the escalator, 'How deep is it?', past the illuminated photographs of bold-bosomed girls advertising anything from sherry to knickers that make commuting in London a voyeurist pastime, and into the tiled dungeon of the platform, an example of neo-lavatorial design that contents itself on being superior to the grubby Paris metro and New York subway, but doesn't seem to have changed much since the world's first underground was built from Paddington to the City in 1863.

She met a further twenty people before giving a speech. 'So far as my family and I are concerned, this is almost a domestic undertaking. It is some years since you first started burrowing underneath the Mall, and your progress has been of constant interest.' She recalled that her great-grandfather, Edward VII, opened the Central London Railway, known as 'the twopenny tube', in 1900.

Another introduction, to the train driver, and off she went in the cab to Oxford Circus, where she met fourteen officials and inspected the ticket office before travelling to Victoria for a champagne and canapés reception on the platform.

'This is really amazing. It was a very smooth ride,' she said.

'At least you can say this for our royals,' muttered an M.P., 'they make sure things get completed. What would have happened if the Queen wasn't coming here today? Tiles would be cracked, nothing would be finished.'

Any problems were drowned by champagne. Six months later, though, the proud new line was described as a mess, and the Consumer Council complained about its narrow platforms, noisy trains, inadequate indications, and un-functional design.

'The well-meaning efforts of the royal family's image makers to turn them into a with-it crowd seem to have got out of hand,' wrote a newspaper.[2] 'The Queen on an underground train . . . who do they think they are kidding?'

[2] *Sunday Mirror*, 9 March, 1969.

The Cost

'They're very good value. What do they cost? A penny a month, a day . . . ? You won't even be able to pee for that when decimals come in.' Duke of Bedford.

'Our Monarchy costs more than all the other European Monarchies put together.' Emrys Hughes, M.P. *The Crown and The Cash*, Civic Press Ltd., Glasgow.

'There is great danger in allowing room for misunderstanding about the cost of the institution of Monarchy. It is dangerous to allow public money to be spent on it unless the manner in which it is being spent is explained and is capable of being controlled by Parliament.' *An Evolving Monarchy*, Bow Group pamphlet, March 1968, p. 20.

NO ASPECT OF MONARCHY is so secret as its true cost. For years there have been inaccurate statements from Buckingham Palace, combined with inspired newspaper stories about the Queen's thrift, designed to elicit sympathy for her financial position. Government pamphlets, officially distributed abroad, also give a misleading impression.

The cost provides a classic example of how an old-fashioned Court can entwine itself in excruciating double-think, side-track legitimate enquiry, and become involved in complicated arrangements that in any other sphere would charitably be called hanky-panky. Sometimes it may have seemed that the Keeper of the Privy Purse, Lord Tryon, was too aptly named, but fortunately during the year there were signs that previous inaccuracies were being rectified.

The Government had agreed to review the Queen's whole financial situation after the election. This would have been done quietly, and without much fuss, if it hadn't been for an ingenuous remark made by Prince Philip on American television. It was one of those nightmares of inopportune timing that in isolation could be mistaken for machiavellian planning – or extreme naïveté.

Newspaper stories about the Queen's money usually appeared about Christmas time, when the 'family' aspect of Monarchy could be exploited.

'The finances of the British Monarchy, hard hit by inflation and new taxes, are now a cause for concern to the Queen's advisers at Buckingham Palace,' said the *Sunday Express* on 8 December, 1968.

'Unless there is a revision of the Civil List – the annual sum paid by the Treasury to meet the Crown's expenses – cuts may have to be made in royal spending on traditional ceremonial and on other aspects of the Queen's national role.

'Meanwhile, there is reason to think that the Queen has had to use some of her private wealth to fulfil her public commitments.'

In 1969, it seemed as if the poverty-stricken season was starting earlier than usual when *The Times* 'revealed', ironically on Guy Fawkes day, November 5, that 'the Queen is spending more than the £475,000 annual allowance made to her by the Government, an official at Buckingham Palace said last night. He said that it might be time for the situation to be reviewed.'

This would have soon been forgotten, except for the fact that a few hours after it appeared Prince Philip, in Washington, recorded a television interview for the National Broadcasting Company's *Meet The Press*. He was asked about money and he replied, as he had done privately for over twelve months: 'We go into the red next year, which is not bad housekeeping if you come to think of it. We've in fact kept the thing going on a budget which was based on costs of eighteen years ago. So there have been very considerable corners that have had to be cut, and it's beginning to have its effect.

'There's no question of just we get a lump sum and we can do what we like with it. The thing is that it's allocated for particular purposes. Now, inevitably if nothing happens we shall either have to – I don't know, we may have to move into smaller premises, who knows?

'We've closed down – well, for instance, we had a small yacht which we've had to sell, and I shall probably have to give up polo fairly soon, things like that. I'm on a different allowance anyway, but I've also been on it for the last eighteen years.'

The interview was considered innocuous by Prince Philip's secretary, James Orr, and others watching. The references to money were not thought shattering and they were said in an obviously light-hearted way. However, when they were relayed to Buckingham Palace later in the day, there was a feeling of numbed anticipation, premeditated misery. Attempts to suggest cuts in the tape were abandoned when it was realized British journalists had been present as observers.

After the interview was shown on British television a few days later, an astonishing furore took place in newspapers, illustrating the lack of proportion and humour allowed in the incendiary discussion of Monarchy and money. Eventually, the Prime Minister was forced to make a statement in the House of Commons explaining that a Select Committee would be set up at the beginning of the next Parliament to examine the Civil List. He added that various expenses, previously paid for by the Monarch, had been transferred to the Government, and he mentioned £40,000 'for certain expenses in relation to State entertainment, for example during State visits, which in previous reigns would have been borne on the Civil List'.

The ambiguity caused some worry at the Palace, in case it was thought the Prime Minister was referring to banquets. The Queen personally pays for all entertaining at Buckingham Palace, whatever the occasion. It was simply one more small confusion in an unnecessarily involved situation.

The reality is quite simple. Monarchy is vastly more expensive than other forms of Government, maybe justifiably, maybe not. That is a matter of opinion. It cannot, anyway, be judged on a cost-effective basis. In some ways it is desirable that the royal family should be the last stronghold of romantic extravagance and the grand gesture against technological mediocrity, management consultants, Prices and Incomes boards, and other utilitarian kill-joys of the seventies. Why shouldn't they provide a show?

On the other hand, the reality should not be concealed and it is still impossible to say accurately how much Monarchy costs because it depends on the items you take into account. It is anything between £2,500,000 and £7,500,000 a year. This compares with £6,548,300 that Government departments spend on advertising, a £1,069,500 budget for advertising Guinness, or £770,000 for Ford (Appendix).

Comparison with other countries can be misleading because the British Monarchy is unique. It has more prestige than other Monarchies, more importance than the average constitutional President of a similar-sized country such as Italy, and does not fulfil the same functions as an American President. A frequent justification for the British Monarchy given by Buckingham Palace insiders is 'it costs much less than the American President'. This is like comparing crossing the Atlantic by liner with travelling to the moon. The American President is Head of State *and* Chief Executive. The Queen is only Head of State. Even so, the President's basic cost is not much different:

	£	$
Salary	83,332	200,000
Expenses	21,000	50,000
Travel	17,000	40,000
White House budget	1,345,000	3,229,000
TOTAL	1,466,332	3,519,000

The President also has three Boeing 707 jets, a cargo plane for his armoured car, several Lockheed Jetstars, four helicopters, twenty cars, the use of a ninety-two-foot yacht and a sixty-foot cruiser – both maintained by the Navy – and a 'special projects' fund of £625,000 ($1,500,000) to be spent at his discretion.

The Queen has several obvious, and well-known, items in her allowance. First, the Civil List, which was agreed by Parliament in 1952 and, traditionally, was supposed to remain unchanged throughout the reign:

	£	$
Privy Purse	60,000	144,000
Household salaries	185,000	444,000
Household expenses	121,800	292,320
Royal bounty	13,200	31,680
Supplementary provision	95,000	228,000
TOTAL	475,000	1,140,000

The Privy Purse allowance is for the Queen's personal expenses and could be called her salary. Supplementary provision is designed to combat inflation, and until 1961 there was a surplus in the Civil List which was invested and then drawn upon until 1970 when the savings were exhausted. The Queen also pays £25,000 to members of the family other than the four who receive an allowance from the Consolidated Fund, the nation's central financial pool:

174

	£	$
Queen Mother	70,000	168,000
Prince Philip	40,000	96,000
Duke of Gloucester	35,000	84,000
Princess Margaret	15,000	36,000
TOTAL	160,000	384,000

Also charged to the Consolidated Funds are Civil List pensions, inaccurately named – as much as £5,000 a year granted by the Queen on the recommendation of the Prime Minister to people 'who have just claims on the royal beneficence or who, by their useful discoveries in science, and attainments in literature or the arts, have merited the gracious consideration of the sovereign and the gratitude of their country'.

Princess Anne will receive £6,000 a year when she is twenty-one, and £15,000 a year upon marriage. The Queen's two younger sons, Andrew and Edward, will have £10,000 a year at twenty-one and £25,000 on marriage. None of this is excessive, and could even be described as niggardly considering the Queen's importance, and the value placed on her family as an image booster for Britain's tourist trade. But, like the iceberg, it is only a small part of the truth. With Prince Charles's income, the first manifestly inaccurate statements begin to appear.

Until he was twenty-one, on 4 November, 1969, he was receiving £30,000 a year from Duchy of Cornwall revenues. Most of the land was taken on 17 March, 1337, by Edward III for his favourite son the Black Prince, then six years old, and has been inherited by the eldest son of the Sovereign ever since.

It covers 130,000 acres, and includes nearly all the Scilly Isles, the Oval cricket ground, Dartmoor prison, and about forty-five acres in Kennington comprising 850 tenancies of flats and shops. Tenants used to pay rent in a number of ways:

roses, a grain of wheat, pepper, a greyhound, pair of silver spurs, as well as money. Scilly Isles rent was three hundred puffins, decreased to fifty during the reign of Henry VI. Whenever the Duke visited his domain, one tenant greeted him with a bow and twelve arrows, another baked a pie of raisins, herbs and limpets and others had to carry cloth capes in front of him for forty days.

If there was no eldest son, the land belonged to the Sovereign. George IV paid off some of his debts by making over the income during his lifetime to banker Thomas Coutts (the family still bank with Coutts, in the Strand, using ordinary cheques embossed with individual monograms topped by a crown or coronet). But it wasn't until Queen Victoria's reign that the Duchy was really made to pay, largely because of Albert's business ability. Edward VII was able to buy Sandringham for £220,000 with the accumulated profits.

Nowadays the Duchy of Cornwall provides a glimpse of Monarchy in its squire–tenant guise, a fascinating combination of commercial application and feudal glory unmatched throughout the world....

11 July, 1969, was the last time the Queen would visit the estates as trustee for Charles. Although, in law, the Sovereign is always 'of age', the heir apparent could perform only a few adult functions – such as becoming a Councillor of State – on his eighteenth birthday. In other ways, until the age of majority was lowered to eighteen at the beginning of 1970, he was still a minor.

Dorset, in the south-west of England, is an example of England's heritage at its most schizophrenic. Neolithic man first inhabited the area four thousand years ago, followed by Romans, and then Saxons. Dorchester, ancient capital of Wessex, was a Parliamentarian stronghold during the Civil War, and was also prominent in the Puritan emigration to America. The Reverend John White, rector of St. Peter's Church, organized a Charter from Charles I to enable colonists to settle in New Dorchester, near Boston,

Massachusetts, and told them to build a church as soon as they landed. They did. The church at New Dorchester is known today as Daughter of John White. During the Civil War, White had to flee to London when royalist troops recaptured the town. It became, in 1685, the centre for the Bloody Assize when Judge Jeffreys sentenced 292 prisoners to death, some of whom were charged only with being 'absent from their habitacions from and att the tyme of the Rebellion'. The heads of victims were impaled on the railings of St. Peter's where they stayed for several years blistering in the sun and blackening in the wind as a warning against disloyalty to the Sovereign.

The warning seems to be remembered. When the Queen and Prince Philip arrived by train for their six-and-a-half-hour visit, station sidings had been cleared of all unsightly mess. For two days, coalmen had worked to remove seventy tons of coal from twelve-foot high piles the Queen might have seen. Schoolchildren, whose parents had been told to dress them in Sunday best, stood in front of smaller four-foot mounds waving regulation-size Union Jacks. A London express left early to make way for the royal train, and late-comers were taken by taxi to the next station along the line. The royal couple stayed at the station for under five minutes being greeted by officials, and then drove to the first of three farms in the Manor of Fordington, granted by Charter to the Black Prince on 9 July, 1342, and still retaining a number of ancient customs.

Each year, on St. George's Day, villagers roast a sheep on the green, and send Prince Charles a leg as rent for the annual fair. The vicar, Canon Edward Brooks, usually posts it to wherever Prince Charles is staying. This year it was Aberystwyth College. On a previous year Canon Brooks had met a commercial traveller on the green who said he was driving to Windsor next day, and would deliver the meat to the Castle. Having done so, he returned home late. 'Where have you been?' asked his wife.

'Delivering a leg of roast sheep to Windsor Castle.'

'Why don't you admit you were drunk?'

'It is,' says Canon Brooks, 'something that has no deep significance, except a bit of jollification. We usually have a tug of war as well and we auction the sheep for charity. It goes for about £30. We do other things. On Oak Apple day, 29 May, we heave an oak bough on to the top of the church. It's a royalist thing to do.'

He stood now on the mower-caressed lawn of Fordington Farm with the tenants, their children, the farm workers in neat suits, waiting for the landlord's mother and father. The Duchy flag fluttered one side of the gate, opposite the Union Jack. All was still, with expectant breathlessness. Hardly a wisp of air brushed the tranquillity. Solitude was so much more satisfying than the make-believe absurdity of government red boxes, the petty squeaks of self-important ministers.

A tent of eloquent complexity and grandeur had been erected in case of rain. More tenants waited inside, around a table with the visitors' book. Some of the Friesians, disrespect-fully curious, leant over and mooed into the manicured geraniums.

The Queen arrived, looked out over the flat, rich culti-vation to where Thomas Hardy lived at Max Gate, was interested, was watched, was given three cheers, and left after twenty minutes for Poundbury Farm that had been let to the same family for three generations. Schoolchildren cheered along the route – except for one solitary little girl with chicken pox who peered at the Queen over the gate by the cattle shed, unnoticed by city officials in their clattering shoes and bowler hats on their way to inspect the miracles of modern farming methods.

The third visit was to a stud farm, where a red carpet was placed from the drive into the ring so the Queen could see the foals and mares without dirtying her shoes. On the lawn, sitting down, holding Union Jacks, middle-aged women fluted patriotically. Boy Scouts had their scarves adjusted, and were reminded to cheer.

Then the usual royal motorcade – to Winfrith Atomic Energy Establishment, where the manhole covers had been freshly painted black and she was shown a steam-generating heavy water reactor and other items of feminine interest before lunch.

Another drive, along lanes lined with men in gumboots, housewives in bathing costumes, motorists picnicking beside the road with folding chairs and tables – pitchfork rurality and urban absurdity – to Poole General Hospital, which needed opening. This meant she had to be presented to twenty-four people, surrounded with mace-bearers, make a speech, be accompanied round the hospital by sixteen people, and meet a further fifty-two on the way, each of whom had been issued with white, grey, yellow, blue, green, or pink admission tickets depending upon their place of meeting.

'Now do you know who this is,' said a nurse to a four-year-old in the children's ward.

The girl looked at the Queen, puzzled, then smiled. 'Yes, it's granny.'

In the evening she went to Cranborne Manor for the twenty-first birthday party of Richard Cecil, grandson of the Marquess of Salisbury, senior member, by repute, of the British 'Establishment'.

'I like the hereditary system because it works,' says Lord Salisbury. 'But I think the House of Lords is impossible logically to defend in the modern world. The Monarchy, though, stands on its own, and the Queen has become one of the great personalities of the world. It's very important that she should remain above controversy, and the veil of mystery should remain. On the other hand, showing her to be ordinary might be a good thing. The English like people who are just like them. That was the trouble with Winston after the war. I think he was too high-powered, like a powerful car you couldn't control. Baldwin made the people think he was just like them, but he wasn't. He was far cleverer than average. A valuable piece of constitutional machinery, the Monarchy. But there should still be something of a veil. . . . '

Until the beginning of September 1969, Buckingham Palace authorities were underestimating the revenue from the Duchy, and claiming publicly that it was subject to tax. A Central Office of Information booklet, *The Monarchy in Britain*, which is 'intended to be used for reference purposes in preparing articles, speeches, broadcasts etc.', also propogated this idea, and grossly misjudged the real income.

'. . . the eldest son of the Sovereign is entitled by ancient inheritance to the revenues of the Duchy of Cornwall (which amount to about £90,000 a year).

'The Queen does not pay income tax on the Civil List, but does on income arising from her private estates. The estate of the Sovereign is not liable to death duties. All other members of the royal family pay income tax and death duties.'[1]

This is incorrect.

The net revenues for the Duchy of Cornwall amounted to £220,000 in 1968. The Prince of Wales does *not* pay income tax on them.

Early in the year, meetings between Treasury representatives and the Queen's Privy Purse officials took place to discuss how this situation should be overcome. The Duke of Windsor, when Prince of Wales, paid about thirty per cent of the revenues to the Consolidated Fund. In 1969, the Government wanted more, and eventually it was agreed that fifty per cent would be reasonable. So Prince Charles receives £110,000 a year tax free. The other half goes to the Consolidated Fund. If Prince Charles did have to pay tax, he would need to earn £2,478,035 a year before being left £220,000. Tax on a gross £220,000 would be £197,578.

Another misconception Palace authorities have not discouraged, even though many don't believe it themselves is

[1] *The Monarchy In Britain*, C.O.I. pamphlet, revised September 1968, p. 11.

the imaginative whimsy that the Queen really pays for herself.

Interminable arguments swirl around the origin of Civil List. Princess Margaret provides one of the more realistic comments. When told that George III had given the Crown lands to Parliament in 1761 in return for a fixed allowance, she said: 'Silly ass. The land would be much more valuable today.'

Money is the main ingredient in the rise and fall of the Sovereign's real power. Until the restoration of 1660 he paid all civil and military expenditure from the Crown's hereditary revenue: land, fines, taxes on ale, cider, and other oddments. An economist, Robert Heilbroner, has calculated that Queen Elizabeth I paid off all Britain's foreign debts and balanced the budget with her stock-holding share of the *Golden Hynd* voyage.

But as expenses increased, and Monarchs became corrupt, Parliament granted an allowance in return for the surrender of hereditary rights. The Declaration and Bill of Rights, which is still in force, set out fundamentals of the constitution imposed upon William III and Mary in 1689, and prohibited the levying of taxes for the Crown without Parliament's consent. Eight years later, the first Civil List Act allowed William £700,000 a year. This excluded military costs, but included civil expenditure such as salaries of judges, ambassadors and civil servants, and the upkeep of royal palaces and households. At the beginning of George II's reign it was increased to £800,000.

George spent a lot of the money on bribes and miscellaneous corruptions and agreed to surrender, during his life, most Crown revenues. £800,000 was insufficient for George III, and Parliament had to pay his debts on ten occasions. For the first twenty-five years of his reign the Crown Estates were virtually bankrupt. George IV gave up all land in England and Scotland except the Duchies of Cornwall and Lancaster in return for an extra £50,000, and increasing unpopularity:

'George I was reckoned vile
Viler still was George II
And whoever heard any good of George III?
When George IV to hell descended
God be praised, the Georges ended.'[2]

The ultimate move towards the present Civil List was taken in William IV's reign when he surrendered the hereditary revenues in Ireland and Parliament took over the salaries of judges, ambassadors, Civil Servants, and all public expenditure except £23,000 Secret Service money, and reduced the King's allowance to £510,000.

Now, upon accession, the Soveriegn automatically surrenders hereditary revenue, except for the Duchies of Cornwall and Lancaster, in return for a fixed Civil List. Queen Victoria received £385,000, and voluntarily paid income tax. Since then, it has been broken down in the following way:

	Edward VII 1901	George V 1910	Edward VIII 1936	George VI 1937	Elizabeth II 1952
Privy Purse	£110,000	£110,000	£110,000	£110,000	£ 60,000
Salaries and retired allowance of h'hold	£125,800	£125,800	£134,000	£134,000	£185,000
Expenses of household	£193,000	£193,000	£152,800	£152,800	£121,800
Works	£ 20,000	£ 20,000			
Royal bounty, alms and special service	£13,200	£ 13,200	£ 13,200	£ 13,200	£ 13,200
Unappropriated	£ 8,000	£ 8,000			
Supplementary provision					£ 95,000
	£470,000	£470,000	£410,000[3]	£410,000	£475,000

George VI paid money to the Exchequer saved through not entertaining during the war, but at the end of his reign

[2]Thackeray.
[3]Of this amount, £40,000 in respect of the king's possible marriage, and £79,000 representing the revenues of the Duchy of Cornwall, were undrawn.

the Privy Purse allowance had a deficit of £30,000 a year. The Queen was able to save money during the early years but at present she is subsidizing the Civil List at the rate of about £100,000 a year.

Much of the land she 'surrendered' was stolen from the Church at the time of the Reformation, and other property could only 'belong' to her by the most fanciful stretch of imagination. It includes 180,000 agricultural acres in England, 70,000 acres in Scotland, and 260 in Wales producing a total gross revenue of £1,200,000 a year; and valuable urban property worth £3,750,000 a year. In London, the Crown Commissioners, who handle the estate, have bought heavily in the Carnaby Street area, and now own most of Regent Street, which produces a rental of £764,950 a year. Lower Regent Street and the Haymarket add another £388,405. Various other parts of London include St. James's (£259,053 a year), Victoria, Hyde Park Corner, Millbank, Carlton House Terrace, flats in Fulham and commercial property in Southwark (a mere £5,431 a year). Then there are housing estates in Hackney, Tower Hamlets, and Camden. The London properties make an annual profit of nearly £3,000,000.

Outside London there is valuable property in Ascot (632 acres), Windsor (12,153 acres including parks), Datchet (78 acres), Bagshot (90 acres), Eltham (1,006 acres) and Richmond (408 acres).

Total profit on Crown lands, which is paid to the Exchequer, was £4,050,000 in the year ending 31 March, 1969 – an increase of £500,000 on the previous year, and twice as much as ten years ago. The commissioners still have certain privileges. Any development carried out by them on their own land is not subject to normal planning permission. Nor do they pay rates on property occupied by themselves. Like the Duchy of Cornwall, they make a contribution to the local council instead.

In addition to property, the Crown still has ancient rights –

treasure trove, wrecks, ownership of the foreshore, all mute
swans and, by an Act of Parliament in Edward III's reign,
sturgeon caught in the sea or below London Bridge in the
Thames. Now that London Bridge has been sold to Arizona
there is an added constitutional problem.

Because the Monarch is exempt from death duties, the
Queen's estate and capital is vast. She pays taxes on private
property under the Crown Private Estate Act, 1862 – but this
does not include about £220,000 a year from the Duchy of
Lancaster. Money is invested in England and, presumably, in
the United States as well as other countries. It is impossible to
guess accurately the Queen's fortune in cash, although it
must be several millions. Her art collection – worth about
£50 million – cannot fairly be included in any assessment of
her personal wealth, as she could not sell the most valuable
pictures without threatening her position. There would be
discussion as to whether they really 'belonged' to her, or to
the nation.

Other members of the family are not in the same class.
Princess Marina, who died in August 1968, left £54,121.
Queen Mary left a sizeable £379,864, Princess Royal
£328,224, Princess Arthur of Connaught £6,217 and
Princess Marie Louise £104,515.

Nearly all the Queen's money and most of her valuable
possessions, will be inherited by Prince Charles, as royalty has
a strong tradition of primogeniture. Unless customs change,
he will have to pay for a strange collection of gifts.

Every Christmas the Queen presents a hundredweight of
coal to the needy over 65 years old in Windsor – eight
hundred to nine hundred people, surprisingly. Her staff
members (not Household) all have a plum pudding. She no
longer pays the royal bounty of £4 for quads and £3 for
triplets, contrary to popular belief. This was discontinued in
December 1957. Queen Victoria had introduced it for
triplets whose parents were in 'necessitous circumstances'
when she visited Ireland in about 1849. In 1938, the condition

was abolished and all triplets born alive, in wedlock, with both parents British or naturalized, received the bounty if notification was made within twelve months. During the reign of King George VI and Queen Elizabeth there were nineteen sets of quads and one thousand four hundred and fifty-one triplets – a £4,429 bonanza for fertility. Nowadays the Queen sends telegrams – as she does for hundredth birthday celebrations. 'The Queen is much interested to hear that you are celebrating your one hundredth birthday, and sends you warm congratulations and good wishes.' Another message is automatically sent at 105, and thereafter one a year. In 1968 there were nearly one thousand messages, and three thousand six hundred and sixty-six for diamond weddings. The Queen's telephone bill and mail is paid for by the State, and given priority. Letters sent to her at Buckingham Palace while she is away are escorted to the railway station by police car.

The Queen pays for all presents she gives on Commonwealth tours and all pictures distributed on English visits – unlike the Prime Minister, whose official portrait costs the taxpayer £150 a year.

She also takes her own food and servants to the Opera when she attends charity galas. Head Steward at the Palace telephones the Opera House head waiter to ask for a table, chairs and napkins to be provided. Sometimes they bring soup in a container, but usually it's a cold meal – salmon or something. There is one waiter for every four people.

The royal box replaces sixty seats in the grand tier. Part of the crush bar is roped off, and ten blue chairs, originally from Buckingham Palace, are set out for the royal family who always enter through the private entrance in Floral Street. Security is minimal. About two hours before the Queen arrives, Special Branch officers inspect the theatre, and remain there until the end of the performance. One sits in the balcony, another in the stalls, and the officer in charge circulates. All are issued with special passes.

The picnicking aspect illustrates in a small way the most important dilemma of the Civil List. It is supposed to pay for the Queen's private and public expenditure, but which should be which? Surely if she attends a charity performance it is somewhat melodramatic to take her own food?

Clearly, she cannot manage on her allowance from the Government and, although it would be absurd to suggest she finds it necessary to economize, it is noticeable how often she wears the same clothes to different public functions during the year. She has vast housekeeping bills: the three hundred and fourteen staff at Buckingham Palace alone are paid £300,000 with an additional £5,000 for S.E.T., and another £5,000 for National Insurance stamps. Three garden parties a year cost a total of £15,000. Groceries could amount to £50,000, and wine another £6,000. Then there are quirky expenses like the Poet Laureate's pay.

Some Palace advisers think mystique will be even further shattered if the Queen is salaried and given a tax-free expense allowance. Inevitably this will happen. There is no reason, too, why the Queen should not be taxed on her private income such as the Duchy of Lancaster, or pay death duties.

The opportunity to completely re-style the form of the Queen's pay has been presented, however inadvertently, by Prince Philip. If it is not taken confusion will continue as it does now – and notably over the cost of the Palaces.

The Queen divides her year between five residences. Autumn at Buckingham Palace, Christmas at Windsor and Sandringham, Easter at Windsor, part of the early summer at Holyroodhouse, and summer at Balmoral. The royal standard, which is never half-masted, flies wherever she resides and is floodlit by eight lamps until midnight at Buckingham Palace. Sandringham and Balmoral belong to her personally, but the rest are paid for by the Government and in the year until March 1970 cost £660,000.

In addition, the Government pays for three other royal palaces: Kensington Palace, St. James's Palace, and Hampton Court – which include grace and favour residences. Kensington Palace is for members of the royal family and the Household, St. James's for members of the Household, and Hampton Court has grace and favour residences for about thirty-six people, mainly widows whose husbands have been of service to the State, such as Lady Baden-Powell and Lady Ironside. Many flats are of dubious value because they haven't been modernized. Tenants pay rates, but no rent.

Buckingham Palace is naturally the most expensive royal residence and costs about £310,000 a year to run. During the year there were two expensive items – a new lift to the State Rooms and a reorganization of the kitchens, both of which cost £12,000. A further £3,000 was spent modernizing staff toilets, £3,400 for supplying minor new works, and £4,000 for furniture. Another £9,000 was spent cleaning the outside front of the building.

The Queen pays for her own domestic staff, but the Government contributed £21,500 for cleaning services. Fuel was another £34,750. Last year the chandeliers were overhauled at a cost of £5,500.

Windsor also had a new lift, for £2,000, and the central heating was extended for £5,200. The fuel bill was larger than at Buckingham Palace – £44,274. Altogether, Windsor cost £275,000.

Holyroodhouse was cheaper – £74,000, and that includes £8,000 for renewing part of the floor and roof. By comparison, one of Britain's most popular stately homes, the Duke of Bedford's Woburn Abbey, costs £140,000 a year. The Duke could do with another £10,000 but can't afford it.

Total cost for royal palaces increases by about £100,000 a year:

	1962/63	1967/68	1968/69	1969/70[4]
	£	£	£	£
New Building Works	197,702	70,648	101,107	135,000
New Supplies	2,156	5,236	12,560	10,600
Rents	209	260	330	331
Maintenance of Buildings	409,814	595,548	687,320	770,000
Maintenance of Supplies	56,066	67,012	58,508	74,500
Fuel	498,910	109,189	122,050	125,000
Grant-in-Aid	33,000	38,000	38,000	38,000
Gross total	797,857	885,893	1,019,875	1,153,431
Appropriations-in-Aid (i.e. sales of tickets, publications etc.)	59,387	83,048	82,077	97,000
Net total	738,470	802,845	937,798	1,056,431

The 'Grant-in-Aid' is money the Queen spends from her Civil List on private apartments. It is paid to the Ministry of Public Building and Works, and indicates one way that misunderstandings arise.

Various items, originally paid for by the Monarch, have been taken over by the Ministry since 1947 when the gardeners became their expense. In April 1951 the electricity costs were added to the bill. Because of confusion over the Queen's private and public duties, it is impossible to judge accurately unseen rises in the Civil List that have taken place in this way. If President Nixon has tea in a private drawing-room, does that make decorating it the Ministry's responsibility?

A member of the royal family told me there had been help over the years paying for items that had previously been the Queen's expense. No figure was given, but it could mean subtle Civil List increases of up to £50,000. There was a look of horror on the face of a Ministry official to whom I put this suggestion. At first he denied it. I mentioned the source of information.

'He shouldn't have said that. I'm sure he didn't mean it. It

[4]Estimated.

was a silly thing to say. Neither he, nor us, would want that sort of information made public.'

And yet, this is exactly the sort of information that should be made public, if confusion is not to arise. In a public opinion poll during the year, more than half those between 16 and 24 thought a lot of money is wasted on the Monarchy. It was generally considered good value among higher social classes, and throughout the country 51 per cent thought it money well spent – compared with 39 per cent who didn't.[5]

The Queen's travel is also a combination of private and public cost.

CARS

There are four official maroon Rolls Royces, all insured but un-taxed and, therefore, without number plates. Each one has a royal shield that can be illuminated, and a small blue light on top, used as an unobtrusive warning to police. One silver mascot, of a naked St George with a dead dragon at his feet, is transferred to whichever car the Queen is using. Usually, if she is on a provincial trip, one of eleven royal chauffeurs drives up overnight so the car is spotless for her use.

The oldest car is a Phantom IV, one of only twelve made for heads of State, given as a wedding present by the RAF in 1950. A second-hand Phantom IV was bought in 1954. The Phantom V's were bought in 1960 and 1961. In addition there are two semi-official Austin Princesses (NGN 1 and NGN 2) acquired in 1958.

There is a pool of about eighteen other cars, including a Renault from the French Government, in the royal mews. Whenever one is sold, it is given a new registration number, so it will not be identified as a former 'royal' automobile and fetch an inflated price. The Queen's personal transport is a 1961 Rover saloon (JGY 280); Prince Philip has a 1961 three litre Alvis (OXR 1); Charles has a blue MGC GT (FGY 776)

[5]Published in the *Sunday Times*, 23 March, 1969.

fitted with a bull horn: Anne was given a Rover 2000 TC as an eighteenth birthday present from her parents. It has a cassette tape recorder and a number plate (1420 H) bought from a United Dairies milk float in Ealing by the 14th/20th King's Hussars of which the Princess is Colonel-in-Chief.

TRAINS

Since the first royal train journey was made by adventurous Queen Victoria 120 years ago, it has been a favourite form of transport. The royal family do not suffer the usual deprivations of British Rail. Tunnels are inspected before they pass, and automatic level crossings are specially roped off with red and white pennants.

The Queen pays for all her journeys, but rolling stock is provided by British Rail – i.e. the taxpayer. There are two royal trains, both painted purple.

The first, formerly owned by the London Midland and Scottish railway, is used for overnight journeys and has a maximum of twelve coaches, including a special play room, with bathroom, for the young children. The Queen and Prince Philip both have a lounge and bathroom; the Household have three bedrooms and a small lounge. The second train, used for day journeys, has six coaches and was owned by the London and North Eastern Railway.

Whenever the Queen is scheduled to start a tour away from London early in the morning, she travels most of the way during the evening, and stops overnight at a siding. Returning from Balmoral, she stops outside Northampton to wash and change. There is a special telephone switchboard with twenty-eight lines, so she can remain in contact with the outside world.

BOATS

Britannia, paid for by the Government, costs approximately £500,000 a year (see page 27). The Queen and Prince Philip own several sailing dinghies. Their yawl, *Bloodhound*, became

too expensive during the year, so they sold it for £250,000 –
making a profit of £15,000 since it was bought in 1962.

PLANES

The Queen's Flight of three immaculate red Andovers, two
luxurious twin-engined Westland Wessex helicopters, and a
£45,000 six-seater Beagle Bassett acquired for Prince
Charles in July 1969, operates from a hangar at Benson,
Oxfordshire, and is cared for by 140 people – including eighty
of the RAF's top technicians. It was founded on 20 July,
1936, by Edward VIII, and now costs £450,000 a year to
run.

There is an unspectacular royal flight lounge sparsely
decorated with a Union Jack that went on the Gemini Seven
mission in December 1965, and a Maori Diggers' swimming
club pennant brought back by Prince Philip from one of his
journeys.

Technically, anyone wanting to use the planes needs
written permission from the Queen. The Queen Mother
applies. Philip doesn't. Other users, apart from members of
the royal family, include Government ministers, overseas
Heads of State, and senior serving officers. The planes are
most in use between March and November but even so they
are underemployed. In 1968, the Andovers flew a total of
1,567 hours 20 minutes – half one commercial Andover's
reasonable expectation.

Contrary to belief, there is no Government rule stating the
Queen cannot travel in helicopters. She can, but doesn't like
to.

Maintenance is cautious to a neurotic degree. Engines have
increased tolerance and are made to double inspection
standards. In other words, they are built, stripped down,
inspected, rebuilt and reinspected. Even then, they have a
half-life system so that every part is changed long before
really necessary.

The interiors, with blue curtains chosen by the Queen, have

twenty-two different styles covering three separate compartments. Compartment 'C' is the Queen's and has six changes depending on the length of journey: a couch and four seats, four seats only, two seats and a couch, twelve seats, and so on. Compartments 'B', for staff, and 'C' both have eight changes. Air Commodore Winskill, Captain of the Flight, has a special seat with radio controls built into his table.

According to instructions, the 'C2' layout must have two near forward facing seats of 'the Princess Margaret type'. The Princess Margaret seat is specially designed with a low back, because Her Royal Highness, being somewhat short, kept knocking off her hats on the back of previous seats.

It is possible, therefore, to calculate with reasonable accuracy the annual cost of the Monarchy paid for directly by the Government, even though departments tend to become indignant when asked to supply figures.

	£	$
Civil List	475,000	1,140,000
Consolidated fund	160,000	384,000
Palaces	1,056,431	2,535,434
Britannia	500,000	1,200,000
Royal flight	450,000	1,080,000
Telephone bill	51,000	122,000
Postage	6,000	14,000
TOTAL	2,698,431	6,476,234

Some sort of perspective can be given by comparing one other royal family, and the President of a similar sized country.

Changes in the Dutch constitution may mean that Queen Juliana will be taxed on her allowance – which she isn't at present. She herself pays the two hundred and seventy-nine staff at three Palaces – Soestdijk, Amsterdam, and the Hague – and maintains her own motor yacht. The family have the use

192

of a Fokker Friendship aeroplane, paid for by the Government.

	Fl.	£	$
Queen Juliana	4,750,000	546,695	1,312,150
Prince Bernhard	475,000	54,660	131,215
Princess Beatrix	300,000	34,522	82,873
Prince Claus	300,000	34,522	82,873
Palaces:	825,000	94,937	227,900
TOTAL:	6,650,000	765,246	1,837,011

Italy has about the same population as Great Britain – 54 million. Until June 1946, it was a Monarchy, but a Referendum gave a two million vote majority in favour of a Republic. The royal family left the country on 13 June, and there has been a President since 28 June, 1946.

The President of Italy's allowances are:

	lire	£	$
Personal allowance	30,000,000	20,000	48,000
Dotazione (expenses)	180,000,000	100,000	240,000
Residences	100,000,000	66,600	160,000
Plane	Nil		
Yacht	Nil		
TOTAL:	310,000,000	186,600	448,000

Hidden costs of Monarchy are the most difficult to assess, but they provide an interesting sidelight on its reality. When the Queen travels anywhere, it is certain somcone is going to have a four-figure bill, an inch-thick file of plans, and need at least a week's holiday afterwards. There are numerous examples similar to the opening of a new wing at King's College Hospital, London[6] – a ceremony for which there is ample precedent and one that provided no obvious difficulties.

[6] 23 October, 1968.

About a year before the wing was completed, Lord Normanby, chairman of the Governors, wrote to Sir Michael Adeane saying it would be a great honour if the Queen would be present at the opening. It had cost £1,400,000, two-thirds of which had been provided by the Government. 'The hospital endowment fund contributed £300,000,' says Lord Normanby. 'That was all the money we had. It was the biggest moment in our history, so we thought it would be nice if the Queen could come. Everyone likes a bit of a do. Nobody can give glamour like our royal family, and that's what you want. The cost was negligible. I didn't enquire about it. I don't believe you want the Queen to wander in unannounced. The cooks love to do a special tea. and the fact that the passages are a little cleaner is a bit of fun for everyone.'

If the Queen hadn't been able to attend, they would have invited the Queen Mother, but on 10 July a letter was sent from the Palace accepting the invitation, and twelve weeks of planning began. A circular went to all departments for suggestions, and returned with vital questions such as 'Will a Royal Cloakroom be required?' Yes, and the bathroom floor of Sister Jones's flat was specially cleaned with Tik-Et, in preparation. It was never used. What sort of bouquet should the Queen be given? Can wives be part of the act? Should flags fly? How many people should be introduced?

A gold-plated microphone, kept for special purposes, was hooked up to the patient's broadcasting system. A two hundred and fifty yard route was organized for the Queen and, by 18 September, draft arrangements went to Sir Michael Adeane at Balmoral for the summer holidays. He replied with various recommendations: the visit should take place from three until five, rather then three-thirty until five-thirty, no wives should be presented, the royal standard shouldn't be flown unless there was a vertical flagpole, and the Queen likes any flowers in season (but not wired because she once cut herself).

Detailed planning began. 'There could be thirty introductions,' said Lord Normanby. 'But thirty doesn't go a long way when you have a Board of twenty-eight. I split them into various groups, and tried to limit outside people like architects, but Philip Moore (the Queen's assistant private secretary) said they had to be brought in. There were five.'

John Collinson, hospital secretary, found himself enmeshed in protocol of complexity necessary to maintain the structure of British society. As the hospital is split between two boroughs, both mayors have to welcome the Queen. The Mayor of Lambeth was first on this occasion as the new wing is in his territory. Collinson spent a day trying to persuade the Southwark mayor's secretary that there wasn't room for both dignitaries on the pavement, and it would be easier for one of them to go somewhere else. No luck. Protocol, administration's answer to a harsh world, insisted. Both had to be there. *And* the lady mayoresses.

Another problem. Who is officially host when the Queen visits a hospital? Chairman of the Governors or the Minister? Lord Normanby, puzzled even at the need for two mayors, thought the Minister would not be coming. A draft programme went to the Palace omitting him. When Collinson telephoned to ask if the Ministry would like to send a representative, they were astonished. Of course, the Minister would be there. Former Health Minister, Enoch Powell, had issued an edict making this quite clear. 'I tried to work out whether the National Health Service was analogous to the Army or to the nationalized industries,' Powell told me. 'I came to the conclusion that the responsibility of the Minister was no different from the Minister of Defence for an artillery battery – therefore he has the right to be present when the Sovereign visits.'

For two weeks Collinson and two secretaries worked day and night on arrangements. At the last minute it was remembered the local M.P., Marcus Lipton should be presented. Five separate invitation cards – six and a half inches by four and a half – had to be delivered: two sets of 150 each, *Admission* and *Invitation*, to the opening ceremony and tea; 200 sets for the tea alone; 250 reply cards.

Carriage umbrellas were hired at £1 each, sixty stewards and guides located, an oval table in the consultants' writing room purloined because it was the only one of suitable dimensions for Her Majesty's tea, a sign outside the new ward block saying ADMISSIONS was urgently changed to NEW WARD BLOCK, ENTRANCE, paper labels were torn from walls, lifts were stripped and repainted, tiles repaired, cupboards fixed. The nurses' dining-room floor was sanded and sealed, and altogether sixty-three items of decoration were completed.

Seven copies of details about the hospital were sent to Buckingham Palace, and the weekend before the visit everything seemed prepared. A newspaper, though, publicized a few grumbles to disturb the sweetness:

'Nurses angry at Royal "Clean-up".

'Nurses at King's College Hospital, London, are angry over arrangements for the Queen's visit next week to open a £1,400,000 wing. They say the Queen will not get a true picture of the hospital because of recent extensive decorations.

'They say they have been unable to use their dining-room for the past two days because it is being redecorated. A new carpet had also been fitted in the nurses' home entrance.

'Mr J. D. Banks, secretary to the Governors, denied last night that there had been extensive decorations. "We have 600 nurses and there are bound to be a few who complain. If anybody gets the benefit from all this it is the nurses".'[7]

Finally, the fourth and last draft of the arrangements was sent to the Palace the day before the visit which went, as always, with absolute efficiency. The Queen was *welcomed* by the Mayor of Lambeth, who introduced his wife, followed by the Mayor of Southwark and his wife, and local M.P. Then

[7] *Sunday Telegraph*, 20 October, 1968.

she was *received* by the Minister of Health and escorted through a nurses' guard of honour into the hospital where she was presented to Lord Normanby, who presented a further thirteen people.

She was accompanied round the hospital by these thirteen, photographed in the maternity ward, met another twenty-two staff members before walking to tea. It was planned to have the corridors full of patients and staff, so she could 'informally' meet a few older employees: a mortuary attendant who had been at the hospital since May 1928, Admissions Officer, senior pathology technician, and President of the Student's Union. Unfortunately, seconds before the Queen was due very few people were 'informally' lining the corridors. Officials quickly rounded up another few hundred.

During tea, she was presented to six more people including the engineer, a nervous man, who could have become tongue-tied. 'You're the sort of man who keeps everything going, and doesn't get appreciated,' said the Queen, expertly breaking the ice. He had his memory of the visit. Other people had theirs. A few months later, when accounts were being prepared there was an item of £8 19s. od. for the loss of seven teaspoons, four sugar tongs, five cups, four saucers, and six sugar basins.

Total cost of the visit was £1,111. Most of this, £938 15s. od., came from the Endowment Fund, and was made up in the following way:

	£	s.	d.
Redecorating corridor	78	0	0
Polishing in Main Hospital	83	0	0
Special redecorating in New Wing	72	0	0
Polishing lift entrance and rails	99	0	0
Wall washing for New Wing	56	0	0
Polishing and re-surfacing Nurses dining-room floor	170	0	0
Cleaning and re-naming a statue	103	11	6
Canopy and red carpets	173	15	0

	£	s.	d.
Plaque	205	10	0
Unveiling curtains	49	10	0
Tea for 417 people	57	2	6
Cutlery	92	13	0
Hire of gloves for porters	1	10	6
Admission cards, invitations, car park stickers	58	10	6
Queen's bouquet	8	17	0
Dining-room flowers	5	15	0

'I don't think the visit needs any apology,' says John Collinson. 'It had a morale-raising effect. The budget was never discussed.'

Image and Reality

'The only alternative is to dress it up and call it The Queen Show,' Prince Philip, discussing the problems of the Queen appearing on television at Christmas.

'Everything secret degenerates: nothing is safe that does not show it can bear discussion and publicity.' Lord Acton.

'My husband and I intend to do absolutely nothing in the coming year owing to the dangers of over-exposure. In the past year we have visited with pleasure Brazil, Chile, Austria, and a few other places which escape my memory. The rest of the time we have spent, accompanied by our children, before various television cameras, to the edification and improvement of our loyal subjects.' *New Statesman*, 24 October, 1969, parody of the Queen's Speech to Parliament.

'There is a still greater danger that inquisitions into the intimacies of royal life which profess to be frank and intimate, and cannot, in their nature, be either, will merely encourage scepticism.' *Daily Telegraph*, 3 May, 1968.

THE MOST SIGNIFICANT DEVELOPMENT during the year was the change, initiated by the royal family, that began taking place in the relationship between Monarchy and public. Eventually, though, there were doubts about its value. Was the most prestigious anachronism in the world being replaced by a twentieth-century horror, mystique being quietly smothered by hard-core public relations?

The British royal family is an adman's dream, a unique selling proposition with a pliable market strongly pre-disposed towards the product. To some extent, alas, it had become dull, and was no longer taken seriously. The public attitude to Monarchy had generally been based on emotion combined with selective information supplied by Buckingham Palace. George III appointed the first Court Newsman, at £45 a year, because he felt so many lies were being written. The salary was reduced to £20 in 1909, and a full-time Press Office was started in 1916. It became almost superfluous during Edward VIII's brief reign as he had to be dissuaded from giving press conferences at the drop of every constitutional brick or national problem.

From 1947 until early 1968, newspapers had been fed such a diet of soggy platitudes that everyone was beginning to lose interest. The activities of the royal family had been relegated to the gossip columns, dustbins of social intercourse, and any real discussion about the merits of Monarchy was so hedged with unctuousness as to be meaningless. As usual, gratuitous guardians of royal propriety were pushing the institution further into a twee antiquity than any wild-eyed republican. Reporters, asked for 'summing up' stories about the South American tour, often found their copy mutilated and, in one important case at least, transformed to give a glowing impression when the reverse was intended. Customs officials at London Airport opened packages containing pictures for a magazine feature showing how the Queen could look less frumpish if she dressed more elegantly and used proper make-up. Such *lèse-majesté* was immediately reported to Buckingham Palace, and the pictures held until permission was given to release them. The BBC cut jokes from *Laugh In* – 'I don't care if the Queen does take the Pill. I still refer to Britain as the Mother Country.' (But they did allow satirical references to Prince Philip's nocturnal habits. 'Prince Philip sleeps with a Queen', and 'Prince Philip sleeps in a Queen-sized bed'.)

During 1969, however, there was to be an event of such potential absurdity to anyone under the age of thirty – the Investiture of Prince Charles at Caernarvon – that unfavourable reaction had to be anticipated. How far could the Queen go? At the Palace this has been known as the 'Dimbleby factor' ever since she was criticized for not attending the funeral or memorial service of a popular television commentator Richard Dimbleby, whose words could transform even the most trivial State occasion into an event of awesome majesty.

There had already been one possible mistake early in 1968 when she attended the wedding reception at St. James's Palace of Antonia Palmer, daughter of an extra lady-in-waiting, Lady Abel Smith. The bride's brother Sir Mark Palmer, a former page to the Queen (who lived in a romany caravan and talked about his pot smoking activities), wore orange velvet trousers and a three-quarter length flower-dotted caftan to give away his sister. Mick Jagger was present, with a flower in his hat, and other guests were a mixture of London's more avant garde nobility and pop stars. Next day at the airport, bridegroom Lord Christopher Thynne was discovered with amphetamine tablets in his camera case – and later fined £50. The aristocracy had always had its flamboyant characters, but now their exploits made breakfast-time reading in the newspapers, and snippets in television news. Clearly the Queen didn't have to become a hippie. But, after fifteen years of being easily digestible fodder for women's magazines, a sort of ju-ju figure with a united family binding Britain in vapid maternalism, she decided – reluctantly at first – that a new image was necessary.

The way that newspapers and television were used in this process is a unique example of Monarchy's perennial ability to anticipate change, forestall criticism and accept, at exactly the right moment, contemporary devices previously scorned or patronized. Earlier in the century, commerce had been seduced when royal funds were low. Now, it was the turn of the most potent short-term force in modern life: television. The image of British royalty was to alter. But the reality – well, that did not need be disturbed at the moment.

Prince Philip delivered the warning. 'I think the thing, the Monarchy, is part of the kind of the fabric of the country. And, as the fabric alters, so the Monarchy and its people's relation to it alters. In 1953, the situation in this country was totally different. And not only *that* – we were a great deal younger. And I think young people, a young Queen, and young family is infinitely more newsworthy and amusing. You know, we're getting on for middle-age, and I dare say when we're really ancient, there might be a bit more reverence again.

'I don't know, but I would have thought we were entering probably the least interesting period of the kind of glamorous existence. And I think this follows. This is the way it works. I think there *is* a change. I think people have got more accustomed to us – they take us much more naturally. There used to be much more interest. Now people take it as a matter of course. Either they can't stand us, or they think we're all right.'[1]

In the hushed and reverent atmosphere manufactured round the Queen, a curious journalistic mafia had developed. It was split into three groups, each jealous of its territory and often suspicious of outsiders. The most experienced twosome were also the most pleasant, and they did more than anyone during the fifties and sixties to bolster acceptable acts in the royal soap opera: Godfrey Talbot and Ronnie Gomer Jones. Both were tall, courteous epitomes of pre-war British rectitude, diluted with laconic self-mockery. Godfrey Talbot, who retired during the year, spent a life-time broadcasting evocative paeans on royal progress to British radio listeners, yet retained an unquenchable enthusiasm for taking snapshots of official occasions with his small camera. Gomer Jones, the Press Association's 'Court correspondent', and the only journalist in regular day-to-day contact with the royal family's affairs while they are in Britain, bobbed in their wake with unmutilated sang-froid, his bowler hat,

[1]*Face The Press*, Tyne-Tees Television, 20 March, 1968.

umbrella and pin-striped suit an ever immaculate contrast to
scruffy local reporters assigned to cover royal activities in
their area.

Then there were the dwindling regiment of correspondents
on overseas royal tours, suffering the deprivations of exotic
travel with fortitude and irritability. And, finally, there were
the free-lance writers about royalty, some of whom were
indulging in the most lucrative form of fairy story-telling in
the world. One man, who has convinced American and continental magazines of his reliability earns a comfortable
£5,000 a year inventing stories at home about the marriage
of Tony and Margaret, Princess Anne's latest fracas with a
boyfriend, or Prince Charles's wild oats. He has never
met, or even seen, a member of the royal family. Occasionally, when he wants to check minor pieces of information, he
telephones the Buckingham Palace Press Office under an
assumed name. 'Of course I make it all up,' he says cheerfully.
'What are they going to do? Sue me?'

Others apparently obtain their material semi-mystically,
like the elusive Helen Cathcart, who has written nine royal
books. Miss Cathcart is unapproachable, and her public
utterances are made via an elderly gentleman called Harold A.
Albert. 'She feels the people she writes about are more interesting than her,' he says. 'She prefers privacy, and doesn't
agree with the contemporary idea of publicizing authors. I
act as editor, and do some research. There are certain questions
on her identity that I can't answer, but it is ridiculous to
suggest she doesn't exist.'

Perhaps she is some little old Scottish lady, stringing
together fulsome prose from a mass of press cuttings. Perhaps,
she is a former royal serving wench. But her gratitude to
Mr Albert is undoubtedly immense. He writes to newspapers
on her behalf, and sends copious requests to the Lord Chamberlain's office for information to fill her books.

'Miss Cathcart' has allegedly met the Queen and members
of the royal family. There is no such boasting from Graham

and Heather Fisher, a husband and wife team who have specialized in royal stories for several years. Former footmen are a favourite source of information for them and, at least until the end of 1969, they hadn't found it necessary to check any facts with Press Secretary Bill Heseltine.

Photographers, too, earn an adequate living selling 'informal' pictures of royalty. During the year, one book alone made £30,000 in European serial rights. And, at a time when television was to be used as the main ingredient in improving the royal image, it was a stolen set of still pictures that provided the scandalous *hors d'oeuvre*.

In October 1968 there was an international outcry when *Paris Match* published several pages of pictures, taken by Princess Anne and Prince Philip, showing the Queen in bed after the birth of her youngest son Prince Edward in 1964. She was wearing a negligee, and cradling Edward in her arms.

The Queen heard about their publication on the train travelling from Scotland to London after her holiday at Balmoral. At first, she thought they must have been sold by the relative of an intimate royal servant who had just died. In that case, although they were still her copyright, they were not 'stolen'. They upset her, and certainly lessened the dignity of her position, but what could she do? Bill Heseltine, issued a statement: 'Since the pictures are of such a personal kind, the Queen would naturally prefer that they had not been published. For that reason, we are unable to approve their future publication.'

Had she, at that stage, known the real source of the pictures, and the saga of conning, farce, and deception that surrounded them, it is possible their publication would have been more forcefully discouraged in England. However, the *Daily Express*, who have an agreement with *Paris Match*, decided to publish, thus creating inordinate indignation about 'invasion of privacy' amongst other newspapers. One of the most vehemently self-righteous had, in fact, made an unsuccessful

bid a few days earlier. The Press Council began an investigation into the 'circumstances surrounding their publication',
an American news magazine started a fruitless, weeks-
long probe, and the sanctimonious hullabaloo became so loud
that the *Express* found it necessary to advertise its clear conscience over a full page advertisement in *The Times*:

The royal picture row goes on.

Other papers claim that they decided not to publish the
pictures on ethical grounds.

The fact is that the *Daily Express* was the only British newspaper in possession of the pictures.

They were passed to the *Express* from the magazine *Paris
Match* under the terms of their mutual contract for first
option on each other's material.

Short of 'lifting' the pictures by photographing the pages
of *Paris Match* or photographing early editions of the *Express*,
the other newspapers were helpless.

'Holier than thou' *could* be termed 'sour grapes'.[2]

Some continental magazines did photograph the pages, and
refused to pay a copyright fee, believing the pictures to be
stolen. The editor of the *Daily Express*, Derek Marks, later
excused his attitude to the Press Council:

'When I first saw the pictures, I telephoned the Palace to
inform them of their existence and of the fact that they were
being offered to me. In order that the pictures could be
identified, I sent copies to the Palace.

'I do not propose to go in detail into a series of confidential
conversations. I feel at liberty, however, to say that I
was told, quite understandably, that in the circumstances
approval could not be given for their publication in this
country.

'No specific request was made to me not to publish the
pictures. The fact of the matter is that it was made quite clear
to me that no prohibition was placed upon my publishing the

[2]*The Times*, 4 October, 1968.

pictures. I was told that it was a matter entirely within my own discretion.'

He said he did not know the identity of the person originally responsible for passing on the pictures but thought he was a louse. Once they were passed on, though, they had to be published. This jesuitical argument, which incidentally does not commend very highly the investigatory capabilities of Britain's second largest selling newspaper, is typical of the royalty publicity skirmish. *Paris Match* explained the pictures were taken into their office by a 'mystery man'.'He may have been English, but he spoke very good French indeed. We did not ask him where he got the pictures.' Other newspapers guessed it was 'an English aristocrat', 'a close friend of the royal family', and so on. He was none of these things. He was a timid little man, sitting in a suburban semidetached, terrified by the furore he had caused, and expecting a knock on the door any minute. He had just had a nerve shattering plane journey back from Paris where he had been handed his fee in cash, at a grubby café near the Gare du Nord. It was about ten times more than the £500 he had anticipated for such harmless, rather blurred, ordinary pictures.

They had been gathered over a few years. Whenever royal snapshots are developed, they are delivered to a well-known camera shop by a detective, whose practice it was to stand outside the darkroom door, confident in the incorruptibility of scientists. He was handed the developed films, and returned them to the Palace. No one imagined that copies could have been taken – until they appeared one day at the London office of a man who had a friend, who had a friend, who had kept in touch with an old Royal Air Force buddy, who was in film processing. There was a three inch stack of pictures, taken over several years by various members of the family: one of Margaret lolling against a wall, the Queen the size of a pin-prick against a vast green background – the usual sort of badly focused family snapshots. The friend, who was to act as courier took them to the London office of *Stern* magazine, where the representative had intellectual convulsions, and said he couldn't discuss them in England. He arranged to fly to Hamburg with the courier.

First, though, the courier wanted to call at the *Paris Match* offices in Paris, where the pictures were bought, at a somewhat low figure because they were stolen. One issue of *Paris Match* had been completed that day, and the editors promised, with a handshake over their famous green baize table, not to use the pictures until the following week. The courier flew to Hamburg, where total secrecy was observed. The editor, picture editor, courier, and London representative even used different lifts to avert suspicion, as they rushed late at night to a private room at the top of the building. Just as they were discussing money, a telephone call came through from Paris, saying *Paris Match* had changed their schedules and were already printing. *Gott in Himmel,* you can't trust those French bastards. *Stern* could not compete because their issue was already delivered to bookstalls. At least, though, the Germans had the advantage of time to think about the lay-out. They made sure the best pictures were spread across two pages, so staples would prevent pirates copying them and printing them for nothing. You couldn't trust anyone.

The fracas illustrates again the schizophrenia temporarily adopted by most people when British royalty is involved. On one hand, the Queen is a symbol of dignity and heritage, so 'mystique' has to surround her. On the other, she is a middle class mother who must be seen to be 'normal'.

A hazard of having your feet in two opposing camps is that you may get ruptured. Undaunted, the Palace decided to make the gymnastics even more complicated by allowing a television unit to film the Queen through a year of her life. American magazines, playing a subtle game, hoped for information from this later in the year and at least one to whom the bedroom pictures were offered, declined because they did not want to prejudice future, more riveting material. In the event, it was unforthcoming.

The Queen has always been nervous of television. One Christmas, when commercial television asked to film her going to church at Windsor, she mentioned the request to an adviser. 'I shall have to do it, I suppose, but it's something I can't stand. I'm used to the BBC, and they've made the ordeal easier, but if I say I won't do it for ITV it might sound ungracious.'

Every Christmas, she broadcast to the nation. It was a tradition begun by her grandfather, George V, in 1932. Since 1957, the Queen had appeared on television in a talk pre-recorded about ten days earlier except for the first two years, when it was 'live'. It was a folk custom of dubious benefit but harmless entertainment to a country of tipsy patriots after a good Christmas lunch. The Queen disliked doing it, and squirmed when she saw herself reading stilted from a tele-prompter, or glancing nervously at the additional type-written prompt to her right. It was a performance that always made her miserable, and she wasn't helped by the exotic professionalism of the BBC outside broadcast unit who recorded it with the panache of a circus spectacular. About ninety technicians, designers, make-up artists, furniture removers, sound recorders, interior decorators, cameramen, producers, directors and a retinue of important officials were issued with special passes and descended on Buckingham Palace where they proceeded to redecorate the Bow Room. They removed the Queen's curtains and carpets, and sub-stituted their own. Even the furniture was replaced with antiques from a store, or maybe it was genuine reproduction scenery from the effects department. Finally, the Queen was paraded in front of the cameras for her 'informal' chat to Britain and the Commonwealth:

'Christmas is a Christian festival which celebrates the birth of the Prince of Peace. At times it is almost hidden by the

208

merry-making and tinsel, but the essential message of Christmas is still that we all belong to the great brotherhood of man.

'This idea is not limited to the Christian faith. Philosophers and prophets have concluded that peace is better than war, love is better than hate and that mankind can only find progress in friendship and co-operation.

'Many ideas are being questioned today, but these great truths will continue to shine out as the light of hope in the darkness of intolerance and inhumanity.

'The words "the brotherhood of man" have a splendid ring about them, but the idea may seem too remote to have any practical meaning in this hard and bustling age. Indeed it means nothing at all unless the brotherhood, starting with individuals, can reconcile rival communities, conflicting religions, differing races and the divided, the prejudiced nations of the world.

'If we truly believe that the brotherhood of man has a value for the world's future, then we should seek to support those international organizations which foster understanding between people and between nations.

'The British people together have achieved great things in the past and have overcome many dangers, but we cannot make further progress if we resurrect ancient squabbles.'[3]

Such an ordeal would inhibit the most fervent self-publicist. It did not encourage the Queen to lose her natural shyness, nor did it make the Monarchy seem a particularly relevant symbol to the young people who would be most sceptical about the Investiture. It was dropped in 1969 while a more suitable formula was discussed – to the approval of most, but the indignation of some, notably the *Daily Telegraph*:[4]

'There is really no need for continuous change in all things: the Christmas services themselves are none the less deeply

[3]25 December, 1968.
[4]*Daily Telegraph*, 21 October, 1969.

moving for remaining just as they were centuries ago. A few trend-setting London freaks apart, what ordinary people desperately need in this age of swirling dissolution and transformation, is something constant and durable to hang on to. Is it not part of the Monarch's high function to supply this?

'Perhaps the Queen thinks (or is advised) that she is not a born television performer. Well, perhaps she is not, though it would be easy to name many performers less charming and more inept who make a handsome living from the box. Yet this is not the point. Children value letters from their mother not because she is necessarily the greatest letter writer since Horace Walpole but because she is their mother. In the same way we value a personal word from the Queen not because she is more inspiring than ———— ————, or more amusing than ———— ———— (though she may be both) but just because she is our Queen. As such, she is in a sense the mother of us all.'

Possibly there was an alarming increase in the number of trend-setting London freaks because the next week the Sunday newspaper ran the results of a Gallup Poll survey that showed more than half the country were not disappointed by the cancellation of the speech.[5]

The arrival of Bill Heseltine at the Palace, and the need to retain dignity while stimulating interest, had coincided with a totally unexpected success: the televised autobiography of Lord Mountbatten. When he realized the films were going to be popular, Mountbatten went to the Palace with his son-in-law, Lord Brabourne, a film producer, to suggest a similar

[5]*Sunday Telegraph*, 2 November, 1969 published results of a Gallup Poll which had asked: 'Are you disappointed or not that there will not be a Christmas broadcast (by the Queen) this year?

	ALL	MEN	WOMEN
Disappointed	48	38	58
Not Disappointed	52	62	42

idea to the Queen. For a long time, the Queen thought about the pros and cons. At first, she didn't think the film would be a good idea – apart from which, she didn't want a 'movie star' image. Eventually, she was persuaded it was important to project the 'family life' aspect of Monarchy.

Television often provides a temporarily convincing substitute for life, and when its unreality collides with the unreality of Monarchy, in an attempt to reveal the truth, there can be one result: dramatic immediate popularity, followed by a gradual re-thinking.

The careers of innumerable politicians warned against the fickleness of the electric incubus. President Nixon, questioned in 1952 about irregularities in his Senator's salary, sat in front of the cameras with his wife and children, and admitted he had received a gift. 'You know what it was? It was a little cocker spaniel dog in a crate. Black and white spotted. And our little girl – Tricia, the six-year-old – named it Checkers. And you know, the kids love that dog, and I just want to say this right now, that regardless of what they say about it, we're going to keep it.'

The broadcast was an immediate success, but a few years later it was suggested he lost the presidential election simply because he was worse than John Kennedy in televised debates. There was a reversal in 1968 when it was said a major ingredient in his election was his attractive packaging in the mass media. President Johnson felt television was largely responsible for his unpopularity. In England, Alec Douglas Home was one of television's early disasters, Harold Macmillan's Edwardian showmanship seemed contrived, and Harold Wilson's gritty determination became a stale parody of itself. After a while, mystique vanishes in the make-up room, and adulation can be reversed too soon. 'You have the voice of the people, as well as God,' said a flatterer to Oliver Cromwell when he returned from Ireland. 'The people should be just as noisy if they were going to see me hanged,' replied Cromwell. It hasn't changed much.

Moreover, television trivializes at the same time as it appears to exalt. The Coronation, Britain's longest outside broadcast, lasting seven hours fifteen minutes from 10.15 a.m. until 5.30 p.m., was followed by 'New Elizabethan Age' panegyrics which made the disillusion even more bitter. A film of 'informal royals' could create the same topsy-turvy reaction.

Knowing this, the advisers pondered on the best use of television. One suggestion was to make their own film, and sell it commercially. The profits might be a useful addition to royal finance, but the problems would have been immense. Eventually it was decided to have a joint consortium of BBC and independent TV talents. Prince Philip acted as chairman, and was advised by Press secretary Bill Heseltine, Lord Brabourne, Robin Gill, managing director of ATV Corporation who were to market the film, and BBC Television director Richard Cawston.

Filming began on 8 June, 1968 and by 18 May, 1969 they had spent seventy-five days in 172 locations. Forty-three hours of film had to be cut into what was anticipated as an hour but was extended to 110 minutes in England. *Royal Family* showed the women's magazine side of royalty in a reasonably chatty, but over-long way, and cleverly entwined nostalgia, patriotism, modernity and humour to give an appearance of reality, but the main impact was achieved by showing the Queen as a fairly unremarkable sort of woman. It was greeted with reverential praise. Robin Gill declared it was 'electrifying, the most exciting film ever made for television. Its impact on world markets will be staggering.'

On the first showing twenty-three million people watched – seven and a half million less than for the World Cup football final between England and West Germany in July 1966 and three million less than for *Steptoe and Son*, a series about a rag and bone man. Ironically, it was on the same day Rhodesia announced its intended Republic status. 'Very regrettable,' said Sir Alec Douglas Home. When the film was repeated a week later there was an audience of fifteen million – six million of whom were watching for the second time. The talking point was American Ambassador Walter Annenberg's reply to the Queen when she asked where they were living.

'We're in the Embassy residence, subject of course to some of the discomfiture as a result of a need for elements of refurbishing, rehabilitation.'

This was shortly followed by an aside from the Queen to Prince Philip as she prepared to enter a diplomatic reception.

'He's not here.'

'Who's not here?'

'The American Ambassador.' The Queen was clearly amused, and the implication that she was referring to the pompous Annenberg, added piquancy to the scene. In fact, the film had been shot months earlier, and the remark referred to his predecessor, David Bruce, who had sent a message to the Palace saying he was held up in the traffic.

Another part that showed the family in a 'normal' setting was by a Scottish loch, with them preparing a picnic on the Balmoral estate. It seemed a lovely, airless, cloud-free day and they were a typical, British middle class family enjoying an outing. Unfortunately, immediately after filming ended, clouds appeared, and they had to seek refuge in a nearby farmhouse for a sit-down meal of the 'picnic'.

The film, known as *Corgi and Beth* in some circles, had a £90,000 budget provided equally by the BBC and ITV– that was increased to £150,000 with distribution and ancillary costs. This was covered by the American sale. The Queen had a half share in the profits of approximately £100,000. This was to be added to about £8,000 held in trust by a bank for charities from a previous BBC-ITV consortium film on royal palaces. Total profit on that film had been about £32,000. £8,000 of the Queen's half share

213

had been spent cleaning her Van Dycks and putting new lighting in the Queen's Gallery at Buckingham Palace, which is open to the public.

There were few adverse comments about the *Royal Family* film. Most critics seemed over-awed by the initial sight of the Queen as a human being. 'I think the upper ten per cent have been developing and changing their attitude to the Monarchy over the last ten years,' said Lord Cobbold. 'But the others had their attitude changed overnight by the film.'

After a while, though, doubts began:

'Richard Cawston's film, *Royal Family*, could not have had a better critical reception had it been the combined work of Eisenstein, Hitchcock and Fellini,' wrote Milton Shulman in the *Evening Standard*.[6] 'But the making and showing of such a film with the Monarch's co-operation, may have constitutional and historical consequences which go well beyond its current interest as a piece of TV entertainment.

'What has actually happened is that an old image has been replaced by a fresh one. The emphasis on authority and remoteness which was the essence of the previous image has, ever since George VI, been giving way to a friendlier image of homeliness, industry, and relaxation.

'But just as it was untrue that the royal family sat down to breakfast wearing coronets as they munched their corn flakes, so is it untrue that they now behave in their private moments like a middle class family in Surbiton or Croydon.

'Judging from Cawston's film, it is fortunate that at this moment of time we have a royal family that fits in so splendidly with a public relations man's dream.

'Yet is it, in the long run, wise of the Queen's advisers to set as a precedent this right of the TV camera to act as an image-making apparatus for the Monarchy? Every institution that has so far attempted to use TV to popularize or aggrandize itself has been diminished and trivialized by it.'

[6] 25 June, 1969.

214

Its first colour showing in Britain was transmitted in late afternoon, for the benefit of schoolchildren, who had perhaps the most fascinating preconceptions about Monarchy. According to a survey published in *New Society* in October 1969[7] three fifths of children between eight and twelve thought the Queen was 'the most important person in England', and about half thought she was the most important person in the world. Seven out of ten said she had more to do with running the country than the Prime Minister. Commented *New Society*: 'The child who begins with the assumption that he is the legal subject of a benevolent but unchecked Monarch is not likely, on gradually correcting this impression to develop the further assumption (common among American children) that the government is there for the citizen to guide and influence. And for many working class children, the notion of a royal ruler seems to continue later into adolescence – perhaps even into adult life for a few.'

These attitudes could be subtly changed by the television film, but the danger was in the reaction. 'If she's so ordinary, has a picnic like the rest of us, and is there primarily to keep a check on alternative powers, does she need so much money? And, anyway, do we in England really need such an elaborate system to prevent the Generals taking over?' Was the reality of Monarchy merely a family of ham actors, pre-packed in the flotsam of an imperial past and the jetsam of inherited attitudes, pirouetting in a televised home movie?

'Do we need the Queen?' asked the *Daily Mail*[8] in a series of articles. Overwhelmingly, the answer was still Yes, but the fact that the question was asked at all in a right-wing

---

[7] *New Society*, October 23, 1969 published results of a questionnaire study conducted by V. M. Herman and Robert Stradling of Essex University which took place in spring 1969 and involved interviews with 178 junior school children aged from eight to twelve in three Essex schools. Each school had roughly forty per cent middle class, and sixty per cent working class students.

[8] 31 October, 1969.

newspaper, indicated the change in attitude that was taking place. More invigorating glimpses of the institution would be required if interest was to be maintained, followed by the establishment of new and positive attitudes about the role of Monarchy.

And the focus for these would be Charles and Anne.

Royal Family Inc. - V

Ought we to inflict on a young man of Prince Charles's calibre (or on anybody) a lifetime dedicated to what in essence is a non job? *The Guardian*, 27 June, 1969.

'A twit, I should think,' Prince Charles, being asked to describe himself in the Drummer film, *A Prince for Wales*.

'Fantastic.' An interminably repeated public remark about Princess Anne.

'Princess Anne, the girl who is growing up the wittiest, gayest, and most natural of Royal Princesses.' A *Daily Mirror* special booklet, August 1969.

THE TWIN SENSATIONS of the royal year, Prince Charles and Princess Anne, were launched into public life with the expertise of a new deodorant. At first, Charles was considered pleasant enough, but dull and a bit insipid. Anne was a dumpy schoolgirl interested only in horses, and scorned by the tasteful oracles of international fashion. 'Poor Princess Anne. She's eighteen today, and nobody thinks she's a pretty girl. If I were her mother, the first thing I'd do is slim her down. She has to stop looking like her mother. The frumpy fur stoles, the middle-aged evening gowns. The over-done hair. The under-done hair. The sloppy grooming. It's about time Anne was allowed to bloom on her own.'[1]

By the end of the year both were the apotheosis of British youth, an inspiration not only to their country but possibly the world, examples of Monarchy as a trendsetter. Charles –

[1] *Women's Wear Daily*, August 15, 1968.

dignified, courteous, every mother's ideal son. Anne – well-built, extrovert, with an 'authorized' biography published at nineteen, every uncle's favourite niece. In one autumnal spasm[2] she drove a London bus, a police car on a skid pan, and a fifty-six-ton Chieftain tank at twenty miles an hour across rough ground. The tank was driven at Paderborn, West Germany, where she visited her 14th/20th King's Hussars as Colonel-in-Chief. Elegantly, she also fired a Sterling sub-machine-gun from the hip. 'Even the best in the regiment could hardly do much better,' enthused an instructor, predictably. Every accomplishment of the royal adolescents was greeted with shrill choruses of official wonderment. They could do no wrong.

Charles had the most difficult task. He had to prove himself a potential king for the twenty-first century, yet take part in an ancient pageant in a Welsh ruin, a feat of royal legerdemain that looked virtually impossible at the beginning of the year. 'I think the doubts are not so much allowing him to take part at all but if we had any doubts perhaps to what extent this sort of virtually mediæval revival was relevant,' said Prince Philip.[3] 'I think that probably the final governing factor was that it was quite obvious that a very large proportion of Welsh opinion favoured this.

'I think it (the Monarchy) functions because occasionally you've got to stick your neck out. You can't just be wholly negative about this. I think if you feel strongly enough about it, and you feel that you're doing the right thing and that it is in the interests of people – sensible and intelligent people – you should go ahead and do it in spite of the fact that you may be criticized for it.

'The idea that you don't do anything on the offchance you might be criticized, you'd end up like a living cabbage and it's pointless. You've got to stick up for something you believe in.'

[2] October 1969.
[3] Grampian Television, 21 February, 1969.

Charles had been a late developer. His educational grounding under Miss Katherine Peebles, 'Mispy', was somewhat drab and inadequate by modern standards of primary school teaching. At eight, he spent six months at a pre-preparatory school, Hill House, Knightsbridge, before going to Prince Philip's old boarding school, Cheam, where his academic abilities were publicly acknowledged to be less than brilliant.

With vulnerability and shyness an important part of his personality, attractive attributes in his mother but possibly not so desirable in a future king, Charles was channelled into the hearty, 'hurrah Henry' atmosphere so enjoyed by his father. Gordonstoun, a combination of the more notable Teutonic and English character-building ideas, with a curious philosophical correlation between cold showers and manliness, provided rigorous conditioning in respectable upper middle class attitudes. 'I suppose I could have gone to the local comprehensive or the local grammar, but I'm not sure it would have done me much good,' he said.[4] 'I think a public school gives you a great deal of self discipline and experience and responsibility, and it is this responsibility that is so worth while.'

British public schools do not have a monopoly of the responsibility-giving techniques, but they endeavour to give that impression.

Before leaving Gordonstoun there was a Monarchical gesture to the Commonwealth: two terms at Timbertop, the country annex of Geelong Grammar School, Australia, where Charles could finally develop away from the overpowering influence of home, and enjoy the most rewarding experience of his early life. At last, he could be an individual.

It is difficult enough to grow up. It is even more difficult when the process must be observed by a nation using you as a child substitute to the extent that your birth is greeted by blue rinsed fountains in Trafalgar Square and four dreadful

[4] 6 June, 1969, interviewed by three journalists.

lines of verse from the Poet Laureate. It is hard when you are buffeted from one place to another to satisfy the whims of politicians, and public, as well as the concern of parents, a scholastic scavenger gobbling every potential criticism at its inception. It is hazardous when nearly everyone gives you instant, unearned reverence, so at five years old you are elected one of the eleven best dressed men in Europe, and at ten you hear your mother's tape-recorded voice announcing you are going to be Prince of Wales. It is virtually impossible when, in addition, you are an awkward, jug-eared teenager with a slightly lop-sided grin, quick to blush, trying to mould yourself in the admired image of a debonair father.

The fact that Charles triumphed over his upbringing was a credit to his innate good sense and ability, more than anything else. For a while, in spite of public relations blandishments, he was like a young man trying to find a role. He had the same rolling walk as Philip, with one arm behind his back; the same jabbing right forefinger asking the same sort of questions; the same easy laugh to finish a conversation before walking to the next presentation on an uplifting note; the same way of clasping his hands together and moving an imaginary handkerchief in the sleeve of his left arm. But not yet quite the practised egalitarian attitude. One of the depressing aspects of British middle-class education is that it gives every incentive to understand, but limits the ability to do so. After talking to two children in a pit village in Wales, Charles turned to a matronly woman standing near by, and asked pleasantly, 'Are you their nanny?' In a similar way, his younger brother, ten-year-old Andrew, can be intrigued that anyone actually brushes their own shoes. 'But who *does* them for you?' he asks adults occasionally deputed to look after him while his parents are working on a ceremony.

It was clear Charles needed help in his launching on the British public, and the ideal man was chosen to give self-confidence. Squadron-Leader David Checketts, tough, stocky, thirty-nine years old, director of a public relations firm, Neilson McCarthy, had been Prince Philip's equerry for five years. In 1967, he was deputed to guide Charles through the accumulating problems of life as an undergraduate at Trinity College, Cambridge. 'I've gone to school and University and everything in a much more normal way than any of my predecessors did,' said Charles, adding, 'There have been disadvantages, and moments when I've regretted it.'[5]

In a number of subtle ways Charles, unlike Anne, is not really in tune with the majority of his generation. He has the gentlemanly tranquillity, almost softness, of an intellectual but without the academic qualifications. His clothes indicate squareness of a decade or two earlier – trousers with turn-ups, unlike Philip, even though they both use the same tailor; and he will go on a fishing trip dressed in hacking jacket, thick brown trousers, shirt, tie, and brown brogue shoes. His hobbies – cello playing and polo – are hardly representative, and his choice of a musical concert with Yehudi Menuhin playing a Mozart concerto to celebrate his twenty-first birthday was a more gracious gesture to civilization than would be made by many of his contemporaries, or even his family. His subjects at Cambridge – archaeology and anthropology – suggest a contemplative nature which may provide difficulties in adjusting to the tedious hurly burly that makes up so much of royal duty, and the gossip that provides an essential part of its interest.

'I suppose there will be a lot of balls talked about his possible wife,' said a member of the family. 'But things will die down.'

Other members of the family supplied the initial romantic interest, notably Prince William of Gloucester who was friendly with an inelegantly named divorcée, Szuzui Starkloff, in Tokyo when he was commercial attaché at the British Embassy.

Anne was useful for more general gossip. 'She's the wild one, I'd hate to go driving with her,' said a friend. Her

[5]Drummer Films, *A Prince for Wales*.

221

future presented a problem. She didn't know what she wanted to do, except get married, and her exam results were too awful to enable her to enter university – D and E passes in Advanced level history and geography – and her temperament was not really that of a demure young princess available at any time to add sugar to the life of a nation. She knew her mind, insisted on her own way, was known as 'Madam' by some of the Palace staff and made the best of a somewhat sulky face with a large jaw and jutting bottom lip. She was taller – five foot six and a half inches – than her mother, more assertive than Charles, a girl aware of her sex appeal, and delighted by the publicity she received.

And, at a time when heart-shaped pubic hair was forecast by dress designer Mary Quant as a new fashion, Anne was able to keep a comfortable equilibrium between dowdiness and hipsterism by wearing a large 'mod' watch, shortish skirts, trouser suits, hats that sent milliners into gleeful paroxysms and fashion editors into easily delighted swoons, make a speech confiding where she bought her underwear and other items of clothing, and dancing on the stage at the end of *Hair*, the final play to be banned by the Lord Chamberlain before his powers of theatre censorship were abandoned on 26 September, 1968. Anne's last exploit did not amuse some of the establishment figures who are an integral part of Monarchy.

'I was very surprised with her,' said a senior Duke. 'She's not particularly pretty, yet she was wearing a trouser suit, of all things. I've seen the show myself. Dreadful, dreadful. People doing all sorts of things under that blanket, and standing naked. I left after the first half. I don't know why they allow that sort of thing. Anne, of course, is very like the late Queen Mary. She'll go crazy, and dance around. And suddenly she'll remember who she is.'

To a certain extent, she was protected from flippancy by being given unimaginative chores. Her first solo public engagement was presenting leeks to the Welsh Guards[6] on a

[6]1 March, 1969.

222

bitterly cold parade ground at Pirbright, Surrey – a curious sensation for a young girl, but one that reflected the Queen's own first public duty when, as a Colonel of 16 years old she inspected the Grenadier Guards.

There was another, more sinister, protection in the Statute of Treasons (1351) which concerned itself with the chastity of certain royal ladies, and rendered their seducer liable to capital punishment. As she entered her twentieth year, cool, composed and in command of herself, it didn't seem Anne would need such safeguards even though she was pursued by countless rumours of impending engagements.

Prince Charles's marriage would be more complicated. By an act of 1689 he could not marry a Roman Catholic and there would be uproar if he fell in love with a coloured girl. White Anglo-Saxon Protestant for him, and he had to have his mother's written consent, as did all members of the royal family since George III passed the Royal Marriage Act in 1772 because he was annoyed by two of his sons marrying commoners. 'No descendant of George II shall be capable of contracting matrimony without the previous consent of the King, and signified under the Great Seal, declared in Council, and entered in the Privy Council books.'

Charles himself had somewhat outdated thoughts about a potential wife. 'You've got to remember that when you marry, in my position, you are going to marry somebody who perhaps one day is going to become Queen. You've got to choose somebody very carefully. The one advantage about marrying a princess, for instance, or somebody from a royal family, is that they know what happens.'

His attitude to training in the Armed Forces was also untypical. 'A period in the Services gives you a great experience and responsibility of life, of discipline, and above all of people and how to deal with people, to discipline them, and to be disciplined by them.'[7] It was the upper middle class reflex response, and one that was not popular amongst

[7] 6 June, interview.

223

the rest of the country. Army recruitment figures were dropping by about fifteen per cent a year.[8] Moreover it indicated an inconsistency in Charles's character, a struggle between his real feelings and the traditionally accepted and psychologically important royal virtue of bellicosity. At a centenary concert for Mahatma Gandhi[9] (ironically, a man who had been shoved in and out of prison by the British), he said: 'With the death of Gandhi, a great restraining influence has been removed. Today, violent methods are taken for granted. If only for Mahatma Gandhi's sake, let us have the courage to show that the great majority in this country reject violence.' A few months later, it was announced he was going to Dartmouth Royal Naval College in preparation for a minimum of three years in the Navy – like his father and grandfather. 'I shall have to stock up with plenty of sea-sickness pills,' he said.

A potential king's life must, to some extent, be wrapped in contradictions. It hasn't mattered when there has been unquestioning acceptance of the role, but the problems now were more difficult – as Charles was aware. 'In these times this sort of organization is called into question. It is not taken for granted as it used to be. In that sense one has to be far more professional at it than I think you ever used to be, and I hope that my education and upbringing and all these various schools and establishments will in some way equip me for this role.'

Would he like to change his job?

'No I don't think so. I don't see how I could now, having been brought up and having the background I do have. It would be very difficult doing anything else. I've been, as it were, trained to do it and I feel part of the job. I have this feeling of duty towards England, towards the United King-

[8]Men recruited in Army:

	1966	1967	1968
	25,610	21,313	17,125

[9]22 October, 1969.

dom, the Commonwealth, and I feel that there is a great deal I can do if I am given the chance to do it.'

For guidance, he went to a source that was in increasingly uncommon use: the Church. One of the Queen's senior religious advisers travelled on several occasions at Charles's request to Cambridge and Aberystwyth to discuss the future with him. 'He's a believing Christian, very keen to see the reformation of the church,' says the clergyman. 'Within the next fifty years, the Protestant church will be united, and the Roman Catholic and Anglican churches will be reconciled. Then the Monarchy will have a chance to liberate itself from the past. Charles is very aware of this.'

His sense of humour about the job is particularly attractive and it was on this auspicious note that he really began to enter public life at the end of February 1969,[10] when he appeared in fourteen of forty items in the Trinity College revue, *Revulution*. One of the most publicized sketches was of him sitting in a dustbin being interviewed by a reporter about a well-known new University student called 'Reg Sprott' – a reference to Charles's description in a University magazine of a dustman who sang beneath his window early in the morning.

In a skit devised by himself he came on stage, put up an umbrella, and whispered to the audience, 'I lead a sheltered life'. In another, he marched on, flexing his muscles, and shouted, 'I wreak vengeance'. A second actor ran past, holding his nose, 'So that's what it is'. Later, with a lecherous grin, Charles walked off stage arm in arm with a pretty girl, saying, 'I like to give myself heirs'.

Such undergraduate humour was so popular, with Prince Charles as a member of the cast, that four-shilling tickets were sold for £2, and the wrath of the Lord's Day Observance Society was cracked heavily on to the heads of the heathens who wanted to entertain on Sunday. The performance had to be cancelled, under an Act of 1780.

[10]26 February to 3 March.

The unpremeditated success of Charles in *Revulution* was a bonus in a masterfully understated campaign to make him a nationally respected and popular figure. Practical experience in administration had begun in the summer of 1968 when he visited seven Government departments and saw employees on location. But the first attempt to show his character on a national scale was a lunch-time interview on Saturday 1 March, on the two least popular channels of BBC radio: Radio 3 and 4, a few minutes after Anne had successfully presented her leeks.

It was a caressing baptism by Jack de Manio, avuncular compere of an early morning radio talkshow, *Today*, that scatters millions of bleary-eyed English off to work with a self-satisfied giggle and renewed feelings of faith in the old country, a man of unpretentious mental ability who has made something of a trade-mark of frequently misreading the time. He appeared to demonstrate that the English love a man who has no mind, and speaks it. He was also, a director of Neilson McCarthy, with David Checketts.

For the first time, most people in the country heard Prince Charles speak, and his pleasant, lively and articulate replies had the expected effect. He was enthusiastic about his part in *Revulution*:

'It's the most awful sort of Beyond the Fringe type of revue, you know. We've about 40 skits and I take part in about 16 of them. And most of the jokes are the most awful sort of groan jokes, you know. Everybody goes "Ooh", and there's one complete one where it's called The All-in Groan and we just walk across making idiotic jokes "I say, I say" jokes – that sort of thing.'

'Your investiture as Prince of Wales has obviously been in everybody's mind. Do you feel any sort of apprehension about the whole thing?'

'It would be unnatural, I think, if one didn't feel any apprehension about it. One always wonders what's going to happen in this sort of thing. But I think if one takes this as it comes it'll be much easier. I expect at Aberystwyth there may be one or two demonstrations, and as long as I don't get covered too much in egg and tomato I'll be all right but I don't blame people demonstrating like that. They've never seen me before, they don't know what I'm like. I've hardly been to Wales, and you can't really expect people to be overzealous about the fact of having a so-called English Prince to come amongst them and be frightfully excited. Once I've been there for eight weeks things might improve.'

'When did you first realize as a little boy that you were heir to the Throne and not just an ordinary chap?'

'I think it's something that dawns on you with the most ghastly inexorable sense. I didn't suddenly wake up in my pram one day and say "Yippee I ... " But I think it just dawns on you, slowly that people are interested in one ... and slowly you get the idea that you have a certain duty and responsibility, and I think it's better that way, rather than suddenly someone telling you, "You must do this" and "You must do that" because of who you are. I think it's one of those things you grow up in.'

'Well, we all hear about students today, and you are still a student, and thank heavens not all students demonstrate. But in your view, why do they do it and how can one solve the problem?'

'I can't help feeling that because students and many people feel so helpless and so anonymous in life and society that demonstrating is one useful way of making known your own particular opinions about world affairs, and domestic affairs and things like that. It may also be because perhaps it's enjoyable, a lot of other people do it. I have a feeling that a lot of people are very serious about it – a lot are not so serious about it, and it develops into sheer mob hysteria, which is very frightening I would think. As to solving it, this is, I should have thought, a very very difficult problem. At Cambridge at the moment they've set up several working parties between dons and students, and I think this is a great help.'

Aberystwyth is a pleasant seaside resort on the hilly west coast of Wales, with a kaleidescopic jumble of boarding houses curving round Cardigan Bay in a homely, uninspiring way. At the left, looking out to sea, stands the University College of Wales which boasts, among other things, the most competent tiddlywinks team in the British Isles, and whose two thousand three hundred students make up a quarter of the town's population. Behind, about a mile up the narrow streets, is Pant-y-Celyn hall of residence, prettily landscaped to detract from its grim, grey stone exterior.

It was here, into a room fifteen foot by ten, that Prince Charles was shunted to satisfy Welsh nationalist feelings by learning their language in a term. He had at first been allocated a warden's double room, but this was vetoed by Palace officials because it was not 'normal' accommodation for a student. It was, therefore, reserved for a personal detective. Charles arrived in his MGC on 20 April, 1969, leaving a Chipmunk aeroplane a few miles away at the Aberporth RAF base so he could continue learning to fly. It was his first real experience of the political ping-pong and public relations humbug that are a necessary aspect of a future Monarch's life.

The Welsh office of the British Government had insisted he should go to Aberystwyth, an idea of patronizing arrogance that gave him a disadvantage among fellow students from the start. Either he should have spent the whole of his university education in Wales – or none. It might have been acceptable if he had chosen it as a college himself but it seemed, to the Welsh at least, as if the Monarchy did not have the courage of its own attitudes, and was being used as a bribe to soften feelings of independence in the principality.

'They really loaded the dice against him in Wales,' said a senior politician. 'The Household should have advised much earlier on the way he should be made Prince of Wales. But it was a gimmick he overcame.'

Historian A. J. P. Taylor wrote in the *Sunday Express*[11] 'The prestige of the Monarchy and its secure position above the parties are injured by this sordid exploitation of the Monarchy for party reasons.'

The Free Wales Army, a silly season joke of self-publicizing fanatics inspired by an idealism (sanctified as 'patriotism' by previous generations) made plans for his assassination, an insulting record was released, and demonstrators girded themselves with placards. To minimize the possibility of unfortunate incidents, a bomb disposal expert was brought in from Chester, and one hundred Special Branch plain clothes policemen were billeted in the town, heavily disguised as students in tweed suits, trilby hats, brown shoes, and nonchalant watchfulness. They sauntered inconspicuously into pubs and coffee bars to eavesdrop.

Frequently, they were greeted with cries of 'Good evening, officer'.

Perkins travelled twice to Aberystwyth to give concise, detailed instructions for action to be taken during bomb hoaxes, saw the double room offered to the detective, and exclaimed to an official: 'Good heavens no, he can't have better accommodation than Prince Charles.'

One of the few privileges enjoyed by Charles was a personal laundry service, following an unfortunate incident in Australia when his underpants were put on view in a shop window. Otherwise, he was an ordinary student, being tutored by a Welsh nationalist parliamentary candidate, and driving to college every morning at 10 o'clock along a route lined by up to a thousand people.

There had only been a vague idea about his curriculum before he arrived. 'There was a certain coyness about the object of the exercise, and it was never made clear,' said the registrar Arfon Owen. 'If he'd been thoroughly stupid it

[11] 12 May, 1968.

229

would have been awful. But he kept up with his British history, and studied Welsh history and literature, as well as the language. No one but a gifted mimic could have learnt to pronounce it so well.

'In effect, his time in Wales was an extended Royal Tour, but there's no class consciousness here which makes it rather difficult for the Monarchy.'

Nevertheless, outside the college there was always a small group of women with shopping bags, ready to chorus 'Oooh', and 'Aaaah' – particularly in the lunch hour.

'I'm sorry to disappoint you, ladies, but His Royal Highness will not be down today. I have just been in communication with his secretary,' said a porter dramatically, as if releasing a state secret.

Turning aside, he added: 'A proper fan club, he's got. Some of them come here every day.'

A warden, passing by, was not so impressed. 'My god, it's exactly the same crowd as went to watch a public hanging. Is it a good thing this should happen?' A few weeks after arriving, Charles overcame nearly all the residual dislike of himself as a person, rather than the institution he represented, by making a five-minute speech in Welsh at the National Eisteddfod of the Urdd in Aberystwyth. 'Ardderchag, excellent', they said, and nicknamed him 'Cariad Bach' – little darling.

Later, he was taught to salute, had a hair cut, and presented colours to the newly formed Regiment of Wales as their colonel-in-chief.

More important, he spoke eloquently about the countryside. 'My object is to be alarmist and to say that there is a very small line between extinction and survival – and this applies to the country as well – and that legislation should be enacted now and not vaguely in the future.

'In South Wales nearly an acre disappears under mine wastage every three days. I could go on until I am blue in the face and you are, I hope, aware of many of the problems. An

230

enormous percentage of the population of Britain and of Wales seems to be totally unaware except when it is too late. The most distressing aspect about the whole question is the dormant state of public opinion in this country. If it could be awakened somehow, the whole task of making our environment habitable would be immeasurably easier.'

By the time he left Aberystwyth on 22 June, his stay had been transformed from potential disaster into an enormous success. The University ran out of prospectuses, and there were 10,000 applicants for the 670 available places – an increase of two thousand on the previous year. Charles paid his bill – £65 for accommodation and £20 for tuition – with a personal cheque, and left to prepare himself for Monarchy's biggest stunt of the decade, an event for which his whole year, perhaps his whole life, had been a series of rehearsals: the Investiture.

'I look upon it, I think, as being a meaningful ceremony. I shall also be glad when it is over because, having spent a year in the midst of controversy and talk, between one side and another, it has become a friction point for many people.'

There were to be deaths, bombs, hysteria, temper, humour, tension, and a great deal of energy expended before it finally came to a nervous climax.

Advice to Prince Charles was always forthcoming from members of the family firm about his future. The Queen could tell him about duty. Prince Philip could talk about the occasional screeches allowed to a man trussed in constitutional fetters. The Queen Mother could talk to him about 'image'. Lord Mountbatten could deliver a long lecture on what 'the people' expect. Princess Margaret could talk.

The more noticeably fringe members could also be helpful, and particularly Lord Harewood and Angus Ogilvy, who had different temperaments but understood the reality of Monarchy better than most, and thought it was a 'tolerably acceptable' system.

'It does involve being all things to all men, which is very difficult,' said Lord Harewood. 'If you're a member of the family, you have the entrée in certain circles, but it's far more difficult to get people to think you're talking sense. I think being royal is a very professional business though, of course, it's not mine. The advantages of a Monarchy are that it gives confidence, a lack of controversy, and something you can believe in without your own political outlook being specially involved. And if you have a disastrous point of crisis, it helps there. Of course, it can lead to apathy. Anything that has positive advantages has the adverse side.

'It's a terribly difficult thing to make the balance between being so representative that the Crown is wholly removed, and so keen to be involved that it becomes cheap. If you carved out a new country, I think Monarchy is a system you would discard at the outset. It's not intellectually justifiable. Kings used to come about because someone was needed to unite a country. Only a "tough" could do it. Now there's unity by consent.'

Lord Harewood, eighteenth in line of succession, a man with a drooping Hanoverian face and baggy eyes, is the only member of the royal family to become directly involved in a political issue. In 1965 he made his maiden speech in the House of Lords in favour of the abolition of hanging.

He embarrassed the family when he was divorced from his first wife, and had a child by his second before they were married. But that was in 1967, and British royalty had not yet begun to discard its mystique. Lord Harewood was, anyway, considered a bit outré in his pursuits. He wrote a book about opera, was director of opera planning at Covent Garden, travelled second class on the train to Glyndebourne, condemned the philistinism of political leaders, contributed to a television programme on the arts, spoke against the two-class society established in England because of public schools, and disliked the national anthem being played after cinema performances.

Angus Ogilvy was slightly more acceptable, although regarded by some as churlish for declining a title on his marriage to Princess Alexandra – behaviour that was not really expected from the son of an Earl. Maybe he even tarnished his wife with watery radicalism because she insisted on being known as Her Royal Highness Princess Alexandra, the Honourable Mrs Angus Ogilvy. That upset the heraldic experts. It didn't really make sense. How could a Princess be plain 'Mrs'?

Others were upset, too. A man who was in love with Alexandra kept threatening to kill her husband. 'If someone blows you up, they blow you up,' was his philosophical attitude.

Ogilvy is a director of Lonrho, a mining company, and resigned all his directorships of their Rhodesian subsidiaries, so as not to 'embarrass the Queen'.

'It's bound to be inhibiting. One has to be much more careful. If I got caught in a normal business risk, it would be difficult. Big money is in my view made by backing small men who are going to be big, but imagine what would have happened if I'd backed a crook. You have to be fairly careful, otherwise one could inadvertently damage the Monarchy. You can look very clever, but so what?'

There are difficulties in remaining ultra-discreet at the same time as not appearing to be a complete fool. A week before devaluation, he was asked to talk to two thousand businessmen in Canada. Anything he said could have been misconstrued, particularly if it was known the Governor of the Bank of England had been to dinner the week before.

'I thought devaluation was on the cards, but I had no special knowledge. I had to give them a lot of light platitudes, and a few irrelevant stories. I refused a question and answer thing. I knew I was evading the issue, and so did they. I don't always like to behave myself, but for obvious reasons I have to.'

Interlude-4

'A new commandment I give unto you, that ye love one another; as I have loved you, that ye also love one another.' St John 13, 34 – the opening words of the Maundy Service.

'Today will be THE day in the history of Selby. Selebians, especially those who have played a part in the preparations, will feel proud when they see a reigning monarch in their town. What other town anything like the size of Selby can boast such an honour?' *Selby Gazette and Herald*, 3 April, 1969.

MAUNDY THURSDAY, an ancient ritual obligation, where God, Mammon and the Monarchy collide in splendid magnanimity, took place for the first time in a parish church – Selby Abbey – on 3 April, 1969, as part of the 900th anniversary celebrations. It was an occasion that obviously demanded special preparations.

Each year, on Thursday of Holy Week, the Queen distributes money to as many poor elderly men and women as the number of years in her age. It is done as a symbol of humility and derives from Jesus washing the disciples' feet. It was begun by the English Monarch at least as early as the twelfth century and there are continuous records dating from Edward I in the late thirteenth century. Several court officials used to wash the feet of recipients in preparation for the Monarch's dab with scented water, but this aspect was discontinued in about 1730. As a remembrance, the Lord High

234

Almoner and his assistants still carry linen towels (dating from 1883) and nosegays of sweet herbs, that were first used during the Plague.

Since the Queen came to the throne the ceremony has alternated between Westminster Abbey and other churches.[1] 'A London production on tour to the provinces,' thought the Vicar of Selby, the Reverend John Kent, a tall, aquiline man with mutton chop whiskers and an unusual lack of pomposity, for an Anglican Minister. He wondered at first if the fuss was worthwhile in a fairly prosperous Welfare State, when children were starving in Biafra and real poverty was an enormous problem throughout the world. Still, this was an historic occasion, and eventually he was persuaded to have a cope specially made with £100 donated by an admirer. 'When it comes to church furnishings, I consult my architect. So I asked him about the cope,' said Mr Kent. 'He told me not to go to a shop. I said I like green. He said, "Well, let's have a green one, then. That will look very nice." '

A lime green cope of Thai silk was accordingly prepared for the vicar. His wife, an American, wanted to visit Scotland during April, and she couldn't really understand the significance of Maundy Thursday. She asked friends if they thought she should cancel the trip and remain in Selby. Of course, they said. This was an *event* for a town of not quite eleven thousand.

Six different organizations were concerned with the arrangements: the Urban District Council, the County

---

[1]In the intervening years it has been held at:

St Paul's Cathedral	1953
Southwark Cathedral	1955
St Albans Cathedral	1957
St George's Chapel, Windsor	1959
Rochester Cathedral	1961
Chelmsford Cathedral	1963
Canterbury Cathedral	1965
Durham Cathedral	1967
Selby Abbey	1969

Council, railway police, civil police, Abbey officials, and representatives of the Festival that was taking place as part of the anniversary celebrations.

The Urban Council spent £297 15s. 6d. on bunting, and hired two hundred and fifty crush barriers at ten shillings each.

A bank manager, who was also a sidesman at the Abbey, bought a special pen for the Queen to sign the visitors' book. He planned to present it to his wife afterwards to mark his retirement. 'Here is a pen that the Queen has used.'

The normal police force of thirty was multiplied ten times to a total of 366, including twelve plain clothes men in the Abbey, sitting amongst the choir and guests. At least twelve meetings took place to discuss security and other arrangements.

Car parks were organized at two wartime aerodromes, Riccall and Burn, several miles from Selby, with a bus shuttle service for some of the anticipated 100,000 spectators.

Even the high tide was taken into consideration. There is only one toll bridge on the tidal river flowing through Selby, and it is normally closed to traffic at eleven o'clock each morning so ships can pass. Police asked the Ouse River Board not to use the bridge for the first time in history, because it would have interfered with their intricate one-way system.

Forty-three men and forty-three women recipients of Maundy largesse were gathered from the Archdeaconry of York. 'They didn't have to be Church of England,' said the Vicar. 'In fact, others must be brought in. Everybody wanted to take part, except the Quakers who explained it wasn't their line, thanks very much.' Names were kept secret to prevent pestering from coin dealers who would pay up to £75 for the Maundy money set – particularly as this was one of the last issues before decimalization.

The Lord Lieutenant, the late Lord Scarbrough, had his problems. 'The great question as far as I was concerned, was where the Queen would lunch. She decided eventually to fly back to Windsor.'

To ensure the nosegays were fresh, a mother and her son sat up through the night making them. A charlady deputized for the Queen during rehearsals. 'It is very exciting, but I am a bit nervous,' said sixty-seven-year-old Cora Haynes. Final touches were added to the town's decorations – even oranges in greengrocers' shops were covered with plastic union jacks.

'I was staggered by the amount of work involved,' said Mr Kent. 'At times I thought to myself, "Is it worth it for a one hour service?" What a nonsense. When the thing was over, though, it was a great sense of achievement, and in spite of the quite archaic wording, I think the idea of service as a thing to aim for does get across.

'Against this, you've got the status seeking for places in the church. People were weeping because they hadn't got a seat.'

Most of the congregation were women, and the crowd outside numbered 10,000 – ten times fewer than the most ambitious estimates, and only a third of the number the police could have controlled comfortably.

The Queen and Prince Philip were presented with nosegays at the door. Philip sniffed his, muttered to the Queen, who didn't answer, and then they walked in procession down the aisle behind the Archbishop of York, and in front of the almoner's procession. Two Beefeaters, dignified, and solemn, carried above their heads dishes of green, red, and white purses. The considerable weight gradually began to over-balance one of them, and the tray (bearing the cypher of William and Mary, although it dated back to Charles II), slipped backwards slowly, ever so slowly, and there was fascinating, appalling anticipation of a tragi-comic event.

'Rejoice, rejoice, rejoice,' sang the Chapel Royal choir, their scarlet tunics with gold braid, neatly complementing the Beefeaters' ancient costumes. Spectators, bent themselves double from the hip to watch the Queen, not noticing the imminent disaster. Then suddenly, at the last minute, the tray was given a tap from behind by another Beefeater, and corrected.

There are two distributions of the money. First, the women receive £1 15s. 0d. in a green purse, and the men £2 5s. 0d. in a white one. This is in lieu of cloth, replaced by cash for women in 1724, and for men in 1883 when it was found they often could not afford to have the cloth made into wearable articles. In the second distribution, each recipient has two purses: the red one contains £2 10s. 0d., and the white one has the Maundy coins in silver pennies, twopences, threepences and fourpences making a total of as many pence as the sovereign's years. They are minted specially for the occasion, and are legal tender, although rarely, if ever, used as such.

The Queen is preceded by a nosegay bearer, walking backwards, into the nave. The purses are taken from the tray by an almoner, who passes it to one clergyman, who passes it to another, who passes it to the Queen, who passes it to the pensioners.

Then comes the ceremony of the visitors' book. At the back of the church, a woman in a brown coat is nervously testing the pen. She scribbles once on a piece of paper, puts the top back on, thinks, tries the pen again, replaces the top, worries some more, and tries it again, and leaves the top off. Perkins, creeping around in his well-practised ecclesiastical hush, tells her to replace the top. She tests it once more, then does so. The vicar passes by, a vision of verdant piety, and suggests she take off the top. At last, the Queen arrives, is handed the pen, smiles, signs, and walks out into the sunshine, remembering that she has been asked to pose for a picture to go in the Abbey records. But where is the photographer? He has been assigned to a mound behind the guard of honour of Beefeaters, and the police won't let him move under any circumstances.

Then a sherry party at Selby Grammar School. 'You look very different,' the Queen tells the vicar, now dressed in a suit and tie. He had previously asked Lord Scarbrough if it would be considered impertinent for him not to wear a dog collar. He thought they were ridiculous.

'Why don't you wear one?' asks Prince Philip.

'There has to be a reason *for* wearing it, rather than not wearing it,' replies the vicar.

'Well uniform is very useful. All sorts of people wear it, postmen . . .'

The Beefeaters are given a cheer as they clamber into their coach. The Queen and Prince Philip fly to Windsor.

And, on the same day as this quaint and harmless bolster to Britain's tourist image was taking place, the country's commercial reputation was having another battering. BOAC was unable to fly about fifty leading businessmen and industrialists on their scheduled first flight to Japan over the North Pole because pilots were on strike, demanding an increase of £5,000 a year.

It was about time the Queen was used again in the cause of international goodwill and trade. Soon she was off to Austria. First, though, there was a home game.

The Home Team - I

<hr>

'There have been occasions in the past when Londoners, unable to get from one part of their city to another because the President of Ruritania was driving through its streets for a luncheon at the Guildhall, have said hard things about State Visits in general. The state visit of the Italian President, Signor Saragat, was not of the sort to provoke this reaction,' *The Times*, 30 April, 1969.

'I believe in tradition, but this is ridululous.' Letter in *Evening Standard*, 17 July, 1969, commenting on policemen wearing ceremonial uniform to line the route for President Kekkonen of Finland.

STATE VISITS are produced in Britain by the Lord Chamberlain's office, with aplomb and dedication, almost as if they were a finale for the apocalypse. There were two during the year. President Giuseppe Saragat of Italy from April 22 – 30; and the President of Finland, Dr Urho Kekkonen from July 15–19. Both showed how people who care about tradition and ceremonial and who have the setting, money, and dramatis personae to match their own entrepreneurial ability can make republicans wilt under the nonchalant weight of historical play acting, and even old time Hollywood envious with the lavishness of the show.

A special programme, about seventy pages long, is printed, a superior time-table showing all aspects of the ceremonial and people involved, with alternative arrangements for wet weather.

Usually there is a set routine with coaches, horses, welcoming committees, morning dress, bands, soldiers, police, roads temporarily closed to traffic, familiar duties such as wreath laying, dinner at the Palace, and lunch with the Prime Minister. A full cast list for the first day appears over three columns of the Court Circular published in *The Times* and *Telegraph*, and then gradually recedes in importance.

For President Saragat there was a special treat, an experiment that had not taken place since King Manoel visited Edward VII in 1909. As a concession to London traffic and a convenience to the Queen, the State Visit took place at Windsor. Princess Margaret, in shocking pink, and Lord Snowdon, met him and his daughter, Signora Santacatterina at London Airport and drove in two of the Royal Rolls Royces, followed by nine other cars, to Home Park, an expanse of playing field, fringed with cherry blossom, below Windsor Castle.

A Royal Pavilion had been erected in the middle of two rugby football pitches (which had involved the moving of the Berkshire seven-a-sides to another pitch a few days earlier), and on it stood a posse of dignitaries – The Lord Lieutenant, Prime Minister, Foreign Secretary Michael Stewart, Home Secretary James Callaghan, chiefs of the three Services, chairmen of the County and Borough Councils, and Chief Constable of the Thames Valley. They were moved into line by a small bespectacled man with a clipboard, Ronald Hill, Secretary in the Lord Chamberlain's office. A red mat was placed in front of the dais, and kept swept, because the field was muddy. To the left, a row of VIPs in morning dress, or military uniform, sat on collapsible wooden chairs placed on a red carpet. Some had blankets on their knees. To the right, there was a Press enclosure. And in front the Guard of Honour took up position.

Quarter of a mile away, two hundred schoolchildren waited in a temporary car park. They, and a few adults were the only outside witnesses to this self-perpetuating affectation to international goodwill, this merry frolic. It seemed a little odd, even narcissistic. Salutes fluttered in constant yo-yo profusion.

'Don't they look splendid, absolutely splendid,' said Lieutenant-Colonel Eric Penn, Comptroller in the Lord Chamberlain's Office, referring to the Irish Guards. Stiff-backed, tall, handsome, father of one of Princess Anne's boyfriends, a man of exquisite courtesy combined with unmilitary romantic gestures. His wife, Prudence, had a personalized number plate on her MG – PRU 365 – because, it was said, he loved her three hundred and sixty-five days of the year. His own Bentley was PEN, followed by another number.

As the Queen arrived, he handed her a list of names in the ceremonial line-up, which she studied while Prince Philip chatted to Harold Wilson and Michael Stewart.

'He's coming,' she said finally to her husband.

Prince Philip took note, turned his back, and continued talking. The Queen played with her gloves and watched the President's car coming down the road, into the field. He was a small man in an ill-shaped suit covered by a grey overcoat, looking dumpy and businesslike amongst the splendour of a British state occasion. He spoke to the Queen in French, beamed happily as the commanding officer of the Guard, Major Richard Hume, announced, in Italian taught to him by the Embassy: 'The Guard of Honour of the First Battalion of the Irish Guards is present and ready for your inspection.'

This accomplished, Signor Saragat was accompanied to the first of eight open carriages by the Duke of Beaufort, Master of the Horse. He clambered in, next to the Queen, and a two-mile procession to the castle began, watched by several thousand people lining routes specially decorated by the Council. Behind them came cleaners with shovels and bins to pick up horse manure. 'It was something we hadn't had to cope with before, and I appreciated the problem during the rehearsal,' said town clerk George Waldram. 'We tried to follow up at a discreet distance.'

'Pronto, pronto, pronto,' screeched an Italian journalist into a telephone, attempting to browbeat the bland British post office into allowing him to relay a report of this historic British pageantry to Rome.

At the castle, Signor Saragat met other members of the royal family and was made a Knight Grand Cross of the Civil Division of the Most Honourable Order of the Bath. He saw the Queen Mother in the afternoon, was presented with loyal addresses from the Council, walked round the gardens, and in the evening was guest of honour at a State Banquet in the Grand Reception Room for one hundred and fifty-four people.

They sat at the Queen's longest table – one hundred and sixty-seven feet of solid mahogany, eight feet wide, that had been in preparation since 11.30 in the morning. The candelabra had to be placed in position by three men standing on the table, and the gold plate and cut glass was meticulously wiped before being laid out.

The meal of asparagus soup, flètan au vin blanc, caneton à l'orange, and ananas glacé royal were washed down with Hattenheimer Mehrholzen 1964, Mazis Chambertin 1961, Louis Roederer 1961, and Dow 1945, and digested to the sounds of appropriate music from the Scots Guards: *Wine, Women and Song, Nights of Gladness, Mary Poppins, Highland Mary,* and *Blaze Away.* A pipe programme followed – *Lochiel's Away to France*, and so on – before speeches that were given added piquancy because General de Gaulle was on the point of resigning, Britain's hopes of entering the Common Market would thereby be improved – and then what would happen to the Queen's position?

'We both want to see Europe develop and prosper so that our peoples can live without anxiety and with the greatest individual freedom of movement,' she said to the Italian President. 'To this end, we stand together in the North

Atlantic Treaty Organization and as members of the Western Europe Union and we greatly appreciate and value your unswerving support and encouragement in our approach to the European Economic Community. We believe, with you, that the closer integration of the countries of Western Europe represents the best hope for their future.'

To a number of people in Britain, the Common Market was a subject of compelling boredom, an endless game played by politicians. But for others, the implications were immense.

'I happen to believe we are supporting the most important political cause of this generation,' said Lord Harlech at a Common Market banquet.[1] 'It is becoming increasingly clear that developments in our political and social structure have failed to keep pace with radical changes in man's environment.'

And, a few days after Signor Saragat left England, the Queen spoke at an anniversary lunch for the Council of Europe: 'The setting up for the Council of Europe was a milestone on the road to European unity. The organization of eighteen countries, representatives of all of which are here today, symbolizes that desire for unity and the rejection of national isolation which characterized post-war Europe, and which has been the motive force behind so many subsequent developments in European Affairs. My government will continue to play a vigorous part in the movement towards increased European Unity.

'Many people may accept the ideals of European co-operation in their minds, but we must all accept them in our hearts as well.'

Many British businessmen had also accepted it as a fact, and started continental subsidiaries that made a mockery of tariffs. Ironically, much of the activity was taking place around Calais and Lille, and had Peter Townsend as public relations adviser. More and more British holidaymakers were

[1]Guildhall, 29 July, 1969.

thinking in a less insular way, and the Costa Brava was virtually as accessible as Blackpool.

'If the European Economic Community proceeds as is implied in the Treaty of Rome, to a closer political union, this would affect national sovereignties,' said Foreign Secretary Michael Stewart. 'This, however, would be simply explicit recognition of the fact that in the modern world they are nearly all limited by the facts. If, at some future date, the peoples of various European countries come to feel that their primary loyalty is to Europe rather than a particular State, this would affect the position of all Heads of State – whether they were monarchies or republics. But membership of the EEC has not affected the Monarchy in Belgium, the Netherlands, or Luxembourg, and I do not see why it should affect the British Monarchy.'

Conditioning to the idea of political unity had begun, and it was clear the Monarchy would have to adapt more rapidly than most sections of society especially as regards cost, attitudes, ceremonies, and use.

'The Queen cannot reverse the logic of independence nor perpetuate a happily diminishing delusion,' says Enoch Powell, a politician who has built himself a vast popularity largely by emotive appeals to Anglo-Saxon prejudice. 'Sooner or later she must come home to us; for to us she belongs. The Monarchy is an English Monarchy. Its origins are English and not Welsh, not even Scottish, despite inheritance.

'"Head of the Commonwealth" is essentially a sham we have invented to blind ourselves to the reality of the situation. You don't have to *justify* monarchy. The necessity for a priest king is very deep in humanity. Men lose the satisfaction of these instincts at their peril. Our monarch is not a crowned president. She is anointed. She represents a supernatural element in the nation.'

Whatever the future, surely there will be less excuse to impress foreigners with a full-scale State visit – particularly if

245

we become part of the same group? Eventually it could appear as absurd as the Mayor of Southend making a majestic peregrination round Surbiton.

Or maybe international swank is an integral part of human nature? It seemed so in Austria, which the Queen was now visiting.

The Road Show-IV

'It may seem strange that no British sovereign has paid a state visit to Vienna since my great grandfather came here in 1903, but it is so easy to forget what a tumultuous century this has been for Europe.' The Queen at a State banquet in Vienna, 5 May, 1969.

'I am made even more angry by the state visit to Austria than that to Germany. If the Germans are piggies, the Austrians are piggier still. The British, of course, in their simple, misty way, love Austria with its dirndl, lederhosen, and Kuss die Hand – who said American tourists are the only suckers?' Lord Arran in the *Evening News*.

VIENNA, city of dwindling romantic memories to an imperial past, awaited the Queen with a mixture of sceptical indifference, atavistic envy, and competitive protocol. At one of the planning discussions, which took place casually for three years and earnestly for five months, British Ambassador Sir Anthony Rumbold suggested the Queen should be driven in a Rolls Royce. The company had offered to supply as many as were needed. This idea, intended helpfully, so outraged the Austrians that they determined to provide her with a vast Mercedes, and cram the five-day tour with every conceivable tourist trick – brass bands, tinkling bells, pom-tiddly-om-pom hats, cacophonous blunderbuss salutes, schnapps at breakfast-time, bridges, farms, operetta, crown jewels, horses, receptions, housing estates . . . so much that the Queen once had to circle Graz airport for an hour in order to have a peaceful lunch.

Austria's arrogant past may have been reduced to an economy largely based on ski-ing holidays and a day's sightseeing for Americans on a European tour, and the Habsburgs may be only of equal interest to the Lippizaners on the tourist's cue-card, but the seven million inhabitants have a pride and dignity that remains intact. Their history is testified by innumerable ornate palaces, their present role as political buffer between East and West becomes more important each year, and their future – who knows? Perhaps Vienna could take over from Geneva as the centre of Europe.

'The Russians and Americans encourage our neutral attitude,' said Foreign Minister Dr Kurt Waldheim. 'We are convinced that if Austria disappeared from the map, the consequences would be very great for the whole world. If we become a nuisance factor to one of the two powers, we'll be heading for trouble, but we do believe we have an important stabilizing function.'

Unlike her South American tour, the Queen's visit had few political or trade implications. There was only one obvious commercial aspect: Prince Philip asked British European Airways to take them in a BAC 1–11 because the chairman of BAC, Sir George Edwards, had mentioned they were trying to sell planes to Austria as a replacement for Viscounts. The BEA pilots would have preferred to use a Trident, but they spent two days in a simulator practising landings, and learnt survival technique. The plane was converted, at a cost of £14,000, to include among other things a flush toilet and bedroom – even though all flying was during the day and of short duration.

Basically, it was a period-fun tour for Civil Servants, an intertwining of gemütlichkeit and jolly good show, a Volks-fest. Sir Anthony Rumbold, the third generation of his family to be Ambassador in Vienna, borrowed silver plate from Buckingham Palace so he could return the President's hospitality. This rather awkward habit of Ambassadors requesting the use of the Queen's plate began with the state

248

visit to Germany in 1965 when it was essential to create an impression of urbane wealth.

The silver, worth about £200,000, was flown to Vienna in a BEA Viscount, along with a Johnny Speed giant racing car, an electrically controlled dolls' house, and a battery-operated cooker bought from Harrods as presents for orphaned children in an S.O.S. village that was to be included in the itinerary at the Queen's request. The Central Office of Information distributed flags and five thousand six hundred posters (to be re-used for British week later in the year). Viennese protocol officials, in a tizzy of contradictory postures, announced that 'the cream of Viennese society' would be at Schönbrunn Palace for a reception – yet advised women not to curtsey. 'I am a good republican, and I like my people to be the same,' said President Franz Jonas, a seventy-year-old former printer. 'We love to look at the Queen, but no curtseying.' Austria, centre of the Habsburg empire, and ruled by the same family from the end of the thirteenth century until 11 November, 1918, had just celebrated fifty years as a republic, and did not indulge in antiquated behaviour to support a class system. Oh, no.

Most excitement was generated because Princess Anne was accompanying her parents for the first time on a State visit. To mark the occasion, she had been presented with the family medal on 23 April: a painted miniature portrait of the Queen on a border of brilliants and baguette diamonds, worn on the left shoulder at formal gatherings.

But then, on the eve of the visit, she fell ill with flu and had to cancel her trip. Would she come later? That depended on how soon she recovered. This news was accompanied by the sudden, upsetting revelation in Austrian newspapers that the Queen was importing her own Malvern water, in preference to using the clear Alpine brand. 'We export water to England because of its excellent tea making quality,' sniffed City Councillor Hubert Pfoch. And, for a few moments, it seemed as if all Vienna had been insulted.

Meanwhile, the Queen was delayed by an overturned lorry on her way to London Airport, and arrived nineteen minutes late. The procedure for departures is always the same. About a month in advance, the Lord Chamberlain's office warns the airport's Special Facilities Officer who then issues a 'battle order' planned to the last second. One of five V.I.P. lounges is prepared, but the Queen rarely uses it. Barriers are placed exactly fifteen feet from her path to the aircraft, so that photographers don't come too close. The welcoming committee can be dispensed with in a few seconds, and the BEA crew hoped to make time on the journey. They could only manage ten minutes because of a southerly head wind instead of the usual westerly – a one in seven chance.

The Queen arrived at Vienna's Schwechat airport in eighty degree heat, traditionally called Kaiserwetter as a reference to the sun that always seemed to shine for Franz Joseph, to be met by officials in morning dress and top hats. Prince Philip was in Field Marshal's uniform. There were the usual polite claps, hand shaking, national anthems – while the retinue wilted with jovial masochism. There weren't so many as for South America: Lord Chalfont, Marchioness of Abergavenny, Lady Margaret Hay, Sir Michael Adeane, Philip Moore, Bill Heseltine, Lord Plunket, James Orr, Air Commodore Winskill, Bobo Macdonald, Perkins, various secretaries and clerks, maids for the ladies-in-waiting, the Queen's page and hairdresser, six footmen, eight Household Cavalry troopers, the Yeoman of the Glass and China Pantry, and Yeoman of the Plate Pantry.

A fourteen-mile drive to the city from the airport, escorted by sixty 'white mice' police in black leather uniforms with white helmets, past the largest brewery in Austria, the largest cemetery in Vienna (a huge, gravestone-speckled park where the Viennese are allowed to shoot rabbits once a year as a special concession to their hunting instincts), past dirndl-skirted mädchen, and an old man in a hairnet.

The royal party were staying in forty rooms of the

Imperial Hotel on Ringstrasse, a boulevard of lilac and linden trees in spring blossom that followed the route of walls erected to keep out the Turks. It was built as a town house for Duke Philipp of Württemberg in 1865, became an hotel eight years later, and was the only one to be given the title Kaiserlich-Königliches Hof-Hotel – by Royal Appointment. Doorhandles are still engraved with the Württemberg crest of three antlers.

At first, the Queen and Prince Philip had been allocated a seven-room suite on the first floor, and Princess Anne a different one. But Palace officials said Anne would prefer the midde of the seven-room suite – a surprise the Austrians were too polite to mention. Furniture, taken from Government store, was part of the imperial collection: Persian carpets, white and gold chairs with red and blue damask covers from the second baroque period of the eighteenth century. Candle sticks, ink stands, porcelain and china sets were from the Maria Theresa collection. A direct telephone line to Buckingham Palace was installed as a courtesy, and two sentries stood guard outside the hotel twenty-four hours a day.

After a quick change into morning dress, Prince Philip accompanied the Queen on a formal visit to President Jonas at his official residence, the Hofburg. They had, of course, been met by him at the airport, but no matter, this was protocol. He showed them round the former winter palace of the emperors, and pointed out in particular the Imperial Presentation clock, given to Maria Theresa in 1750. It is the height of a man and has a complicated mechanism that depicts homage to her and her husband, Franz I, followed by the Archangel Michael defeating an evil spirit. Until the Presidential offices moved into the Hofburg in 1946, it had been disused for a hundred years.

A Press reception, a change into evening dress, and return to the Hofburg for a state banquet:

'The word "welcome" is often used without much feeling. The kindness of your words this evening together with the deeply moving reception given to us by the people of Vienna have reminded me what welcome really means,' said the Queen. 'In greeting us you are also greeting my people and their hearts will be as stirred as ours have been by this great demonstration of friendship. Your invitation to visit Austria naturally gave us very great pleasure. We are particularly touched that you should have included our daughter in the invitation and we are most disappointed that she cannot be with us today.

'A glance at the map of Europe would not suggest any particular affinity between island Britain and land locked Austria. This appearance is deceptive. We have both shared the experience of Empire, both countries have long been predominantly industrial, and in recent years we have followed much the same path in social welfare legislation.'

Etcetera.

Schönbrunn, one of the rococo spectacles of the world, was built as a summer palace for the son of Leopold I, but he died before it was completed in 1713. It was not until Maria Theresa became Empress that it was finally furnished and made habitable. She ordered tapestries from the Netherlands, mirrors from Italy, clocks from Paris, carpets from Persia, miniatures from India, porcelain from China. It is surrounded by beautiful parkland, dominated by the Gloriette, designed by Ferdinand von Hohenberg, known as the 'poet in stone'.

It was here that Marie-Antoinette danced.

It was here that Mozart played for Maria Theresa when he was six years old – and promised to marry Marie-Antoinette.

It was here that Haydn rehearsed.

It was here that Napoleon made his headquarters during the French occupations of Austria.

It was here that Emperor Karl, the last of the reigning Habsburgs, formally renounced his title and authority.

It was here, in the forty ceremonial rooms, that tourists had wandered since the collapse of the Monarchy. It was a museum now, with exotic memories.

It was here that the Queen was coming after the state banquet, for a reception.

It was here that one thousand of Vienna's 'high society' crushed each other, drank watered orange juice, and ate marmite straws and oatmeal biscuits, as they waited.

The Queen was preceded by a state theatre actor dressed as a herald and carrying the Imperial stave of the Austro-Hungarian Monarchy, mounted by a double-headed eagle, that is now only brought from store to honour the few remaining crowned heads of the world.

'Get out of the way,' hissed the Queen to someone who was blocking her entrance into the long gallery, suddenly lit with television strobes. Then, becalmed, not a hair out of place, not a smudge on her make-up, not a worry in her eyes, a porcelain figure with head nodding in practised, rhythmic gentility, she walked through the ranks of this fluorescent trough to a specially prepared side room. People were presented, wine was at last served, and a buffet was eaten.

No music. No pretty girls. A stingy accumulation of government officials and their wives chortling self congratulatory remarks.

'Merry making in Ruritania,' said one weekly newspaper. And the Roman Catholic paper, *Furche*, added: 'Bureaucracy has achieved a new victory. Austria as a republic has remained as it always was. Even socialist women functionaries radiantly sank into deep curtsies. Fanatical republicans of the socialist camp indulged joyfully in the vanity fair.'

Tomorrow what was there? Imperial splendour, church, perissodactyl quadrupeds, Parliament, opera, and dinner at Sacher's hotel. It could be worse.

The day began propitiously at five past ten with an hour's semi-private Gala performance at the Spanish Riding School, the world's most famous haute ecole horse establishment, founded four hundred years ago and saved from extinction during the war by an American, the late General George

Patton. Lippizaner stallions, used for the intricate prancing, are descended from Roman ceremonial horses crossed with those belonging to the Moors, when they invaded Spain. Movements are based on two thousand five hundred year old ancient Greek ideas suggested by Simon of Athens and Pliny the Elder. No handbook is available, and instructions have been passed down by word of mouth.

In 1562 the Emperor Maximilian II, proud of the Habsburg reputation as owners of the world's finest horses, started the Imperial stud in Bohemia, and eighteen years later his brother set up a stud in the barren, gorse covered country at Lipizza, near Trieste. With the disintegration of the Austro-Hungarian Monarchy at the end of the First World War, some horses went to Italy and some to Yugoslavia. A former cavalry stud at Piber became the Lipizzaner headquarters, and the horses toured Europe giving shows to pay expenses. During the Second World War they were evacuated to Scharding in Upper Austria, where they were found by the advancing American forces. An officer persuaded General Patton, himself a former Olympic horseman, to fly down from Frankfurt and, after an improvised demonstration, he arranged for their evacuation under armed guard.

The school where they perform in Vienna was built in the 1730s by Fischer von Erlach and is a huge, white room with a ceiling sixty yards by twenty unsupported by pillars, an ambiance of grandeur where Beethoven once conducted a concert with over a thousand musicians. Crystal chandeliers illuminate the scene, and the only colour is a portrait of the founder, Emperor Karl VI. It is this that the riders saluted at the beginning of each act – not the Queen.

The white Lippizaners simply decorated with narrow gilt reins and red and gold saddle cloths performed their usual movements from the quadrille to the more dramatic capriole (a leap off the ground on all fours followed by a swift back leg kick, a mediæval battle technique), and courbette (leaping forward on hind quarters without touching the ground with front legs).

There were only two differences to the normal daily routine: an orchestra was concealed in the upper balcony instead of a gramophone, and Vienna's élite horse lovers looked at the Queen through opera glasses – instead of the horses.

Afterwards, there was a presentation of two Haflinger ponies (Appendix), a plebeian strain, destined for Balmoral as pets for Prince Andrew and Prince Edward.

Next, a visit to the Holy Roman Empire crown jewels. Lunch as guest of the Government, a talk to British Embassy staff, a tour of St Stephen's Cathedral, and a forty-minute visit to the Houses of Parliament. It was here, at about tea-time, that the Queen began to feel the strain and eased one foot from her shoe as Dr Alfred Maleta, the Speaker, illustrated some of the more esoteric points of interest in the apparently empty Chamber. Gently she rubbed her left foot against her right leg, holding on to a desk in front, and looking intently at Dr Maleta, nodding now and again. He continued to speak, pleased by her interest. She squeezed her foot back into the shoe, and repeated the process with the right foot. Then she walked on, chatting. Next day, a picture of the Queen shoeless appeared in most British newspapers. She could never relax in public.

No day of old Viennese schmaltz, protocol and official sightseeing would be complete without a visit to the opera – which has a larger budget than the Austrian Foreign Office – and is housed in a mongrel building that was originally so unpopular that one of its architects committed suicide and the other died of ill health before it opened in 1869. It was bombed during the last weeks of the war, but reconstructed by 1955 at a cost of four million pounds.

In such a splendid setting, with a reputation as one of the world's finest music centres, what can you perform for a Queen whose love for opera is known to be less than enthusiastic, and whose attitude towards the arts in general could be called apathetic. The English themselves had long ago decided mediocrity was usually the most satisfactory solution, and some of the Queen's more arduous annual tasks were consequently called 'fun': The Royal Variety Performance, two and a half hours of repetitive tedium that first took place in front of a reigning Monarch in 1912 and remains apparently unchanged; Royal Film Performance of *Chitty Chitty Bang Bang*, adequate for children under twelve with nothing else to do, a cute treacle spectacle chug-chugging its way to a £70,000 charity donation from the evening; or *The Prime of Miss Jean Brodie*, in which a ten-second sequence of two girls giggling over a drawing of a naked man was cut out in case it offended the Queen Mother.

How could Austria compete? They chose *Die Fledermaus*, an operetta with a complicated story, ponderous jokes, and a few light waltzes. As a special honour, the orchestra played the instantly unmemorable Windsor Melodies composed by Johann Strauss for Queen Victoria, ostensibly as a mark of respect. It was not a particularly good performance, but the white-tied audience laughed with the Queen, and clapped as she walked through a bar during the second interval. It was always pleasant to re-live the elegance of the past. And where else, after such an evening, could one have supper but the hotel Sacher, opposite, where high society always went after the opera, and were magnificently catered for by cigar-smoking Frau Anna Sacher and her faithful pug-dog?

At midnight, the Queen returned to her hotel. Tomorrow, having recovered from flu, Princess Anne was arriving and some youthful zest was anticipated to help old Vienna off her imperial knees.

Dramatically, in a fierce thunderstorm, Princess Anne arrived by executive jet borrowed from the Board of Trade, and was immediately given two bouquets before being driven to her hotel. Prince Philip, meanwhile, talked to the British Trade Council, and the Queen crossed the Danube (which is on the outskirts of Vienna and is not blue, but grey) to visit a housing estate. She met Walter Chlumetzky, a municipal draughtsman, signed the red leather visiting book he had bought specially for the occasion, looked at his flat, and returned to the Imperial to be driven round the Ringstrasse with Princess Anne and Prince Philip. A few drenched onlookers lined the route to the Town Hall, but an anticipated protest about Biafra was abandoned 'out of respect for the Queen'.

After lunch, the traditionally undignified Commonwealth reception. A local Konzerthaus floor had been marked into sections with white sticky tape, and instructions issued to two thousand five hundred invited guests: 'Different areas will be assigned to the various national groups. You are particularly requested to remain within your area and *not to walk on or cross the carpets* until the Royal Guests have left. No smoking will be permitted until the Royal Guests have left at approximately 4 p.m.'

White Commonwealth citizens were herded into one room, coloured into another, by officious young men with short hair cuts, and badges, and minds addled with a Boy's Own Paper conception of England. The Federal Army Band played Army tunes. It had been decided there should be three and a third people per square metre, but bad weather ruined these plans and, as the Queen was about to arrive, only about one thousand five hundred guests milled in their allotted squares.

'Oh, my god, it's a balls up,' muttered one senior British Embassy official, as the Queen started her march past, and occasional chat. A drive in pouring rain through the Wiener Wald followed, with stops at the English school and Klosterneuburg Abbey. In the evening, a return banquet to the President and, at midnight, the royal party left by special train for Innsbruck, capital of the Tyrol.

In Innsbruck, the previous week, brass bands and Schützen companies of volunteer riflemen dressed in the uniform of their particular valleys with white cock feathers and red and white carnations in their black hats, had been rehearsing at five o'clock in the morning to ensure a picture postcard glow for the beginning of the Queen's two-day tour of provincial Austria. A public holiday was proclaimed, and exuberant, ear-splitting hospitality began as the Queen stepped from her train at ten o'clock to a volley of rifle shots and an offer of schnapps. No thank you, she said. But Princess Anne tried some.

Sixty triumphant bandsmen, except one drummer who stepped from the ranks to take a picture of the Queen with his box camera, played the British National anthem followed by the marching song of their own Andreas Hofer who led the nineteenth-century struggle against Napoleon. The Austrian national anthem was not played.

Then a five-hour sightseeing tour commenced. First, the Europa bridge, highest in Europe and eight hundred and ninety-seven yards long, where the Queen was driven up a small hill for a better view, and members of the Household walked, panting, behind; a visit to a farm at Sistrans where she ate peasant bread, sipped red wine, and discussed dairy farming; a stroll through old Innsbruck; another Commonwealth reception – and this time she was temporarily stuck in a lift; lunch given by the Landeshauptmann; posies from children; enough brass bands to satiate the most ardent fan; a military march past; and off by special train for the three-hour journey to Salzburg.

'It may be difficult for you and the people in Tyrol to appreciate the impact which your glorious mountain scenery can make on someone seeing it for the first time,' said the Queen. 'Added to this has been such a warm-hearted welcome from so many people in this ancient city of Innsbruck that I am sure you will understand that this has been a most moving experience for us.

'Queen Victoria commented in her journal on the magnificence of the scenery when she passed through Innsbruck in

1888. And I have now been able to see for myself why she was so impressed. It has been such a colourful morning, and I have greatly enjoyed the famous Tyrolean singing and the proud feathers of the Schützen. I raise my glass to your health and the prosperity and happiness of the people of Innsbruck and the Tyrol.'

More gun salutes at Salzburg railway station, another set of national anthems and, later that evening at a banquet, the second speech of the day:

'To most of my countrymen, Salzburg means music; thousands of them come here every year to the birthplace of Mozart, to enjoy the wonderful music festivals and some even come to perform in them.

'What is perhaps not so well known is that it was the English Saint Boniface who became an Archbishop in Germany and who, in 738, organized the church of the Southern Empire with a Bishop at Salzburg.

'These are only added reasons for my pleasure at being able to see for myself tomorrow something of the natural and man-made treasures of your famous city.'

Wolfgang Amadeus Mozart died broke at the age of thirty-five, but later generations are always adept at turning tragedy to romance, and capitalizing on past mistakes, so his birth-place is now a tourist shrine, where the Queen was taken to see the spinet on which he composed *The Magic Flute*. 'They made a different sound in those days, didn't they,' she said. 'It was more, er . . .'

There was little time to discuss technicalities. She had to walk through Salzburg for thirty minutes, drive to an S.O.S. village for destitute children at Seekirchen where ninety-five children live in a thirteen-house community, and had devised a little show as part of her forty-minute visit. A Peruvian Indian banged the cymbals, shy nine-year-old girls danced to a special tune, their teacher prompted from behind the Queen's chair, a phalanx of officials beamed, presents from Harrods were stacked on the veranda of a house, the Queen looked round and said: 'Such a frightening mêlée for them.'

As she was leaving for Salzburg airport, several children thrust ragged flowers at her for a make-shift bouquet. She passed them immediately to a lady-in-waiting.

Lunch was taken as the aeroplane circled Graz airport, and was followed by a forty-five minute drive to Piber Federal Stud where the Queen watched horses for an hour and a half before attending a reception of local worthies at nearby Schloss Eggenberg, another baroque museum. It began to drizzle, but the band oom-paaah'd bravely in the mud as she departed once more for the airport.

At the aeroplane steps she stood talking while weary Household members clambered in, and schoolchildren waved flags. Ubiquitous Perkins, carrying a bunch of flowers, a fur coat, a handbag, and a heart-shaped pastry cake, looked on, never varying his all-seeing glare.

'Can I have a bite?' a photographer asked him.

'You can have the whole bloody lot.'

Auf wiedersehen, Königen. We have enjoyed you.

The plane left for Vienna – Schwechat and the final and, only private, evening of the visit. Crowds outside the hotel shouted 'Lizabette', and the Queen waved from a balcony. Next day, in a BAC 1-11 deodorized luxury, she returned to London. A planned appearance at the Windsor Horse Show was cancelled because of rain.

Austrians returned to their republican present, and a bill of about £1,660,000 ($398,400) for five days of imperial make-believe. They sat in cafés, and the park where a statue of Johann Strauss, with violin, looks down on misspelt notices 'Consumation obligatory', and orchestras remember him daily through the season with the true, unpretentious sound of Vienna, casually, as the sun sets, in the open air, with the hollow cry of a Kauzchen owl whispering like a cuckoo from the linden trees, lovers sipping their wine to the future, and pensioners contemplating the turmoil caused to their lives by politicians, and thinking it could never happen again. People are more sensible now.

'I'm very upset I didn't get a CVO,' sighs a senior Austrian Embassy official, fingering his less grand MVO (Appendix). 'It's something nice to go round your neck.'

God *v.* Scotland–I

<hr>

'Despite the Ministry of Technology and all the wonderful things in the world, it does still appear that God has the last word from time to time.' Prince Philip, delayed by a blizzard, Sheffield, 8 February, 1969.

'I was one of the many who went to watch the Royal Family attend Craithie Church last Sunday. Standing next to me was a little girl. She kept asking her father how long it would be before the Queen would come. "Won't be long now," said her daddy. "I suppose," said the little one, "she would take some time putting her crown on properly!" In my own excitement when the Queen did arrive, I forgot to take note of that little girl's reaction when she discovered the Queen wore no crown. I hope she didn't feel let down.' Three guinea prize letter in *Sunday Express*, 22 September, 1968.

EVERY YEAR, the Queen makes an official visit to Edinburgh, capital of Scotland, and resides at Holyroodhouse for a few days where she gives a garden party, reviews troops, tours factories, and performs other functions considered necessary for the correct functioning of Monarchy and the alleviation of Scottish inferiority. This year, though, with nationalist feelings becoming more pronounced, and Caernarvon's mammoth spectacular planned as a tourist boost to Wales, the rival limb of the United Kingdom, her trip had more religious and social significance than ever before.

A week after returning from Austria, the Queen, Prince Philip and Princess Anne flew to Edinburgh for ten days mainly to attend the General Assembly of the Scottish Kirk, the country's nearest equivalent to a Parliament. It was the first time a Sovereign had done such a thing since the Act of Union, in 1603 – and it caused some rumblings in the Church of England. 'Why isn't she getting involved with us if she can give a week to Scotland?' asked one of her religious advisers. 'She's frightened of it, that's why, and dear old Michael (Adeane) won't let her. I say fiddlesticks. The Sovereign needs to be brought back into the non-political life of the nation. The concept of a super person exercising a para influence is not going to last.'

The Queen's relationship to God changes as she moves over the Scottish border. She becomes less important. In England, the custom of bishops being appointed by the Monarch developed from the dark ages, and was made statute law during the Reformation in the sixteenth century. When Henry VIII broke from the Church of Rome, the Annates Act was passed in 1534 depriving the Pope of his power to appoint English bishops. The King was declared 'the only supreme head in earth of the Church of England'. Elizabeth I modestly altered 'head' to 'Governor', and that is the position of the Queen today, although a large minority of the British seem to feel otherwise. In 1956, thirty-four per cent thought she was specially chosen by God, and eight years later the number had only decreased to thirty per cent.[1]

At the start of the Hanoverian dynasty, the Church's influence was low, and the practice of the State making ecclesiastical appointments was gradually established. Bishops are appointed by the Crown, on the advice of the Prime Minister – who has personal responsibility for the nomination. He cannot be questioned about his choice in Parliament.

Bishops still pay homage to the Queen, usually at Buckingham Palace, and always in the presence of the Home Secretary. The bishop kneels, the Queen folds her hands over his, and he repeats the oath: 'I acknowledge that I hold the said bishopric,

[1] *Long to Reign Over Us?* by Leonard M. Harris (William Kimber, 1966, p. 43).

263

as well as the spiritualities as the temporalities thereof only of Your Majesty and for these temporalities I presently give my homage to Your Majesty.' Then he kisses the bible, and leaves. It takes about five minutes.

Many senior churchmen, including the Archbishop of Canterbury, the Most Reverend Arthur Ramsey, would like the Church to have a more substantial say in its own affairs, such as the power to elect bishops. Eventually, the only alternative to the present system would be disestablishment. This is unpopular because church leaders are myopically considered to be men of national importance who are kept under control as part of the State machinery. To some extent, establishment also has the reverse effect: a few of Britain's more dynamic and liberal church leaders would probably languish in a vacuum if the ecclesiastical hierarchy was solely responsible for appointments. 'Chaps like you, for instance, would never become a bishop,' Prince Philip told Mervyn Stockwood, Bishop of Southwark.

However, with only two million Anglican church-goers in the country – seven per cent of those baptized and slightly less than the number of Roman Catholics who attend mass – the Church of England can hardly be helped by being an appendage of the State, and it doesn't flatter the Queen to be titular head, ineffective Defender of a diminishing Faith. Moreover, the continuation of eighteenth-century religious intolerance embodied in the 1701 Act of Settlement, mocks two institutions trying to grapple with the 1970s:

'That all and every Person and Persons that then were, or afterwards should be reconciled to, or should hold Communion with the See or Church of Rome, or should profess the Popish Religion, or marry a Papist, should be excluded, and are by that Act made for ever incapable to inherit, possess or enjoy the Crown and Government of this Realm and Ireland, and the Dominions thereunto belonging, or any part of the same, or to have, use, or exercise any Regal Power, Authority or Jurisdiction within the same; And in all

264

and every such Case and Cases the People of these Realms shall be and are thereby absolved of their Allegiance: And that the said Crown and Government shall from time to time descend to and be enjoyed by such Person or Persons, being Protestants, as should have inherited and enjoyed the same, in case the said Person or Persons, so reconciled holding Communion, professing, or marrying as aforesaid were naturally dead. . . .

'II. Provided always, and it is hereby enacted, That all and every Person and Persons, who shall, or may take or inherit the said Crown, by virtue of the Limitation of this present Act, and is, or shall be reconciled to, or shall hold Communion with the See or Church of Rome; or shall profess the Popish Religion, or shall marry a Papist, shall be subject to such Incapacities, as in such Case or Cases are by the said recited Act provided, enacted, and established; and that every King and Queen of this Realm, who shall come to and succeed in the Imperial Crown of this Kingdom, by virtue of this Act, shall have the Coronation Oath administered to him, her or them, at their respective Coronations, according to the Act of Parliament made in the first Year of the Reign of His Majesty, and the said late Queen Mary, intituled, An Act for establishing the Coronation Oath, and shall make, subscribe, and repeat the Declaration in the Act first above recited, mentioned or referred to, in the Manner and Form thereby prescribed. . . .

That whosoever shall hereafter come to the Possession of this Crown, shall join in Communion with the Church of England as by Law established.'

In perverse Scotland, Jesus Christ is considered sole head of the Kirk. There, the Reformation was carried through by clergy and nobles who forced Parliament to accept the Confession of Faith in 1560. Although John Knox and other leading reformers had no real objection to episcopacy, bishops were considered to be predominantly 'King's men', so they were abolished in 1592 and the Presbyterian movement began. Nine years after the Act of Union,[2] James I of England (James VI of Scotland) had bishops reinstated. He was the last king to attend an Assembly of the Scottish Kirk, but when he tried to expound the Divine Right of Kings he was reminded by the Presbyterian Party leader, Andrew Melville, that he was 'only God's silly vassal'. Bishops were abolished again in 1639, restored in 1660, and were removed finally thirty years later by William and Mary as 'contrary to the inclinations of the generality of the people'. Since 1921, the Church of Scotland has been governed by an Act that gives them complete freedom in spiritual matters, and the only signatures legally required at the Accession Council of a new reign are on two copies of the Monarch's declaration to maintain the Presbyterian Government of the Church of Scotland.

Every year, the General Assembly of Ministers meets. It is the Supreme Court in spiritual matters. An elected Moderator presides, and the Sovereign appoints a Lord High Commissioner to report on proceedings. The Queen's personal attendance was considered by some church leaders as a magnificent opportunity to oil divisions between people who inoculate themselves with the same God, but have different methods of injection. 'There's a great deal of scope for her in these spheres,' said one of her religious advisers. 'Within the next fifty years the Protestant Church will be united.[3] The Roman Catholic and Anglican church will be reconciled. The Monarchy itself can't be liberated, until the churches liberate themselves. I saw the speeches she gave in Edinburgh, and I thought they were a bloody disgrace, because they said so little. I complained to Adeane. He said the ecumenical movement was quasi-political.'

The visit did arouse suspicions of yet another political stunt, that the Queen was attending in order to calm nationalism.

[2] 1603.

[3] Perhaps this was optimistic. On 8 July, 1969, the Convocations of Canterbury and York refused unity with the Methodists.

Some Kirk ministers had prepared strong rebukes in their speeches in case she spoke too much about ecumenicism or nationalism.

'The business of the Queen coming to the General Assembly is not a thing somebody said last week, "Wouldn't it be a good idea",' said Prince Philip.[4] 'In fact, we have been discussing this suggestion for at least five or six years, which is really before the sort of development of nationalism on that scale ever occurred. I think the important thing is that the Sovereign is, and understands herself to be, sovereign of Scotland, just as much as of England.

'The point is that if we had waited for that sort of pressure to occur, the event would have been put off anyway for another two or three years, but it would have been counter productive, people would have said this is done deliberately to this end, whereas fortunately in that sense it was thought of before that happened, and this argument never arose.

'In this case, the General Assembly, we thought of this idea ourselves, and we personally have been in a sense progressing it by trying to get various people to agree, gently, by talking to Moderators. We see them every year, and other ministers, sounding them out, asking what they feel about it, and cautiously we got to the point where they said this would be quite a good idea.'

After her Coronation in 1953, when the Queen went to Edinburgh to receive the honours of Scotland, she wore an undistinguished blue dress, bonnet, and black handbag – and looked like a housewife collecting goodies from the supermarket. Today, Tuesday 20 May, 1969 (Appendix), she travelled the cobbled hill from Holyroodhouse in a newly restored maroon and black Scottish State coach. Five carriages followed, flanked by a hundred horses of the Household Cavalry (one hundred and sixty men and one hundred and twenty horses had travelled from London for

[4] Interviewed on Grampian TV, 21 February, 1969.

this one occasion). They stopped for the opening religious service at Edinburgh's High Kirk – named St Giles after an Athenian who lived in France and spent most of his life in solitude with a hind as his only companion.

Then, preceded by an official neatly resting a mace on his knee in the back of an open red Triumph Herald convertible, the procession clattered to the Assembly Hall that broods in solemn grey splendour over the city on a ridge below the castle. Guarding the entrance were the Royal Company of Archers, the Queen's bodyguard in Scotland, equivalent to the Beefeaters in England, in Border green uniform and black Kilmarnock bonnets in which eagles' feathers denote rank. They carried bows, and three arrows tucked in their belts. A clutch of Heralds, looking like an elderly psychedelic Shakespearean pop group in their yellow, purple, and red tabards, began to form a retinue. Lord Cobbold and other members of the Household, in morning dress, took their places. The Secretary of State for Scotland, Mr William Ross, M.P., carried the large red purse, that symbolically holds the Queen's money and the Great Seal of Scotland, should she want to buy or stamp anything. Seven mace-bearers prepared to move forward. The Queen's coach so highly sprung that a wheel knocked against a carriage light, came up the hill. The Archers were commanded to attention by an officer with such an enthusiastic, nerve-twisting bellow that his hat fell off.

'No Popery,' shouted a few extremist Protestants, led by the Reverend Ian Paisley. They were angry because a Roman Catholic observer was being admitted to the Assembly. They didn't want to embarrass the Queen, but Paisley thought she was being used 'to cover up ecumenical machinations and hypocrisy. Admitting a Roman Catholic, even though he is only an observer, is an insult to the memory of John Knox, founder of the Scottish National Kirk.'

The Queen stepped from the coach, wearing a long silver brocade dress trimmed with white mink, and a diamond tiara, and went into the Hall to be greeted in Gaelic by the Moderator: 'Failte chridheil do bhur morache pigheil – a hearty welcome to your Majesty,' and claps from the massed clerical grey.

More prayers, the twenty-fourth psalm ('I've given up the hypocrisy of even mouthing the words,' says a member of the Household), and a speech from the Queen in the jargon of official utterances:

'Right Reverend and Right Honourable.

'Right Reverend Moderator, I congratulate you on your election to the Chair of this Venerable Assembly. Fathers and brethren, since the General Assembly last met, many Ministers and office bearers have died. We remember them with gratitude and affection; their influence, devotion and example will be with you as you address yourselves to your duties.'

'Fathers and brethren pray be seated.

'This occasion brings back many happy memories of the special meeting of the General Assembly held in October 1960 to commemorate the 400th anniversary of the Scottish Reformation. It was my experience of that time and the warmth of the Assembly's welcome which made me resolve to be in Edinburgh at a suitable opportunity for the period of the normal annual General Assembly and to be present at the opening and at some of your regular deliberations.

'Over the years I have had ample opportunity to witness the work of the Church of Scotland among my people in different parts of this country as well as among people in many parts of the world.

'Instead of sending a letter to read out on this occasion I can tell you myself that I remember and renew my promise to preserve and uphold the rights and privileges of the Church of Scotland.

'Christians everywhere are sustained and inspired by the ideal of the brotherhood of man and the commandment to love one another. In this imperfect world the struggle to achieve this ideal is long and hard but we all look to the leadership of the Church and we are most conscious of its unceasing efforts. There may be an inclination to look back at the apparent lack of progress but it is far better to look forward with hope, with faith and with expectation.

'The world may often seem gloomy and discouraging but we should remember that we are only able to witness a very small part of its continuing development; we should remember that with courage and perseverance we can do God's will in the certain knowledge that he expects us to fulfil his grand design.

'In this there is work for the most humble. Injustice, suffering and ignorance cry out for remedy all around us. Church people have every opportunity to set an example of service and self-sacrifice so as to make this world a better place for all people.

'Right Reverend Moderator, as you know, I am pursued by many other duties so that I shall not be able to attend the Assembly as often as I should like. I shall however follow your debates with the closest interest and I expect to receive reports on them both from my husband and from the Duke of Hamilton who will be present on other occasions.'

One of the first duties, after lunch, was to visit the Usher Hall, a building of rococo fussiness rising in tiers like an inverted wedding cake where about three thousand representatives of one hundred and thirty thousand Woman's Guild members of the Church of Scotland waited with unabashed passion. Four diffident clerics sat in the front row of the stage, overwhelmed as petals in a hurricane.

Guild President Mrs Denny Grieve, a homely woman resplendent in a blue dress and white and pink hat, was conducting a medley of hymns. Suddenly she stopped. 'I have just been informed that this is going live on Scottish Television.'

Oooooh. Aaaaah.

'We shall sing the twenty-third psalm.' We did.

The psalm finished, and the Queen still hadn't arrived.
What could we do? Luckily, an additional item of praise was
printed on the back of the programme, another hymn, four
verses long.

> 'Crown Him with many crowns,
> The lamb upon his throne . . .'

'We had this terrible gap,' explained Mrs Grieve, 'the
Moderator was too short. We expected him to speak for ten
minutes, and he only went on for about four. We were live
on Scottish TV. I should have known, but I forgot. Ghastly,
my dear.'

The additional item of praise ended, rousingly.

'I think we might sing the last two verses again,' suggested
Mrs Grieve, and at last, in the middle, Her Majesty arrived.
Perkins and Sir Martin Charteris were still in morning dress.
Sir Martin even carried his black top hat. Willie Ross clutched
his purse. It looked like a conjurer and his mate come to
transmogrify the rapturous femininity into instant gloom.

Mrs Grieve made a speech. 'I had a dream, and together we
women laughed at this dream because it was that the Queen
would be here, at this meeting of ours. But then . . . we were
all thrilled to find out that it was true.' She paused. 'For the
first time in my life a dream has come true. We could have
filled this hall forty-three times over. Your words,' she
assured the Queen, 'will reach every corner of the land.'

The Queen's words on this occasion had been written by
Sir Martin Charteris, with a vain attempt at lightness:

'It is becoming more generally recognized that the home
is not the only place for women' – not a sound – 'and the
ladies of the Manse are leading the way in bringing christian
support to the social and charitable works of the community.
'The conventions and prejudices which have for so long

dictated the limits of women's activities are slowly breaking down. The pioneers have shown conclusively that women are capable of making a valuable contribution in a great many spheres without for one moment losing their essentially feminine qualities. Indeed the growing opportunities for women means that their special qualities of gentleness and sympathy can find expression in a much wider variety of religious and social work. Particularly important is that special brand of feminine tenacity and sense of continuity which has played and will certainly continue to play such a vital part in the life of the Manse in dense urban communities or in remote country parishes.'

Polite claps. Not so much a blast, alas, more a toot of the trumpet from John Knox's monstrous regiment of women.[5]

[5]John Knox wrote a pamphlet in 1558 called *The First Blast of The Trumpet Against the Monstrous Regiment of Women.*

God *v.* Scotland-II

'What do you do when you're having a forenoon stroll in Holyrood Park, walk over the brow of a hill – and come face to face with a real Princess? Stammer "Good morning", of course, and then try to get your breath back after that dazzling Royal smile.'

'I was coming out of Hunter's Bog when the Princess suddenly came over the ridge in the opposite direction. She and her companion immediately greeted me with a smile, and I blurted out an embarrassed "Good morning". The Princess returned the compliment and added: "I want to enjoy the sunshine so I'm going for a walk on the hill."'
Report in the Edinburgh *Evening News*, 22 May, 1969.

EDINBURGH IS PERHAPS ONE OF THE MOST PROUD and arrogant cities in Britain, impervious usually to Sassenach marauders who provide it with an Arts Festival, or Americans spending dollars on ancestral excavation. After a day or two even *their* royal family become part of the scenery, and guests staying overnight at Holyroodhouse – from the Prime Minister to Sir John Wheeler-Bennett to Lord Reith (Appendix) – are given no more than cursory stares. In order to fully satisfy Scotland that real government could take place in the capital, the Ambassador of Lesotho (formerly Bechuanaland), created a precedent by being flown north in an aircraft of the Queen's flight to present his credentials with all the ensuing diplomatic hullabaloo. A Privy Council meeting also took place, in between other more traditional engagements.

Glasgow, glaring sulkily from forty-four miles away, was granted a four-and-three-quarter-hour visit. Open a fruit market. . . .

Sign the visitors' book – Philip, holding the page with his left hand, a thick gold ring on the little finger, makes a big loop for the 'P' and casually dots the 'i's' when he's finished. The Queen, more cautious, a smaller signature, dots the 'i' before completing the name, Elizabeth R. . . .

Dedicate a chapel at the Cathedral. An old gentleman, in morning dress, tries to take a picture. Perkins taps him on the shoulder. The man looks sheepish, hides behind a pillar, peers shiftily round and tries again, as a memento for the congregation, but he can't focus before Perkins, now wearing half-moon spectacles, explains: 'I'm sorry, but you can't take pictures.' Heavies from Glasgow CID look on. Apart from them, the Heads of both the CID and Special Branch, plus the Chief Constable and his deputy, are in attendance. . . .

Walk informally across the park, barricaded from spectators by crush barriers, to the Town Hall, where twenty-four magistrates, enchained, are presented to the accompaniment of pipe music. . . .

Lunch with the Lord Provost. . . .

Visit publishers William Collins where actor David Kossoff, commentating on closed circuit television, is inadvertently overheard. 'There's Philip, going dutifully behind his wife, the great Royal wisecracker' . . . .

Tour the Design Centre. . . .

Return to the station for the journey to Edinburgh and a performance of *The Gondoliers*. Lean out and wave as the train departs. . . .

Next morning, the Queen heard part of an Assembly debate on self-government in which the convenor of the church and nation committee, Rev. George Balls asserted: 'Some of the power and choice must lie in Scotland, in a Scottish parliament answerable to the Scottish people. They will not be fobbed off any longer by delays and evasions.'

274

They wanted to remain part of the United Kingdom, and the Queen's position would not be altered, but it was a suitably dour note on which to cross the road to visit the smaller Assembly of the Free Church of Scotland at St Columba's Church.

Most of the Ministers represented Highland communities where religion was still the most powerful force in people's lives. Perhaps because of harsh weather, perhaps because the twentieth century hadn't yet penetrated, perhaps because it made them happy, they seemed to have an uncompromisingly drab version of Christianity. It was reflected in humourless lips, righteous glints in their eyes, baggy black suits, the stiff confidence of their bearing, clipped coldness in their voices, the rigidity of their rules. Love was discussed. Tolerance was neglected. Even though the room was small, and people could be clearly heard without moving from their seats, they were required to address the meeting from a lectern equipped with a microphone.

'We are expected to be upstanding as soon as this door opens,' said the Moderator.

A messenger entered. The Queen was about to arrive. A procession began to form outside, visible through the frosted glass windows. 'Here's the Mace,' a whisper shuddered round the gleamingly polished wood. A woman nearly fell out of the low balcony in her anxiety to see what was happening. The royal party entered, Prince Philip sat rigidly in front of the Assembly thinking – who knows what? These people had criticized his polo playing on Sundays. Surely there was something wrong when religion was such a humourless pastime?

The Queen was speaking. Could she be lecturing them?

'Fathers and brethren pray be seated.

'Reverend Moderator, you referred with sympathy and understanding to the contradictory pressures which surround the Crown. They are indeed none other than the difficulties which confront countless people in their search for a christian way of life in the present-day environment, but perhaps they are more obvious. The principles of christian living, as none know better than the Free Church of Scotland, have not changed over the years but, as the old conditions of life change, so we must always be looking for new ways to put these principles into practice. This is where we need the daily renewal of strength, wisdom and compassion so that God's will may be done.

'It is, of course, right and proper that you should meet here in the Capital, but I cannot prevent my thoughts turning to the Highlands and islands where I have seen so many of your churches and members.

'In these distant churches you serve a people whose steadfastness and loyalty has given them a very special distinction for many generations...'

When she left, the Assembly returned to form. There were attacks on nationalism, transplants, abortion, the Roman Catholic Church, the Church of Scotland, and so on.

It was time for a rest. After visiting a factory and attending a white tie reception given by the Queen at Holyroodhouse, Prince Philip caught the 11.20 p.m. sleeper to London, and a game of polo the following afternoon.

There were more engagements the following week before the Queen could leave, on Thursday, for a long week-end at the Queen Mother's estate, Birkhall, seven miles from Balmoral. June was to be a fairly easy month, with Ascot, Goodwood, Trooping the Colour and three minor military events. She had to prepare for the major set piece royal spectacular of her reign. All strands of the country would be involved, – Church, Army, Government, tourism, television, the family, show business, politics – and to what purpose? Could the Investiture of Prince Charles be a success?

Interlude - 5

'So morning dress is in and lounge suits are out for Royal Ascot this year. What a relief – for the relaxing of this age-old rule of formal dress was a complete failure and no one, the ladies least of all, liked the sloppiness of informal men's wear. With so many of our British traditions fast disappearing in this age of "change for change's sake", it is comforting to know that good sense sometimes prevails and people can still have the pleasure of dressing-up for an occasion.' Letter in the *Daily Telegraph*, 24 March, 1969.

'At Epsom, where everything is ready for the Derby, the sun burst through when the Queen and members of the royal family arrived.' BBC 1 radio news bulletin, 2.30 p.m., 4 June, 1969.

'I saw the Queen at Ascot wearing a simple coat. She gave me a smile which I will never forget. I burst into tears as she reached my heart. How many women will you find like her? One in a million.' Letter in the *Evening Standard*, 13 August, 1969.

LANDMARKS IN THE BRITISH HORSE CULT are eagerly patronized by the Queen each year and, in a curious way, provide perhaps her single most emotional and deeply felt contact with the majority of 'my people'. A shared enthusiasm for the exploits of dumb animals seems to provide a tangible bond that is frequently missing on formal occasions. When she meets children in public, for instance, the Queen is noticeably tense, as if knowing she should provide a façade of imperious majesty yet not knowing quite how to cope.

But to see her walking through the crowd from paddock to grandstand, is to watch a woman at last able to communicate, and almost enjoying the role.

There are several types of horse event: shows, trials, races, point to point and fox hunting. The Queen attends them all, except fox hunting because that would involve her in controversy. 'I know she'd love to hunt, though,' says one of her hosts. 'But she is very conscious of what people would think.'

The three-day Badminton Horse Trials in April take place on the country estate of the Duke of Beaufort, Master of the Horse. The Gloucestershire village, sardonically called 'Beaufortshire' is another relic of England where feudalism appears to serve an emotional necessity. The Duke himself, known as 'master' to inhabitants, has held the trials on his estate for twenty-one years, and was given a plaque in 1969: 'To Master, for his support and encouragement over twenty-one years.'

The Queen usually spends a couple of nights at the Duke's house, taking with her a footman, chauffeur and detective. And 'Bobo' of course. In the evening she watches a film – this year the equestrian events at the Mexico Olympics, and two other horsey epics to illustrate the development of different riding styles.

During the day, in heavy coat, thick stockings, long tartan skirt, headscarf, and sensible low-heeled shoes, she mingles with the predominantly upper middle-class audience paying homage to the ability of horses in dressage, speed, endurance, and jumping. Asprey's, Garrard, the Bristol Evangelistic Centre, and hot-dog stands vie with each other for custom. The Queen watches the horses intently. Prince Philip veers between grim boredom and flip heartiness. Princess Anne wears a new hat and provides the photographers with their picture for the day.

Racing is more of a leveller, allowing all classes to unite in support of one pastime – gambling – and the subsidiary attraction of watching well-bred animals being manipulated by experts. No wonder it is the sport of kings. The fact that the Queen had to limit her flat racing activities to fourteen horses in 1969, compared with twice that number the previous year, is of interest only to economic pedants.

It is important, though, that she allows more animation to show during a race than on any other public occasion – and this provides the Monarchy in general with a source of lower middle-class support, offset by intellectual derision, particularly when she names one of her horses Charlton after two footballing brothers she saw playing for England in the final of the World Cup. Her interest is seen to be genuine and innocuous and allows racing to remain one of the harmless vestiges of class-ridden amateurism, a leisurely sporting activity controlled by the Jockey Club, a self-perpetuating aristocratic group who have three royal dukes as honorary members, and a committee of officials that includes four ordinary dukes, two marquesses, six earls, three viscounts, eight miscellaneous lords, and nine generals.

Such obvious elegance inspires its own attitude towards duty, and it is not considered strange that the Queen should hold a Privy Council meeting in the drawing-room of the Duke of Norfolk's country house, Arundel Park, when she is in residence for Goodwood week.[1] Some Privy Councillors, though, are not happy. 'You can't get it into her head that she's supposed to be working, poor thing,' said one. 'She finds it a bore, and I don't blame her. We barge in on her privacy. She can't see how royalty can travel up to London for the sake of a meeting with politicians. She feels there's no distinction between Labour and Conservative. They're all below her anyway.'

The Duke of Norfolk would not agree. He had a black and gold wooden plaque put on the wall of his drawing-room to commemorate the occasion.

[1] 31 July, 1969.

Of all racing events, perhaps the Derby[2] at Epsom is the most symbolic of England: a myth clinging to the past with easily invoked soporofics to excuse the frequently squalid reality. Yet it has a sort of ironic and self-critical charm.

'Up the workers. Down with the privileged classes,' a young man shouts at the Queen, to the massed glares of onlookers, and the admiring glances of his two pals. He is, of course, wearing morning dress, such is the egalitarian nature of social protest.

'Anne is very jowly, isn't she?' says one woman.

'I wanted to see what she was wearing. That's the only reason I came,' replies another.

On the grandstand side of the course, where tickets can cost up to £10, racegoers are predominantly in morning dress. The English accept the dank toilet facilities, the seedy bars, and decaying atmosphere with a stoicism that equates elegance with cissiness, and squalor with manliness. Deprivations of the Second World War are still being guiltily invoked as a comparison in many English public places, and the 'you should be grateful for what you've got' excuse is happily accepted. Foreigners, who would not tolerate such conditions at home, shrug it off as English perversion.

The downs, opposite, provide even more of an air-raid shelter mateyness as fifty-yard queues develop for the converted yellow buses that act as temporary toilets, the fun fair begins its activities, and thermos flasks and sandwiches are laid out on the grass for picnics.

'This is something to be believed,' shrieks a man in a white stetson, holding an outsize cigar in one hand, and banging a drum with the other. He stands on a makeshift stage advertising a knife-throwing striptease. Two skinny girls wearing white pants and bras flecked with red tassels which they occasionally twirl in a drab effort at titillation, shiver in response, and flick their pale shoulders with indifferent sexiness. 'This is cold steel against warm flesh,' enthuses the

[2] 4 June, 1969.

280

man. 'You'll see her naked as the day she was born. There's a hundred pounds to any charity you care to mention if this young lady wears a stitch of clothing.' He bangs the drum again, and hits a cymbal for added effect. 'Okay, follow the crowd, folks.'

Chubby girls with their acned boyfriends slurp tea from cardboard cups, and eat ersatz food, while they wait for the next race. Freshly permed matrons, out for the day, shopping bags stuffed with groceries, drink stout in a grey beer tent, the lucky ones sitting on torn canvas seats, as they contemplate a view of their Queen and her family. Soon they will stagger through screwed-up racing forms, serenaded by pop music, dodgem noises, gun cracks, to have a look at the royal box. After the next drink.

A gipsy, who claims to have X-ray eyes and is 'patronized by royalty and the leading stars of the film world', promises to guess your age correctly – or forfeit a lucky black cat plastic charm. He steps dramatically on to an orange box to begin his act. It splits in two.

In one tent, fuzzy centre-spreads from *Playboy* decorate an improvised screen provided by a youth equipped with an old projector and oil can, and earning a shilling a time from hundreds of raincoated men. Farther along, real flesh is being advertised by a man in dinner jacket and frilly white shirt. 'Watch their clothes come down like ... Venetian blinds,' he improvises.

Protecting the grandstand side of the course from such vulgarity is a row of thirty, open-topped, double-decker buses. In front of them, as a last line of defence, are bookies. As you approach the quality of merchandise improves. Fresh Norwegian prawns, two bob each, candlesticks at seventy shillings, and forty-five-shilling Indian carved boxes. Two couples on an exploratory stroll, sipping gin and tonic, gingerly sniff the scent of fish and chips combined with the sweet smell of undercooked onions, and retire to their own side, amused, in a quaint sort of way, at how the others live.

A man in light velvet trousers, flowered hat, yellow jacket embossed with zodiac signs and carrying a red umbrella, announces: 'Always make out you're deaf when anyone talks to you. Where are we now? Who's winning? Are you all right, your Majesty?' he bows to the royal box.

'Give us a kiss. Sod the racing.'

A luminous red and yellow sign moves past on the back of a solemn old gentleman. 'Repent, and turn to God.'

Not yet, not while the racing's still on, and well-bred Anglo-Saxon faces, etched with pink-cheeked prejudice, are rushing forward to collect their winnings. 'It makes you feel so much younger, a great weight off your mind when you've won.'

Up above, in her box, the Queen talks to Lord Porchester, looks through field glasses to the heath and the fun fair apparatus sparsely fringed with coloured light bulbs. From that distance, at least, it looks colourful and enjoyable.

Ascot[3] is one of the last sad remnants of manufactured class consciousness, where privilege can be bought in the form of a royal enclosure badge (£4 per day, £9 for two, £12 for four days – reduced prices for those between seventeen and twenty-five), and fake jollity is given an obligatory lift by over-priced non-vintage champagne poured into smeared whisky glasses.

The four-day royal meeting was begun by Queen Anne in 1711. King George IV instituted a coach procession of the royal family – led by the Master of the Buckhounds – from Windsor Castle to the course in 1825, and he also introduced a separate royal enclosure for his personal friends. Nowadays the royal family make part of the journey by car, and change into carriages for the journey down the royal mile. Anyone except an ex-jailbird or undischarged bankrupt can apply to the Duke of Norfolk for a ticket to the royal enclosure and most – judging by appearances, seem successful. Divorced people have been admitted since 1955.

[3] 17–20 June.

It still has the formality insisted upon by Edward VII when he had nothing better to do as Prince of Wales ('Mornin', Harris. Goin' rattin'?' he asked a peer who arrived in tweeds), and the break with tradition allowed in 1968 was not repeated in 1969. Morning dress, an uncomfortable and absurd anachronism but popular with the upper classes because it is the only uniform servants don't wear when fulfilling their functions, was insisted upon. Trouser suits and micro-skirts were banned, although plastic raincoats generally cover most spectators on the first day when there is a tradition of rain to spite exhibitionists. Which actress has been arrested for indecent exposure? Who is wearing the most outrageous hat? Oh yes, and what about the wretched horses?

The most important race is for the Gold Cup, first run in 1807 and now carrying more prestige than is matched by the prize money of £12,000. Consequently, many owners prefer to send their horses to the United States where they can race for seven times as much.

Until won on the third day, the cup stays in front of the Queen's glass-fronted box. She watches all the races. Prince Philip disappears to play polo. Bowler-hatted stewards keep undesirables out of the royal enclosure. Strawberries and cream, champagne and smoked salmon is consumed, money is lost, money is won. The Queen's house party attend the theatre, play games at the castle, race each other in the early morning down the course and drive in state in the afternoon.

Women curtsy. Men raise their toppers and give a cheer. Who are they cheering? Themselves? The spectacle of an institution playing to its supporters club is piquant and sad. The Stock Exchange remains sluggish on big horse-race days. It used to be the King's friends who vied with each other for a royal enclosure space. Now it is those with money. *Plus ça change.*

Interlude-6

TROOPING THE COLOUR, now held on a June Saturday, is a pinnacle of the British tourist season and as immutable a fixture of the Queen's year as the Lord's test match which she visits for an afternoon later in the month. It is also the most spectacular of the large number of military events she attends – from presenting colours to reviewing ships; from the jingoism and cosy schoolboy commentary of the Royal Tournament, to taking the salute on a freezing Woolwich parade ground and watching grown men of the Royal Artillery salute their guns. As such it deserves suitable preparation, and the Queen spends at least an hour and a half every morning for two weeks at the Buckingham Palace Mews practising to ride side-saddle – an uncomfortable and unnecessary position still required as a tribute to the day when it was considered indecent for ladies to ride astride a horse.

The Queen is Head of the Army, Navy, and Air Force. They owe allegiance to her, not the Government. Fortunately, to save jealousy, the royal family's interest is imaginatively spread through the three Services. The Queen has a preference for the Army and is an expert on various uniforms. Prince Philip is a sailor. And Prince Charles, although entering the Navy has a clearly projected preference for the Air Force.

The ceremony of Trooping the Colour which, besides being an unashamed dollar earner, symbolizes the special position of the Household troops, was first carried out in 1755 and has taken place fairly regularly since 1805. During Queen Victoria's reign, it was held to celebrate her actual birthday on 24 May. It is now held in summer on the Sovereign's 'official' birthday because there are few tourists in winter. Until 1958 it was the second Thursday in June, but had to be changed to Saturday because it caused too much traffic congestion.

Escorted by the Household Cavalry, the Queen rides from Buckingham Palace, up the Mall to Horse Guards Parade. The Household Cavalry is the collective title given to the Army's two senior regiments – Life Guards, and Blues and Royals. The Life Guards were commissioned from royalist noblemen by Charles II in Holland prior to his restoration.

This year,[1] the Queen was on her own horse for the first time – Burmese, a present from the Royal Canadian Mounted Police – and had a new £300 doeskin saddle presented by the Worshipful Company of Saddlers that made the side-saddle posture slightly more comfortable.

A few minutes before she arrived, the Queen Mother and other members of the family clip-clopped over the parade ground in a carriage, waving gently, to their seats in Horse Guards building. The first guardsman fainted, traditionally, making a jagged gash in the line of red uniforms. Morning-coated spectators shifted uncomfortably in the eighty-degree heat. Sheikh Zayed of Abu Dhabi, whose annual income is about £80,000,000, sat to one side, an honoured guest.

The Queen entered the parade ground. The clock, held back or advanced so she is always seen to be on time, struck eleven. Commanders screeched their orders like castrated parrots. 'That's what they need today, that long-haired crowd – discipline,' said an old man admiringly.

'There isn't a finer sight in the world than this,' breathed an American newspaper editor.

The national anthem was played – the first of three times – and a march past began. Burmese drooped his head, wilting in the sun, and possibly tired from the morning's exercise. A police function is to exercise important horses before the

[1] 14 June, 1969.

285

parade so they are not too frisky. The Duke of Kent's horse started to cough, arching its back a number of times.

Another guardsman fainted, another march past, another fainting. The Household Cavalry walked, then trotted past to the sound of *D'ye Ken John Peel*. As the Queen was saluting, Burmese, now more tired, suddenly jerked his head down. She was dragged forward, but without losing her salute or composure.

Then she returned to Buckingham Palace at the head of her troops, gave Burmese a carrot, had a drink, and went on to the balcony for a crowd-waving scene and RAF fly-past. This year, as a special treat, taxpayers were given a glimpse of the Concorde. It was cheered slowly at first, then louder as enthusiasm turned to patriotism and was transferred to the Queen and her family several hundred yards away. A symbolic moment, the new and the old, isolated for one moment in the middle of London on a warm summer's day.

'If this was in America, you'd have police on all the roof-tops, and everyone would be checked,' said a schoolteacher from Boston. 'That is one of the greatest things in your country. You're relaxed.'

He should have stayed awhile, and travelled a few hundred miles to Caernarvon for royalty's biggest show of the decade.

The Royal Vaudeville - II

'You're getting quite good at this.' The Queen to the Duke of Norfolk, discussing ceremonial for Prince Charles's Investiture.

'There will be no monkeying about in the name of modernization.' The Duke of Norfolk.

'Although the Secretary for Wales took the view that the main purpose of the Investiture was to boost the Welsh tourist industry, there was another view that it would give a boost to the Prince, and Royalty, preparatory to a campaign for an increase in the Civil List.' Emrys Hughes, *The Prince, The Crown, and the Cash* (Housemans 1969), p. 53.

PRINCE CHARLES'S INVESTITURE as Prince of Wales, on 1 July, 1969, could have been the last set-piece national extravaganza, the swan song of the royal vaudeville. The next coronation is not likely to take place for at least fifteen years, if the Queen abdicates, and longer if she doesn't. By then, attitudes towards the British Monarchy will have developed and their ceremonial activities modified.

Only the most audacious and gifted antiquarians could succeed in transporting several hundred of the country's important men on a damp Tuesday afternoon to a limestone ruin partially covered with fifty tons of turf specially imported for its uniform greenness on colour television, and sit them on uncomfortable red chairs for four hours or more to watch a twenty-year-old prince with a French fleur-de-lys of African feathers as his badge, and a German phrase as his motto, pay mediæval homage to his Anglican mother under the stage management of a Roman Catholic Duke in a Non-Conformist country whose subjugation was being celebrated, largely for the benefit of American tourists, many of whom cancelled at the last minute because of bomb scares, but also as a sop to fraught municipal pride, national heritage, and genealogical contrivance. Only the English could have made it appear an inevitable consequence of a respected system. The Welsh, with cultivated cynicism, capitalized on the reality of the situation, spat bardic moonshine and Celtic clichés into the eyes of observers, and made themselves a comfortable profit of several million dollars. One man even sold bits of Snowdonia at £4 a square foot, plus an illuminated scroll.

The Investiture, loosely based on a confidence trick, took place in an atmosphere of farce and nerve-racking tension that had been built up for more than a year. Eighteen months previously, the Lord Lieutenant of Caernarvonshire, Sir Michael Duff, had travelled to London to tell Sir Michael Adeane that anything might happen.

'What do you mean, anything?'

'Anything,' replied Sir Michael Duff, who, at sixty-three, is one of the more flamboyant Lords Lieutenant, dresses trendily in King's Road boutique clothes, and was to be host to the royal family immediately before they set out for Caernarvon Castle.

The Queen was apprehensive about the safety of her eldest son and wondered, too, if it was necessary to spend so much money. If there was going to be an interminable row she was quite happy to discard the Windsor greys, and stop at Caernarvon railway station, instead of having a procession. 'She would have said no to the whole thing, if she could,' said one of the people intimately involved in the arrangements. 'But it was entirely a political thing, and she was pushed. The Welsh office and Uncle George[1] insisted on a show.'

[1]George Thomas, Secretary of State for Wales.

Anthony Wagner, Garter King of Arms, also had doubts and at one time was in favour of cancelling the ceremony gracefully when the Chancellor of the Exchequer set a budget of £200,000 ($480,000). Initially, a figure of £500,000 ($1,200,000) had been mentioned.

The Duke of Norfolk wrote to the Prime Minister. 'It was meant to be a help, not a hindrance,' he explained. 'I said that from what I'd heard it might come to more than £200,000 and we may have to have, what's the phrase, a supplementary estimate.'

About half the people in Wales thought it was a waste of money anyway and a third thought the Monarchy should change with the times.[2] Nevertheless, a few months later, Prince Philip talking about his and the Queen's doubts said: 'I think the doubts are not so much allowing him to take part at all, but if we had any doubts, perhaps to what extent this sort of virtually mediæval revival was relevant, and I think that probably the final governing factor was that it was quite obvious that a very large proportion of Welsh opinion favoured this. This really tipped the scales.'[3]

After the show, the Queen became ill with a cold, and cancelled her engagements for four days. Prince Charles toured his new principality. Princess Margaret confided to a friend: 'Non-swanks, I felt some of the wifely pride when I saw the castle.' George Thomas, surrounded by henchmen, sat in his office smoking a cigar and claimed: 'The support of the populace exceeded my wildest dreams. I don't want to be guilty of the Welsh sin of exaggeration, but it was a far greater triumph than we had a right to expect. He really was the Prince Charming. Wales has been in a state of euphoria, and at least a million dollars came to Caernarvon itself.'

[2]In a survey carried out by Opinion Research Centre for the *Western Mail* in September 1968, 44 per cent thought the Investiture and accompanying celebrations a waste of money. In the 21–34 age group it was 53 per cent. 35 per cent said Monarchy should change with the times.

[3]Grampian TV, 21 February, 1969.

Angus Ogilvy travelled to Canada the following day and he thought they would say 'Good Shakespeare'. 'I was staggered by their attitude. They thought it was marvellous.' An eight-year-old boy lay in hospital with his right leg amputated after a bomb explosion, and several recent widows wondered why their husbands felt strongly enough about an English summer sport to blow themselves to pieces.

Caernarvon, standing at the foot of the Menai Straits and overlooking the island of Anglesey, has a long experience of invasion. It was founded by Agricola in A.D. 78 as the fort of Segontium, the north-western limit of the Roman Empire. When the Romans left Britain in 422, a number of rival princes ruled Wales, and Prince Charles of course is descended from the most powerful – Rhodri Mawr.[4] For years, Rhodri's ancestors squabbled amongst themselves and tried to fight off the English. In 1063, surrounded by King Harold's armies, Prince Gruffydd ap Llewelyn had his head cut off by his own men and offered as a token of submission. The Norman conquest didn't help Wales either, but in the second half of the thirteenth century Prince Llewelyn ap Gruffydd managed to obtain recognition for his title Prince of Wales. He was supposed to pay yearly tribute, but he ignored this duty in 1272 when Edward I was on a crusade in Palestine, and did not attend the Coronation two years later. The Welsh lost the ensuing war in 1276, and another in 1282 – when Llywelyn was killed on December 11, his brother executed, and his daughter sent to a nunnery.

The following year Edward began to build Caernarvon Castle as a military fortification, and offices from which his Civil Servants could administer Wales. It cost about £19,000 – equivalent to £2,000,000 today – and was consciously designed to reflect the Roman empire. Their symbol, the eagle, crowned the triple turrets of the most spectacular tower.

According to legend, Edward agreed with the Welsh

[4] A.D. 844–78.

leaders to provide a Prince who had been born in Wales and could speak no English. He then transported his pregnant wife, Queen Eleanor, to a shack on the site of the castle. The ensuing son, also called Edward, was made Prince of Wales. At the time, he was not heir to the English throne but an elder brother, Alfonso, died soon after. Edward was created Prince at the Lincoln Parliament in 1301 when he was sixteen.

For over a hundred years Caernarvon Castle was a walled garrison equipped with sixty-four English burgesses – despite assaults in 1401 from Owain Glendwr, perhaps the most popular Welsh hero from whom, it was disclosed, Prince Charles is also descended. The Investiture, of course, was a magnificent opportunity for genealogists – in particular Major Francis Jones, Wales Herald Extraordinary, and county archivist at Carmarthen, who discovered that Richard II was a direct descendent of the Welsh princes, and Charles himself is related to such luminaries as Gruffydd ap Cynam, Llywelyn, Bleddyn ap Cynfyn, and Hywel Dda, who codified the Welsh laws. His relationship to Owain Glyndwr is through two daughters and two sisters, down to the fifth Earl of Cumberland, the third Earl of Cork, and the Queen Mother.

It was unfortunate, considering this, that during one of his early forays into Welsh life, Charles asked some protesting students about their placards, 'Who is Llywelyn?' It wasn't a mistake he repeated.

Before the twentieth century there was nothing much more than a few mutterings in the House of Lords to invest the King's eldest son as Prince of Wales (Appendix). Then, over tea at Windsor Castle in 1889 Alfred Edwards, newly enthroned Bishop of St Asaph, and future Archbishop of Wales, spoke to Queen Victoria and her eldest daughter, the Empress of Germany, about the need for a ceremony to emphasize the unity of Wales and England. In 1910, when George V came to the throne, David Lloyd George resurrected the Bishop's proposal for an installation of the Prince of Wales. The Liberal Party was still in power, but Lloyd George was worried about his own seat, Caernarvon, and thought a pageant would provide much good publicity.

'This ceremony had been allowed to lapse for centuries,' wrote the Duke of Windsor in his memoirs, 'but surprisingly enough the Welsh radical, Mr David Lloyd George, who only a few years before shocked my family with his famous Limehouse speech attacking inherited privilege, decided that its revival would appeal to the national pride of his people. With an eye to what would please his constituents, Lloyd George proposed that the ceremony be transformed into a spectacular Welsh pageant.'

The College of Arms investigated the precedent and found a description of the 1610 investiture of Henry, son of James I. Virtually the same ceremony was used on 4 November, 1616, for Henry's brother, Charles I, at Whitehall (where he was to be executed thirty-three years later). 'It was fascinating,' said Sir Anthony Wagner. 'Until 1621 peers were always invested, but James I and Buckingham were selling off so many (a barony was £15,000 ($36,000)) that they had to do away with the ceremony. The investiture of the Prince of Wales is a special form of investiture for a peer. It could be done anywhere. Doing it in Wales is purely a political gesture.'

The clothes were not, though. Charles I had worn 'a mantle of crimson velvet, containing eighteen yards, edged with gold lace and furred with ermine; a kirtle or surcoat containing fourteen yards, edged and furred as before and of the same stuff; laces, tassels and buttons of silk and gold, and a girdle of silk for the nether garment: a hood and cap of estate of the same velvet, with edging and furring as before.'

The Duke of Windsor was also made to parade like a pantomime character:

'The ceremony I had to go through, with the speech I had to make, and the Welsh I had to speak were, I thought, a sufficient ordeal for anyone. But when a tailor appeared to measure me for a fantastic costume designed for the occasion, consisting of white satin breeches and a mantle and surcoat of purple velvet edged with ermine, I decided things had gone too far.

'I had already submitted to the Garter dress and robe, for which there existed a condoning historical precedent; but what would my Navy friends say if they saw me in this preposterous rig?

'There was a family blow-up that night; but in the end my mother, as always, smoothed things over. I also got the impression, although the thought was never actually put into words, that if I did what was asked of me it would help Papa in his dealings with the difficult Mr Lloyd George.'

He was taught a few Welsh phrases by Lloyd George, and a processional route was devised from a refurbished railway halt, Griffiths Crossing, two and a half miles outside Caernarvon, so crowds could be spread. The young prince, who was only seventeen, made a speech: 'I have already heard some of your far famed singing, of which I have been told so much. It gave me great delight. It touches all who hear it, coming, as it does, from the heart as well as from the head. As we say, Mor o gan yw Cymru i gyd ("All Wales is a sea of song").

'When I think of the many links which bind me to your beautiful country, the title I bear seems more real to me than ever. You greet me on behalf of all in your ancient mother tongue, Croeso, and so let me end by saying Diolch o waelod fy nghalon i hen wlad fy nhadau (Thanks from the bottom of my heart to the ancient land of my fathers).'

Caernarvon had always imagined itself to be capital of Wales from the time Edward I made it his vice-regal headquarters, and it was described as such in encyclopædias until the early twentieth century. After the last war the borough sent a petition to King George VI which said, in part: 'Your petitioners have always shewn a steady, keen and enlightened

293

interest in all matters concerning Wales; this being the direct and natural expression of that mode of life which has characterized their ancient Borough from time immemorial.

'Welsh is the language of the town. In its corporate and individual life it radiates all that is truest, finest, and noblest in the nation. Religion, art, drama, and music find in it a worthy home. Caernarvon, more than any other town or city in the Principality, can claim to represent truly the Welsh way of life.

'Your petitioners know that the full strength and impact of the national forces and energies will not be realized unless they are marshalled, co-ordinated and directed from an acknowledged centre in the Principality.

'Wales, like every other nation and civilized country in the world, needs a capital town. The absence of such has been a retarding factor in the life of the nation.

'Your petitioners therefore humbly and respectfully submit that a capital town for the nation is an imperative necessity; and that such should be a town which commands the affection, admiration and respect of the whole nation by reason of its history, tradition, culture and mode of life.

'Your petitioners humbly, but proudly, recall that the first Prince of Wales was born in Caernarvon, and that in 1911 King George V graciously acceded to hold the Investiture of the Prince of Wales in their town.

'Your petitioners maintain that Caernarvon is the recognized and traditional capital of Wales, and that the Welsh nation would be pleased and gratified if Your Majesty recognized the right of the Principality to its own capital, and by reason of the prerogative vested in Your Majesty, grant the privilege of Letters Patent under the Great Seal to the Borough of Caernarvon.'

Cardiff, Aberystwyth, and Llandrindod Wells had also petitioned, and eventually a compromise was reached. Cardiff became the capital in 1955, Aberystwyth had the University, and Caernarvon was promised the Investiture, announced three years later, at the British Empire and Commonwealth Games in Cardiff on 26 July, 1958. The Queen was in bed at Buckingham Palace with a heavy cold, so a recorded message was introduced by Prince Philip: 'I want to take this opportunity of speaking to all Welsh people, not only in this arena, but wherever they may be. The British Empire and Commonwealth Games in the capital, together with all the activities of the Festival of Wales, have made a memorable year for the Principality. I have therefore decided to mark it further by an act which will, I hope, give as much pleasure to all Welshmen as it does to me. I intend to create my son, Charles, Prince of Wales today. When he is grown up, I will present him to you at Caernarvon.'

Nationalism has always rumbled in Wales, but if the Queen had known the proportions it would reach ten years later, the Investiture might never have been held. At the time, it seemed a pleasant enough idea and the then Prime Minister, Harold Macmillan, was in favour of providing the Welsh with some drama. The Welsh, though, were to have some justification for their charges that it was a lackadaisical political move, handled with complacent insensitivity. In the next ten years, Prince Charles visited his principality on only two occasions. Nevertheless, the first bickering was a municipal conflict. The Lord Mayor of Cardiff thought his city should be the centre of attraction. A Caernarvon alderman, Jonathan Hughes, replied immediately:

'When we met a deputation from Cardiff City Council at Shrewsbury in 1953, they said that if we supported their claim to capital status, they would concede our claim to be Wales's ceremonial centre. The reply of our deputation was that because of Caernarvon's historical associations there could be no argument about it.'

Five years later,[5] Caernarvon was given another boost. The Queen paid a visit and announced from the Castle: 'Felly penodaf Gaernarfon i fod yn Fwrdeisdref Frenhinol', which

[5] 9 August, 1963.

she translated, 'I therefore declare Caernarvon to be a royal borough'. It didn't actually mean anything, but it made them special like Windsor, Kensington, and Kingston-upon-Thames, allowed municipal dustcarts a new coat of arms, and a charter to be written: 'Elizabeth the Second by the Grace of God of the United Kingdom of Great Britain and Northern Ireland and of Our other Realms and Territories Queen, Head of the Commonwealth, Defender of the Faith, to all to whom these presents shall come, Greeting. Whereas King Edward the First granted by Royal Charter bearing date at Flint, the Eighth day of September in the Twelfth year of his reign, that henceforth the town of Caernarvon should be a free borough; and whereas the inhabitants of that borough are now a body politic and corporate by the name and style of the Mayor, Aldermen, and Burgesses of the Borough of Caernarvon; and whereas for divers good causes and considerations us thereunto moving our will and pleasure is that a Royal Charter shall issue, granting to the said Borough so constituted the title of Royal; now therefore know ye that we of our especial grace do, by this our Royal Charter, grant to the Borough of Caernarvon, the title of Royal.'

Enthusiasm in Caernarvon itself was inspired by the Mayor. Ifor Bowen Griffith, who began as a sceptic and turned into a lilting enthusiastic in the cause of Prince Charles. 'You could put a suit of armour on that boy, and send him to Agincourt. I reckon he's the ace in the royalist pack. Wales has reached a point where we need friends – from Buckingham Palace upwards, or downwards.

'The Investiture is the spur that has got us to do things we wouldn't ordinarily have done. We've put a shilling on the rates, and begun a crash programme for the streets. It's a bit like asking a village to run a cup final, but life would be very dull if we didn't have any pageantry.

'The castle, of course, is not a symbol of oppression, but of our toughness. I love this town, as a man loves a woman. I spoke no English until I was eight. My wife would think I'd gone queer if I went back and spoke English to her. We've seen them all off. There's no oppressor any more. It's a privilege for the Prince, as well as the Principality.'

Municipal pride having been satisfied, historical justification found, and genealogical research having discovered numerous realities, preparations began. An Investiture office was set up in London in September 1967 and a fifty-three-man committee convened.

The ceremony was to be the first State Television Occasion, organized predominantly for the benefit of five hundred million viewers throughout the world by two leading impresarios of Monarchical image: Lord Snowdon and the Duke of Norfolk. It would be difficult to find two more opposing temperaments than the unbending traditionalist who would 'bring back conscription tomorrow', and the apparently fey photographer with a natty taste for the more exotic men's wear. Their amused tolerance of each other, the basis of a successful partnership, was expressed by the Duke of Norfolk when asked what should be worn on the day. Gravely, through hooded eyes, he peered at Lord Snowdon, sitting next to him in a mildly fanciful ensemble of grey jersey suit with zipped jacket, pleated pink shirt, spotted tie, leather belt with huge gilt buckle, and answered lugubriously, 'Well, you know, I think it might be a good idea to wear a tie.'

The Duke of Norfolk, England's senior lay member of the Roman Catholic Church, first heard about the Investiture on the radio as he was listening to a news bulletin to discover the weather situation for cricket, of which he is a devoted fan. It would be another notch in his royal M.C.'s cap – the funeral of George V, coronation and funeral of George VI, Coronation of Elizabeth II, Sir Winston Churchill's funeral – and now this. Experience made him deceptively casual, and at times during committee meetings he would appear to doze off.

'It seemed he was taking no interest at all,' said one

member. 'Then suddenly he would look up, and have a very bright suggestion.'

One, though, wasn't considered so practical. Discussing invitations for mayors, he mentioned that the Mayor of Arundel always had two mace bearers. 'I want the mace bearers.'

The secretary of the committee, Dr Robert Jones, tried to point out that there wouldn't be room – particularly as some mayors also had sword bearers. The Duke of Norfolk insisted, and Dr Jones had to placate the clerks of large councils with perhaps eighty thousand people who could only have the same – or less – representation as boroughs with perhaps one thousand.

'I didn't change one iota of the ceremony from 1911 because that would have been wrong,' said the Duke of Norfolk. 'It's a constitutional act, and as such you can't do it. I frankly believe that it couldn't have gone better. There's still a great sense of pride in this country, thank God.'

He worked out some plans with toy soldiers, and caught a bad cold during rehearsals on Buckingham Palace lawn. 'My standards are high, but it isn't upsetting for anyone. There would have been just as much work if I'd said come in your pyjamas.'

The demands of television, and simplicity, more than halved the number of guests who had attended the 1911 Investiture. Then, the castle was cluttered with 11,000. This time there would be only 4,000. Television? 'We've got to live with these things if people invent them,' said the Duke.

Lord Snowdon was responsible for the castle, which closed six months before the event. He was also secretary of the music committee. 'He was very good at that, because he knew nothing about music,' explained one member. 'But it was a bit difficult over the castle because he was interested – as a part-time architect.'

'The Duke of Norfolk was super,' said Lord Snowdon. 'I was in charge of the aesthetic side of what went on inside –

from the dais to the banners. I got Carl Toms, a romantic designer, and John Pound, a very brutal modern designer, to work with me. I saw it as a kind of operation to improve the castle on a long-term basis.

'I tried to make it as simple as possible, to let the castle speak for itself, and have the dais as a kind of theatre in the round so it would read well on colour television. I may have done it wrong. But if it's going to be televised – and that's up to someone else to decide – you have to do it properly. I don't like working in an amateur way. Morally, the television audience has a right to see it as much as anyone because the money comes from the taxpayer. We worked out, with the television companies, the best place for the cameras. I wanted them below the skyline, so they wouldn't show in the picture. Two cameras that occasionally had to take higher shots were on hydraulic cranes, so they could be moved out of sight after each shot.'

The Duke of Norfolk wanted the Ambassadors to have awnings, and he was keen on red carpets. Lord Snowdon successfully opposed that. If you want it indoors, he said, have it indoors. But he wasn't against more traditional aspects such as red robes. They would look good on television. It would have been better to have someone like Peter Hall do the choreography near the dais, but you can't have everything and the Duke of Norfolk did have some colourful ideas.

'I had what I call my little flowerbeds,' he said. 'I looked at pictures of the 1911 Investiture. The dais was surrounded with people. At three o'clock one morning, I suddenly thought, "I've got it". Two sets of seats for members of the royal family, and I tried it out in Buckingham Palace gardens. That kept the whole stage, so to speak, uncluttered.'

A special canopy of acrylic sheets – a gift from I.C.I. – was designed to cover the dais, tapering from twenty-five feet at the front to nine foot six at the back, supported by steel rods that resembled lances. A scale model was tested in a wind tunnel to make sure it could withstand sixty-mile-an-hour winds.

Because of the Duke of Windsor's well-publicized remarks, one of the most important problems was dress. What was Prince Charles to wear? 'I'd like to have seen him start the ceremony in a lounge suit, and then give him a robe, so we could say, Now we can make him a Prince,' said Ifor Bowen Griffith. 'Call it a gimmick if you like, but I'm not keen on uniform. Once a war is finished, we become pacifist in Wales.'

His suggestion was not accepted, and Charles wore his ceremonial uniform as Colonel-in-Chief of the Welsh Regiment.

What would the Queen wear?

Sir Michael Duff thought it would be nice if she had a tiara. The Duke of Norfolk pointed out that, at the beginning of her reign, she used to wear a tiara in Africa, even in the mid-day sun. 'I don't think you'd like the Queen to appear for the Welsh as she did for the Africans.' Indeed no.

Angus Ogilvy was asked to wear a uniform, but refused and as he thought coronets and robes looked absurd, he used morning dress. Lord Snowdon designed himself a bottle green zip-fronted uniform with a belt of corded black silk and two tassels that made him look like a gnomic page boy. 'Buttons', he was called by some. The Duke of Norfolk wondered why he didn't go the whole hog, have a hat and be Robin Hood.

Meanwhile, vocal opposition to the investiture increased in Wales. It was the first royal occasion in recent years for which a large number of people felt no sympathy, and they were determined no ermine wrap should shroud their disaffection. A senior civil servant, whose job was to publicize the event, admitted privately: 'This gooey mush about royalty. Wales has done very badly under British rule.'

Plaid Cymru, the nationalist party with forty thousand members and allegedly large donations from expatriate Welshmen in the United States, decided to ignore the ceremony – a difficult proposition considering events. English road signs were obliterated with paint, gelignite sold at £3 for a two-ounce stick, 'Revolution in progress' was daubed on bridges, water pipelines were guarded by helicopter patrol, caricatures of Charles likening him to a well-meaning dog were distributed, he was called 'this German oaf' in literature of the Free Wales Army, and a satirical folk song became top of the Welsh hit parade:

'I have a friend who lives in Buckingham Palace
And Carlo Windsor is his name
The last time I went round to his house
His mother answered the door and said:
"Carlo, Carlo, Carlo is playing polo today
Carlo is playing polo with his Daddy."
So come all ye serfs of Wales and join in the chorus
At last you have a prince in the land of song.'

This was augmented by a series of bomb attacks (Appendix) that began on 17 November, 1967, when four hundred and fifty representative Welshmen met at Cardiff's Temple of Peace to discuss preliminary arrangements, and an explosion caused £30,000 worth of damage.

Ironically, important State occasions used to be a time of amnesty, but the Investiture was to be marked by the second longest trial in Welsh criminal history, an elaborate legal charade that parodied a Ruritanian self-protective instinct. In the early morning of 26 February, 1969, nine members of the Free Wales Army were arrested under section two of the 1936 Public Order Act, banning quasi-military organizations. As the subsequent trial showed, they were basically a group of enthusiastic exhibitionist patriots, almost comic desperadoes. The prosecution, however, took twenty-one days and called seventy-three witnesses to prove the point. Eight Q.C.s, nine junior counsel, one hundred and thirty exhibits, and a million words were used in the trial, which continued from 16 April until 1 July with only a short Whitsun recess. The cost was officially estimated as £84,500 ($212,000), plus fifteen months prison sentences for the two leaders, Julian Cayo Evans and Dennis Coslett. They seemed chosen to play contradictory roles, first to illustrate that opposition to the investiture was caused by a few mild eccentrics performing stunts for the world's Press in the hills of Lampeter, and secondly to show they were a dangerous group of crazed Celtic assassins.

The latter possibility was more acceptable to the authorities and several thousand policemen were drafted into Caernarvon where, as in Aberystwyth, they mingled inconspicuously with holidaymakers, licking ice-creams, sucking rock, smoking pipes and taking surreptitious photographs. Arrow slits in the castle were boarded over, manhole covers glued down in the streets, and crush barriers market tested at a local boys' school. Access to the space beneath the seats in the castle was through special doors fitted with MI5 security locks, and Princess Margaret, in Caernarvon with Lord Snowdon, was refused entry to the BBC television compound because she didn't have the correct pass and a security man failed to recognize her. Rumours that Prince Charles was to wear a bullet-proof vest were readily believed, even though he was indignant at the very suggestion.

This was not Dallas. It wasn't even a puny Celtic fleshpot rampant with Mafia, nor a Welsh lido swirling with shady 'businessmen'. Even so, no one took chances, and a by-law was invoked that prevented people waving banners, distributing leaflets, or shouting slogans. Caernarvon was not going to be scarred with the crime of regicide.

Cost was a more delicate, and endlessly arguable item, as with all State occasions. Generally, as much money as necessary is forthcoming. Afterwards it can be concealed in different budgets to save embarrassment. The estimated £200,000 ($480,000) was increased by £50,000 ($120,000) in March, and the final, true expense could be wrapped in certain confusion although the Government said the net cost was only £130,000 ($312,000). Ultimately, arguments about

302

the cost are meaningless. It increases in a number of ways that are not immediately obvious, but are eventually paid by taxpayers. At least £100,000 ($240,000), for instance, could have been saved by better co-ordination between television companies. The BBC provided a six-hour programme, using over thirty cameras and equipment worth £2,000,000. Commercial television had a larger involvement. 'More than fifty cameras were doing the work of twenty-five,' wrote Denis Foreman, chairman of Independent Television's special events.[6] 'Attempts to bring reason to bear upon this absurd situation failed.'

Caernarvon itself was spending £3,000 ($7,200) on decorations (equivalent to threepence on the rates), and inhabitants were provided with 5,000 lb of free paint by a local firm, so the houses looked prim in their greens, pinks and creams, and smelt fresh. Cardiff, adapting May to September into a carnival period, agreed to spend £30,000 ($72,000). The nationalized Electricity Board supplied free electricity to councils wanting to illuminate attractive features of their towns. Police spent an estimated £23,000 ($60,000) on security operations.

A coronet, for Charles, made to specifications laid down by Charles II, was donated by the Goldsmiths' Company. It was a stark circlet with alternate crosses and fleurs-de-lys, spanned by an arch mounted with an orb and cross, made of twenty-four-carat gold reinforced with iridium platinum, and containing seventy-five diamonds and twelve emeralds. It weighed only 3 lb because it had been 'grown' in an electro-plating bath by a new process. The cost to the Goldsmiths' was £3,600 ($8,640), but the real value was nearer £20,000 ($48,000).

Government money was spent in a number of ways: £115,000 ($276,000) for the castle; £4,000 ($9,600) for the Earl Marshal's office expenses; £40,000 ($96,000) to the Ministry of Defence for supplying and housing two thousand

[6] Letter to *The Times*, 31 July, 1969.

five hundred soldiers including one hundred and forty-eight men and one hundred and seventy horses of the Household Cavalry, and equipping Caernarvon with a temporary bridge over the river mouth that had been needed for years but was considered too costly; £36,000 ($86,400) for car parks and mobile public lavatories called rollalongs; £2,000 ($4,800) preparing Griffiths Crossing so 1911 precedent could be observed; and £4,000 ($9,600) transporting ambassadors and Commonwealth representatives to Caernarvon by train. Some of this money was recouped from the subsequent sale of chairs used inside the castle at £12 ($28.80) each, and the rent of seats in the moat for £10 10s. ($25.20). The last price included vermilion cushions in Welsh wool, cost price 27s. 6d. ($3.10), as mementoes.

Individuals also made money. Apart from Caernarvon's inadequate accommodation, which meant landladies could charge £5 ($12) per person (two in a room) for inferior hospitality in terraced houses, and the main hotel was £11 ($26.40) per person (three in a room), there was profit in souvenirs. One hundred and sixty-six officially approved items and dozens of free-lance offerings were on sale – from fivepenny pencils to £105 ($252) commemorative vases and £100 ($240) silver cigar containers. There were tiles, goblets, tankards, cruet sets, pie funnels, money boxes, paperweights, pendants, pill boxes, cuff links, rings, cravat pins, brooches, coffee sets, crystal chalices, tree plaques, napkin rings, model miner's safety lamps, egg-cup cases, calendars, notelets, booklets, red socks, toys, rugs, spoons, dolls, cocktail mats, key rings, cardboard cut-out figures of the Wales Herald Extraordinary and carpets. At one point, though, Caernarvon shopkeepers complained the only Welsh dragon flags they could buy were from Hong Kong and incorrectly printed.

The College of Arms gleefully held their first Press conference – in the London room where heralds were formerly invested by having wine poured over their heads – to explain the detailed significance of the occasion. Four of them changed into tabards, colourful clothing that is passed on until it falls to pieces, as it is provided by the Treasury who have only bought one new outfit in the last fifty years.

Sir Anthony Wagner, sitting in lounge suit under a carving of two cherubs, was asked by an American if he considered himself part of show business. 'I don't regard myself as part of show business at all,' he replied. 'The greater part of my time goes on research. There is nothing showy. It is interesting and serious work. The colourful side comes upon us every now and again, and on the day itself we have to dress up and play our part.'

Later, he admitted he wasn't keen on dressing up. 'I get rather tired of it, because I don't have the peacock instinct. But it is something worth doing. It has an effect in pulling our history together. People think the College of Arms represents some dreadful right wing reaction. We don't at all.'

Excitement increased. Lord Snowdon was nearly capsized in his boat by a shot from Lord Newborough's personal cannon on the lawn of his sca-front house – an incident which also had a 1911 precedent as Queen Victoria's yacht was nearly sunk by a shot from one of his lordship's ancestors.

English newspapers, such as the *Sunday Times*, printed eulogistic leading articles in Welsh; and headlines announced 'Siarli yw ein hanwylyd ni' – Charlie is our darling.

The Welsh Language Society, meanwhile, held an anti-Investiture at Cilmeri, where Llywelyn had been killed, and wore armbands saying 'Special Branch'. It was no longer a joke. The Sunday before the Investiture, a home-made bomb comprised of two sticks of gelignite and a wrist watch, exploded at Cardiff post office. No one was injured but Detective Chief Superintendent David Morris, head of South Wales C.I.D., said prophetically: 'Someone will be killed if these outrages don't stop.'

Caernarvon was sealed off to unofficial traffic at three a.m.

on 1 July, and had an atmosphere of a garrison town nervously twitching itself into a hopeful carnival spirit. Poet Laureate Cecil Day-Lewis had his poem published:

> 'Today bells ring, bands play, flags are unfurled,
> Anxieties and feuds lie buried,
> Under a ceremonial joy. . . . '

Two clumsy village terrorists, a painter and a road worker, with a home-made bomb, blew themselves up instead of the local government offices at Abergele, thirty-five miles away – the seventh bomb incident in three months. 'They hated the idea of the Investiture, so they decided to do something about it,' said Mervyn Roberts, a cousin of one of the victims. 'They were both decent sort of chaps. They just had it in their mind to do something about this Investiture business, like many young people in Wales today.'

One man was hurled forty feet over two houses. Parts of him were found in a garden in an adjoining housing estate.

Fifty jittery soldiers were evacuated from an army camp on the processional route when a brown paper parcel was found behind a tent. Gingerly, it was opened, to reveal a yellow sou'wester.

The royal family's overnight train from London was delayed by a series of incidents – including an hour's wait at Crewe while a bomb disposal team from Liverpool dismantled a hoax package of two plasticine sticks attached to a ticking alarm clock under a bridge outside Chester. Later it stopped at a secret destination near Bangor, in a siding bounded by cliffs into the Menai Straits on one side and a thickly wooded valley on the other. All night, patrols watched the track between there and Griffiths Crossing.

At 10.15 in the morning, the royal party were collected for champagne and coffee refreshments at Sir Michael Duff's elegant house, Vaynol. 'About six weeks before,' explained Sir Michael, 'the Duke of Norfolk came to me and said, "Now look here, for security reasons, the royal train will stop at a siding." Then Johnny Johnston[7] said, "I'm sure you wouldn't want them to wait there." I said, "Certainly not," and invited them to breakfast. The poor little Queen looked tense and nervous. There weren't enough cars, so I sent the vegetable van for my darling Kent family.'

Fourteen members of the royal family arrived at Vaynol – Princess Margaret came by helicopter – for pre-Investiture revels.

'Are you the detective?' Sir Michael asked Prince Richard of Gloucester, who shyly stood in the background.

'I'm Richard of Gloucester.'

Prince Charles strolled in the garden, returned to a lounge to see the television broadcast. 'It's always me,' he said. 'I'm getting bored with my face.'

Princess Margaret and Princess Anne were by now so nervous that they had to keep excusing themselves and going to the toilet.

In town, security arrangements were more apparent than people. Grim-faced constables, with helmets for dignity, uniforms for recognition, regulation blue macs for weather precaution, and orange life jackets for pessimism, shivered along the Menai Straits in khaki rubber dinghies piloted by two soldiers, helplessly looking for a bomb that might blow them to an unrequested death. Two minesweepers patrolled farther out, and the harbour in front of the castle was fringed with bright red buoys, like a cheap necklace round the crusted throat of an elegant hag. An ugly, Cyclopean television camera, perched on top of a police van, swivelled in the damp, grey morning to scrutinize the crowd – numbering half, at most, the expected two hundred and fifty thousand.

The old English topic, weather, was hardly mentioned. In 1911 a fierce heatwave incapacitated many people taking part. Conversely, 1 July, 1968, had been one of the wettest on record. The meteorological officer at a nearby RAF station assured everyone, though, 'We shall be using radar, satellite,

[7]Assistant Comptroller, Lord Chamberlain's office.

and all the usual gubbins to try to get a picture of the weather as accurately as possible to within fifteen minutes.' Not that it would do much good. The ceremony was taking place, regardless. 'If it rains, we all get wet,' the Duke of Norfolk had decreed.

Already guests were arriving, including Tricia Nixon, former Vice-President Hubert Humphrey, Prince Charles's two former nannies, and diplomats with hip flasks and sandwich boxes. They were all searched for gelignite and smoke bombs by morning-coated detectives at the entrance to the castle. Outside, a vehicle stood waiting – EXPLOSIVE ORDNANCE DISPOSAL – and a watercart sprayed disinfectant on the streets.

A television interview with Prince Charles was relayed to waiting fans followed by a tinny recording of *Tales from the Vienna Woods*. The English national anthem, spluttering through occasionally, was ignored. An American in green trousers and purple jacket argued with his wife about the sort of pictures they should be taking. Elderly be-wigged municipal functionaries in velvet suits and black knee breeches, pride cut into their faces with a hundred wrinkles, wearing their dignity in their strut, looked on in distaste. A Welsh poet, with a white beard, and puffy hair, toured the main square on a ladies' bicycle fitted in front with a wicker shopping basket. He was cheered. A hot dog stand and a mobile bar had brisk business. Another American, one of the few spectators brave enough to capture the vaudeville spirit, marched to his ten-guinea seat wearing a Stetson with two flags – the Stars and Stripes and Welsh dragon – stuck in the brim. Wales Herald Extraordinary Francis Jones, gave his signature to a young boy. 'Isn't he flash looking?' said the boy's companion admiringly. Three helicopters observed the scene from five hundred feet. A youth inflated and burst a brown paper bag. He was immediately surrounded by police, and the area sealed off for an hour while buildings were searched.

Outside the County Council offices, starting point for the processions, a clock was fixed to the railings. On the roof, a plain-clothes detective tried to eat a sandwich and observe the crowds, at the same time as holding his binoculars and short-wave radio. At 1.15 the parade (Appendix) began . . . representative youth of Wales . . . then wobbly-kneed, white-moustached, parched-skinned, venerable gentlemen . . . Bards and the Chief Druid, huge, flowing white robes, like an extra in an Old Testament film . . . M.P.s in morning dress except Leo Abse in a chocolate-brown concoction, with no tie, like an old-time Teddy boy gone to seed . . . Harold Wilson, brushing back his grey hair with his hand, smiling to a girl taking a picture . . . Mary Wilson nervously licking her lips . . . grown men in fancy dress wondering perhaps why they were dragging themselves along narrow Caernarvon streets in fretful obedience to the past.

The uncomfortable, jostling, smelly intimacy, the shared discomfort that provides an integral satisfaction of such occasions, and is of dubious necessity, was missing, hocked to the television cameras who were ensuring second-hand reality for several millions.

At 2.15 as Prince Charles was travelling to the castle, a bomb exploded, rocking several cars but hurting no one. Inside the castle, the noise was confused with the twenty-one gun salute. When he arrived at the Water Gate, twenty-four State trumpeters of the Household Cavalry in groups of eight on the battlements, and conducted by a man standing on top of the Post Office three hundred yards away, released a salute. His personal banner unfurled and, while he walked to the Chamberlain Tower, the audience sang *God Bless the Prince of Wales*:

> 'Among our ancient mountains
> And from our lovely vales,
> Oh, let the prayer re-echo,
> God bless the Prince of Wales.'

Ten minutes later the Queen's coach clattered down the hill, the coachmen sweating with the strain of holding back the horses. A youth threw a banana skin under their hooves and was roughed up by crowds before being rescued by police and dragged to the courthouse. Later, he was fined £3 ($6.80) for insulting behaviour.

Lord Plunket knocked on the Water Gate, demanding entrance in the name of the Queen. The door opened, and Lord Snowdon dextrously descended the steps bearing the fifteen-inch long, six-and-a-half-pounds heavy, ceremonial key on an oak tray – an invention of Lloyd George's to add theatrical dignity to the occasion.

'Madam, I surrender the key of this castle into your Majesty's hand.'

The Queen touched the key. 'Sir Constable, I return the key of this castle into your keeping.' The microphones went dead at this stage, so it was difficult to hear what was said – fortunately, for as the Queen climbed the steps, she noticed a smouldering cigarette had been secreted beind a stone pillar. 'Put that out, Tony,' she said.

The Queen was in a slim-fitting coat designed by Norman Hartnell, and a pearl-embroidered silk hat in an updated Tudor shape. She carried a frill-edged parasol, a regal privilege not yet necessary in spite of the drizzle that spat gently from the heavens. No one else in the castle was allowed umbrellas, in case they poked out their neighbours' eyes.

Banners of ferocious giants, severed Anglo-Saxon heads, lions, and other heraldic impedimenta crashed against the walls as the lengthy procession wound to the dais – great officers of State, chiefs of the Armed Services, heralds, Earl Marshal, and the Welsh national anthem added nostalgia.

> 'The land of my fathers is dear to me
> Land of poets and singers, famous and renowned
> Her manly warriors, devoted patriots
> For freedom they shed their blood.'

After the English anthem, sung next, the Queen told the
Earl Marshal to request Garter to collect Prince Charles from
his tower, where he had been watching television. Sir
Anthony Wagner did so, being careful not to knock off his
hat as he climbed the narrow stairs, and returned flanked by
the necessary people: Wales Herald Extraordinary, Chester
Herald, Secretary of State for Wales, two supporting peers
for Prince Charles, and five others bearing various items of
insignia. Earl Lloyd George of Dwyfor bore the silver gilt
sword made for the last Investiture and inscribed with the
name of the Duke of Windsor. Lord Ogmore carried the
coronet, Lord Heycock held the two-feet-eight-inch-golden
rod made from Welsh gold and decorated with cupids and
ostrich feathers. Lord Maelor had the golden ring of two
dragons clutching an amethyst. In the rear was Lord Harlech
(whose daughter, Jane Rainey, was outside the castle walls
breast-feeding her daughter) carrying the 1911 mantle of
purple velvet trimmed with an ermine cape.

Prince Charles, nervous and flushed, bowed three times,
knelt before his mother. Sir Anthony Wagner presented the
Letters Patent to the Lord Great Chamberlain, who presented them to the Queen, who gave them to the Home
Secretary, James Callaghan, to read. The extraordinary
unpunctuated phrases welled from him fluently:

'Elizabeth the Second by the Grace of God of the United
Kingdom of Great Britain and Northern Ireland and of Our
other Realms and Territories Queen Head of the Common-
wealth Defender of the Faith. To all Lords Spiritual and
Temporal and all other Our Subjects whatsoever to whom
these Presents shall come Greeting Know Ye that we have
made and created and by these Our Letters Do make and
create Our most dear Son Charles Philip Arthur George
Prince of the United Kingdom of Great Britain and Northern
Ireland Duke of Cornwall and Rothesay Earl of Carrick
Baron of Renfrew Lord of the Isles and Great Steward of
Scotland PRINCE OF WALES and EARL OF CHESTER

311

And to the same Our most dear Son Charles Philip Arthur George have given and granted and by this Our Present Charter Do give grant and confirm the name style title dignity and honour of the same Principality and Earldom And him Our most dear Son Charles Philip Arthur George as he has been accustomed We do ennoble and invest with the said Principality and Earldom by girding him with a Sword by putting a coronet on his head and a Gold Ring on his finger and also by delivering a Gold Rod into his hand that he may preside there and may direct and defend those parts To hold to him and his heirs Kings of the United Kingdom of Great Britain and Northern Ireland and of Our other Realms and Territories Heads of the Commonwealth for ever. Wherefore We will and strictly command for Us Our heirs and successors that Our most dear Son Charles Philip Arthur George may have the name style title dignity and honour of the Principality of Wales and Earldom of Chester aforesaid unto him and his heirs Kings of the United Kingdom of Great Britain and Northern Ireland and of Our other Realms and Territories Heads of the Commonwealth as is above mentioned. In Witness whereof We have caused these Our Letters to be made Patent. Witness Ourself at Westminster the twenty-sixth day of July in the seventh year of Our Reign.'

While this was being read, Charles was invested with the insignia, helping the crown into place, as his mother fastened and straightened the mantle. It was, for the moment, a family occasion with three lonely figures under a perspex canopy, perhaps being mocked by memories haunting the age-old grey walls.

The Charter was read again, in Welsh, by George Thomas, before Prince Charles paid homage to the Queen kneeling before her with his hands placed between hers:

'I, Charles Prince of Wales, do become your liege man of life and limb and of earthly worship, and faith and truth I will bear unto you to live and die against all manner of folks.'

They exchanged the kiss of fealty, and Charles went to the throne on the right to listen to a loyal address read in Welsh and English by Sir Ben Bowen Thomas, president of the University of Wales at Aberystwyth. He replied, also in two languages:

'It is indeed my firm intention to associate myself in word and deed with as much of the life of the Principality as possible. And what a Principality.'

There was a short religious service, conducted in both languages, with Bible readings in English from Peter:

'Be subject for the Lord's sake to every human institution, whether it be to the emperor as supreme or to governors as sent by him to punish those who do wrong and to praise those who do right . . . Honour all men. Love the brotherhood. . . . Fear God. . . . Honour the emperor.'[8]

And Matthew in Welsh, read from the Bible completed in 1588 by Bishop Morgan that perhaps stopped the language from decaying and is the most important book in the Principality's history:

'Render therefore to Caesar the things that are Caesar's, and to God the things that are God's. When they heard it, they marvelled; and they left him and went away.'[9]

Three presentations followed, at various points in the castle, to the accompaniment of cheers, largely sprinkled with children's hurrahs. The procession departed. The newly invested Prince of Wales gave a dinner party on board *Britannia*. Edited highlights of the ceremony reached number eight in the TV ratings (the actual broadcast had been watched in six million three hundred and fifty thousand homes – thirty-nine per cent of the possible audience). The Investiture Ball at Glynllifon, former home of the Newboroughs but now an agricultural college, over-enthusiastically anticipated as the ball of the decade, or century, started with two misfortunes – daffodils ordered from Molo, a

[8]1 Peter 2: 11–17.
[9]Matthew 22: 15–22.

remote Kenyan village, did not arrive because of an unexpected drought, and overloading fused the first half-hour into darkness. It continued with over-priced and under-distinguished champagne, and the guest of honour, Princess Margaret, arriving very late.

Early next morning, in the centre of town, an army van exploded killing a soldier locked inside for misbehaviour. The first visitors to the castle began to arrive – there were to be three hundred and twenty-five thousand in the next six weeks, more than the whole of the previous year. And Prince Charles began a tour of his Principality at Llandudno where divers had spent the night hunting for bombs under the pier. Flowers planted along the promenade had also been searched. A road near Bettws-y-Coed was closed while a biscuit tin of explosives was dismantled, and Moscow Radio picturesquely announced that bombs were exploding, and houses and cars burning along the entire route.

In reality, the gaunt, mysterious hills of Snowdonia, echoing the days when husky warrior princes were brutally triumphant or defeated, was now surrendering to what was called Operation Enchantment. Charles travelled subtly, in his mother's maroon Rolls, wearing a brown suit with wide bottoms, to captivate the matrons and impress most others.

On Saturday, ending the tour at Cardiff, he met youth representatives on the castle green. At the same time, a quarter of a million of his generation were congregating one hundred and fifty-three miles away in Hyde Park to hear the Rolling Stones give a free concert. How many of them would have crossed the road to meet Prince Charles, or would have travelled half a mile to hear him speak? Hero worship, always one of royalty's more easily exploitable advantages, has always been coveted by others. Now, though, trite as it seemed, conceptions about 'being a gentleman', and 'public entertainment' were changing irrevocably. By careful management, combined with the natural willingness of the British to revere an institution they feel is no threat, a frenzy of interest had been created in the Monarchy. A week earlier, *Royal Family* had been shown on television to deserved praise and overstated significance. This last week, tradition had successfully consolidated the image. But what was the result? Was everyone satisfied? What would happen next? Was the show so good that the reality could be safely ignored?

At the moment, it was advisable to play it cool, and await reaction.

The Home Team – II

'In all, she was on *Eastbourne* for 66 minutes and the visit
went like clockwork, largely because of the forethought
of the squadron's operations and anti-submarine officer,
34-year-old Lieut-Commander Stephen Emberton, of
Plymouth. To make sure the Princess would be able to
negotiate the narrow companion-ways, steep ladders, and
hatchways in a tight skirt, he went through a special
rehearsal – in drag.' *Western Morning News*, 29 July, 1969.

IN THE REMAINING SIX WEEKS of the Queen's year before
she went on holiday to Norway, and then Balmoral, there
were only a few engagements – notably three garden parties
and some rather uncomfortable nautical manœuvring in
Torbay, South Devon.

This was an assembly of thirty-nine ships of the Western
Fleet – a third of the full strength – and the Navy were determined to provide an elaborate show, in spite of delicacy about
the purpose of the visit and comparison with previous naval
occasions. Only three months before,[1] at Spithead, *Britannia*
had steamed for two hours through the swirling, cosmopolitan loyalties of sixty-three warships from twelve NATO
countries, all predictably dwarfed by the United States
aircraft carrier *Wasp*. In addition the Navy, sensitive to the
effect of defence cuts on morale, did not like odious compari-
sons being made with the lusty reviews provided for Queen
Victoria – part of whose diamond jubilee celebration was to
sail in a paddle steamer through 173 ships spread over seven

[1] 16 May, 1969.

miles. In the 1922 Torbay review, there had been ninety-one ships; in the Coronation review of 1953 there were one hundred and sixty, stretching all the way to Cowes.

The Western Fleet, formed in June 1967 as an amalgamation of the Mediterranean and Home Fleets, was virtually the whole of the British Navy, and the Commander-in-Chief, Admiral Sir John Bush, suggested to the Ministry of Defence that the Queen should present the new colour. A draft of the arrangements was completed over Easter weekend, and a comprehensive list of etiquette devised. How do you greet the Queen? If wearing a cap – salute, bow with the head when shaking hands, salute again. If hatless – simply bow with the head.

Crew on the destroyer *Glamorgan*, to be visited by Prince Charles, were instructed to give an idea of 'the bunch of friendly and hospitable people aboard her. It is imperative that his abiding impression is one of friendliness and alertness.

'There are just two simple rules: Look him fair and square in the face when he speaks to you, and simply address him as "Sir". Speak clearly when you reply, and if you don't know the answer, then say so.'

Cheering required a confidential procedure of interesting complexity: 'On the command "Stand by to give three cheers. Off caps", the men drop the left hand to the side and seize the cap at the front with the right-hand fingers on top and together, thumb underneath. On the command "Up", remove the cap and hold up at the full extent of the arm at an angle of forty-five degrees directly to the front, crown vertical and outboard. On the command "Three cheers for Her Majesty the Queen – Hip, hip, hip, Hooray", men cheer Hooray synchronizing with the command order at the same time as rotating the arm in a clockwise direction (viewed from the rear) round a diameter extending no lower than the shoulder and returning to the original position after each cheer. The second cheer is to be given as the ship's bridge comes abreast of Her Majesty. After the third cheer there is a pause of five seconds, then "On caps" – replace caps, hand remains in position until the order "Down".'

'We'd like it to be as informal as possible,' explained Captain Richard Roe, a staff officer at the underground headquarters of the Fleet at Northwood, Middlesex, who was responsible for most of the organization. 'If the Sovereign's going to mean anything, she must have some contact with her armed forces. There are plenty of people who will say "We're too busy. Isn't this a waste of time?" but it's all part of naval life.

'When the time comes, they'll like it. The sailors will be important people. There will be girls. They've got free ten-pin bowling facilities, free theatre tickets, and so on. Nothing but good can come of it.'

In order to make absolutely certain there wasn't a nasty accident with one of the nuclear submarines, a possibility once in every 50,000 years according to statistics, a tug filled with protective clothing was detailed to stand by at all times.

Torbay Council, determined to make their resort even more attractive, spent £1,500 on flags and flowers, British Rail officials weeded the track where the royal train would stop, and motorists provided the worst traffic jam for ten years – eighteen miles between Honiton and Exeter – as they queued for a glimpse of sea.

Unfortunately, on Monday when the Queen arrived it was overcast. Electrically stimulated gaiety was provided by the Council who switched on their fairy lights between the station and the pier where the Queen embarked for *Britannia*. The grey hulks of the ships looked distinctly unimpressive as the Lord High Admiral steamed to the head of the line. During the day, as rain hurtled down, the Queen, Prince Philip, Prince Charles and Princess Anne visited eleven ships.

'If there was a king, it would have been easier to make it interesting,' said one of the organizers. 'You could take him out and show him sea power.'

Princess Anne provided a diversion. She played Giant

318

Uckers, naval ludo, on HMS *Eastbourne*, had some rum, tasted a chip, and told the cook: 'You'll have to come to Buckingham Palace. We don't have any chips there.' This remark prompted an elaborate culinary lesson from the Palace. 'I think that what the Princess said was just one of those remarks. I don't think it's "chips with everything", but certainly I'm sure the royal family do have chips occasionally.

'Of course, there can be all shapes and sizes of chips – little ones, long ones, round ones. I'm sure they must have chips as well as every other form of potato. There must be about 120 ways of doing potatoes.'

Next day, a force six wind made it necessary to present the new colours in a hangar of the aircraft carrier *Eagle*, instead of on the flight deck. The Queen looked queasy, but gave a brave speech:

'By a fortunate coincidence, today is the anniversary of the final naval action in the defeat of the Spanish Armada in 1588. Nuclear propulsion, supersonic aircraft, guided missiles, and computers may have made things more complicated, but if aggressors are to be deterred, and if the Royal Navy is to play its part with our allies in preserving peace, it still needs high standards of seamanship, tactical ability, and technical competence.

'Colours were first introduced for the Royal Navy by my grandfather in 1924. The colour which has just been marched off was presented in 1937, and in its thirty-two years it witnessed events just as dangerous and decisive as the defeat of the Armada.'

She watched a fly-past before returning to *Britannia* which led the fleet ten miles out to sea for a steam-past. The Queen waved from her veranda deck, and sent a message. 'I am delighted to find you in such good heart. Splice the mainbrace.' And the flag signal 'B.X.' was flown from both yardarms.

Afterwards Prince Philip, Prince Charles, and Lord Mountbatten went by helicopter to Cowdray Park for polo;

the Queen and Princess Anne returned to the station and, ultimately, racing at Goodwood. As they left, a ninety-eight-year-old woman, Mrs Jessie Lumley-Ellis, who had dined with Queen Mary eighty-five years ago, clutched a Union Jack and said: 'I had a wonderful view. Now I'm determined to reach a hundred to get a telegram from the Queen.'

Pressures were relaxed, the season of mellifluous, unequivocal flattery had begun. The Queen's year was almost complete, and she was off on her holidays.

Holidays

'I've been waiting for this for thirty years.' Mrs. Eva Hoe, as she sat on a fence, having travelled twenty-five miles from her home to watch the Queen pass through Hull.

'GOOD MORNING! The first members of the public to whom the Queen spoke were Mrs Henry Taylor and Mrs Walter Abrahams, who had been invited to watch the royal arrival in the Royal Station Hotel. "She said good morning to us," said Mrs Taylor delightedly.' *Hull Daily Mail*, 4 August, 1969.

USUALLY A SUITABLE NORTHERN TOWN IS FOUND for the Queen to visit on her way north to Balmoral. This year the route to Scotland was more complicated and circuitous, beginning at Hull's Paragon railway station, where additional mousetraps had been placed for the occasion, and ending eight days later at Stjørdalshalsen in Norway.

At Hull, her arrival was awaited by a phalanx of officials equipped with an artist who had been commissioned to record the Lord Mayor handing over the City's Sword of State, a scene of grim municipal dignity that would later decorate the Banqueting Hall.

She drove a few miles to open a new dock, past sparse crowds and a lot of policemen, past the prison which had been decorated outside with plants to make it look less sombre, past one of the few protests of the year. About a hundred women held placards referring to housing conditions: 'We want something better for our children,' 'Do we have to be

Tory to get a new house?' 'Mice, rats, slugs in our babies' cots. Our houses are wild-life sanctuaries.'

After the dock, she toured a passenger terminal ferry, saw a model of the Humber, visited a Seamen's Mission, unveiled a commemorative plaque, lunched at Trinity House, attended a thanksgiving service, was received by the Lord Mayor at the town hall, signed a visitors' book, posed for a group photograph, attended a reception, and boarded *Britannia* six and a quarter hours later – having shaken hands with one hundred and thirty people.

She spent the next day sailing to the Shetland Islands, off Scotland, for a seven-hour visit to mark the five-hundredth anniversary of British rule. Then another day's sail to Bergen, Norway, for what was optimistically described as an 'unofficial' five-day visit, at the invitation of a cousin, King Olav,[1] who is in distant succession to the British throne. It was the first time the royal family had been together on a foreign holiday. Princes Andrew and Edward were issued with passports for the occasion.

Norway, with a population of four million, less than Scotland, has what the British contemptuously regard as a 'bicycling Monarchy'. This persistent myth is slyly provoked in Scandinavian Monarchies by the adept use of public relations techniques. In reality, members of the British royal family, who are supposed to be more formal, find themselves out-protocol'd, out-saluted, out-be-medalled, and upstaged on every occasion. There is no snobbery or formality like a 'bicycling Monarchy' – as King Olav's son, Harald, discovered. For nine years he battled to marry Sonja Haraldsen, daughter of a self-made businessman and draper, and herself a dressmaker. The Government officially denied the marriage would take place, and many people opposed the Crown Prince marrying a commoner because of the feeling that a President is as good as a king without true, one hundred per cent royal blood. At the wedding, in August 1968, the

[1]His mother was Princess Maud, daughter of Edward VII.

322

stiff, correct Swedish royal family were notable by their small representation; and, even a year later, Norwegian government departments were issuing profiles of Sonja that referred to her by her maiden name.

The first formality of the 'unofficial' visit was noticed when King Olav stepped from his yacht, *Norge*, on to *Britannia* for breakfast. He was in full admiral's uniform, with medals. Prince Philip wore a blazer.

At the quay, a guard of honour from the Navy, Army, and Air Force were being lined up. So was a band, and a red carpet. A hundred and fifty yards away, kept back by police, the Norwegian public and tourists waited to cheer. *Britannia* docked gently, with the Royal Marine band playing on deck. The British Ambassador, in black homburg and Rolls Royce, greeted the Queen. King Olav stepped ashore and saluted four times on the short walk to his *Norge*, anchored astern and looking like a tug in comparison. The yacht was built by Sir Thomas Sopwith in 1937, acted as an anti-submarine escort vessel during the war, was sold to Woolworth heiress Barbara Hutton (who found it too small), and was presented to King Haakon in 1947 by the Norwegians as a seventy-fifth birthday present.

A few minutes later, King Olav, this time without medals, returned to the gangplank of *Britannia* to welcome the Queen, Prince Philip and Prince Charles ashore. Princess Anne wasn't feeling well.

'They want photographs,' said King Olav, turning the Queen to face the cameras, and smiling, before she inspected the guard of honour, listened to the national anthems, and disappeared to tour a stifling hot maritime museum.

After lunch there was an informal visit to Edvard Grieg's house at Troldhaugen. In the fjord below, a police launch waited. Other policemen clambered round the silver birches, walkie-talkies at the ready, and one stood guard on the roof. Inside, the Queen and her retinue listened to the full-throated trill of *Cowcall, With a waterlily, A Birdsong* and *A Dream*, sung by soprano Siff Pettersen. The royal car was gently backed into a wall as it attempted to park, all photographers were massed on to a flowerbed at the left-hand side so that none were visible in pictures of the Queen and King Olav – now changed into a brown-suit with trilby, humorous-looking, with the portly, bluff charisma of an athletic, out-door man. Otherwise, of course, people might have thought it was a stunt organized by the Norwegian Tourist Board instead of an 'unofficial' holiday. Bergen, smirking towards the capital Oslo, provided a municipal dinner that evening, and saved other delights for the morning.

These included visits to the aquarium and Gamle Bergen, an outdoor museum of full-size period houses from the early nineteenth century, the fronts of which had been newly painted for the Queen's visit.

In the afternoon, *Britannia* and *Norge*, accompanied by frigates *Malcolm* and *Stavanger*, each with one hundred and fifty men on board, sailed for Andalsnes (guards of honour, gun salutes), past the island of Veoy where Rollo the Bold, one of the Queen's earliest known ancestors lived when he wasn't terrorizing the Baltic as a pirate or stealing sheep, and on further to Molde (guards of honour, gun salutes).

On Monday, lunch was provided by Prime Minister Per Borten and his wife at their farm outside Trondheim – an invitation virtually issued publicly so refusal was unlikely – and there was another municipal dinner in the evening.

Finally, the Queen could return to *Britannia* and cruise to Scotland. Prince Philip, Prince Charles and Princess Anne sailed the fjords for a while in *Bloodhound*.

At last, in the baronial grandeur of Balmoral, with its light grey Invergelder granite softening under a capricious summer sun, the Queen could relax. Her year was over. In a few days, the Prime Minister and his wife would pay their traditional week-end visit. Government plans and Cabinet papers would arrive in the interminable red boxes. There would be a Privy Council meeting. There would be walks, shooting, swimming, sailing, tennis. She would be piped to her seat in the small Craithie church, lined with fir trees and tourists.

Six weeks later, she would leave the protective scowl of a Scottish autumn, and return to the ardours of a job that often seemed far from the realities of the seventies. By the end of the decade, the British Monarchy would have altered even further. Perhaps this last year's events would be unrecognizable, unremembered and unremarked as the impetus for change.

That was the future, Now was the time for enjoyment.

Epilogue

'A Sovereign and a subject are clean different things.'
Charles I.

'I think this institution functions because occasionally
you've got to stick your neck out.' Prince Philip, Grampian
Television, 21 February, 1969.

'Crowned heads, like everybody else, must meet the chal-
lenge of change. We are all far more conservative than we
realize. Many outmoded rituals connected with royalty
are on their way into limbo.' Duke of Windsor, 1969.

'We know what we represent is wrong. I think we know
this at Eton more than you people outside know it. It's like
the Queen knowing she is irrelevant and unnecessary, and
everyone else wanting her to stay on.' Eton student,
quoted in *Daily Mirror*, 9 June, 1969.

'To neglect, or at worst dismiss as absurd, the opinions of
younger people, which is what the Queen does on occasion,
is dangerous and has resulted in the overthrow of more
than one throne on the continent.' Sir Charles Petrie,
Modern British Monarchy, p. 217.

THE BRITISH MONARCHY IS AN ATTRACTIVE IDEA but
the reality is, unfortunately, out of date. It is working best at
the moment in the imaginations of those who rarely see it
operate. The instinctive, almost neurotic, amiability with
which the British genuflect to their past, is allowing the
Queen to become a convenience for politicians and a frivolity
for the communications industry.

She performs what is required with patience and dignity. It is the requirements that should be re-adjusted. Many, quite simple, changes could make the institution a more vital aspect of British society than it is today. Old justifications, such as the fact that she is a cohesive element in the Commonwealth, are increasingly irrelevant. Even the negative assessments need reappraisal: 'The strength of the Monarchy does not lie in the power it gives to the Sovereign, but in the power it denies to anyone else.'[1] 'It's cheaper than a President.' 'The Queen doesn't do any harm, is good for the tourist trade, and adds colour to people's lives.'

The Queen herself could initiate changes by insisting on more reality in her routine. Why not a few short-notice visits to factories, hospitals, housing estates? Couldn't she give a positive lead in the two most serious domestic problems facing the country: racial discrimination, and the housing shortage? Couldn't she be allowed to give her opinions on other, less controversial matters? Why should she be seen to be a cipher?

She is in an admirable position to modernize State visits. Couldn't she insist more on shorter trips, not so cluttered with protocol? Couldn't she appear on television and limit the banquets? Does the ritual always have to be the same?

Pageantry, too, could become meaningful again. Couldn't the Queen's annual sortie to Westminster provide more than a traffic jam and the satisfaction of political egos? Couldn't she close Parliament instead of opening it? This would take place during the summer, and identify her with actual legislation rather than a few vague promises.

In the seventies, the Monarchy could play a vital role as Britain is forced to stop stumbling between three possible alternatives: an integral part of the United States of Europe, benign independent offshore pantomime, or partner in an Atlantic alliance.

Ultimately, the Queen's greatest contribution could be as

[1] *Royal Family.*

a focus for civilized living. She could set a standard that is a realistic aspiration for the rest of the country and her duties could become less of a prop to the past. But until new functions are found, the institution of Monarchy is in danger of obsolescence by apathy.

Appendix

THE QUEEN'S OFFICIAL ENGAGEMENTS DURING THE YEAR
(p. xiii)

329

19	Opening of National Postal Museum
	Cocktail Party for Army Officers
25	Investiture
	Luncheon for President Nixon
	Visited Clothing Exhibition at Earls Court
March 3	Henry Wood Centenary Concert at Albert Hall
4	Investiture
7	Opening of new Victoria Underground line
11	Investiture
12	Visited National Institute of Agriculture and Botany, Cambridge
13	Reception given for the Society of Women Writers and Journalists
18	Investiture
26	Gala Performance at Royal Opera House
27	Visited Royal Regiment of Artillery at Woolwich
April 1	Lunch for President of Nigeria
2	Visited the Queen's Life Guard at Horse Guards
3	Maundy Service
14	Centenary Exhibition of the Royal Philatelic Society
	Army Benevolent Fund's 25th Anniversary Variety Performance *Fall in the Stars* at London Palladium
17	Inaugurated Terminal 1 Building at Heathrow
22	Arrival of President of Italy
23	State Banquet for President of Italy
27	St George's Day Parade of Queen's Scouts
29	Banquet given by President of Italy
May 1	Toured the *Queen Elizabeth 2*
	Opened Ordnance Survey Headquarters, Southampton
5–10	State visit to Austria
13	Visited Plymouth
14	Visited Royal Botanic Gardens at Kew
15	Visited Bromley Town Hall Swimming and Diving Gala at the Crystal Palace National Recreation Centre
16	NATO Review
19–28	Visited Edinburgh for the General Assembly of the Church of Scotland
29	Visited Dundee
June 4	The Derby
5	Received party of girls from Young Australia League
	Concert at Royal Festival Hall
11	Visited School of Infantry at Warminster
13	Lunch for Ruler of Abu Dhabi
14	Birthday Parade
16	Garter Service
17–20	Ascot Races
23	Visited Ward Royal, Windsor

25	Presented new Colours to the 2nd Battalion Grenadier Guards
	Garden Party given by Grenadier Guards
26	Presented Royal Air Force Central Flying School's new Colour
30	Test Match at Lord's
July 1	Investiture of the Prince of Wales
8	Investiture
10	Garden Party
11	Dorset visit: Duchy of Cornwall farms, Atomic Energy Establishment. Opened new Poole General Hospital
15	Arrival of President of Finland
	State Banquet
16	Royal Tournament
17	Lunch to President of Finland
	Garden Party
	Reception at Guildhall
22	Investiture
	Reception for members of the Canadian branch of the Royal Air Force Escaping Society
24	Garden Party
	Royal International Horse Show, Wembley
25	Test Match at Lord's
28	Visited Assembly of ships of the Western Fleet in Torbay
29	Presented new Colours to the Western Fleet
August 2	1969 Stoke Mandeville Games
4	Visited Hull
6	Visited Lerwick
7–12	Visited Norway
	Balmoral.

THE ROYAL VAUDEVILLE (p. 8)

Fitzalan Pursuivant Extraordinary	Wales Herald Extraordinary
C. W. SCOTT-GILES	FRANCIS JONES
Norfolk Herald Extraordinary	Arundel Herald Extraordinary
G. D. SQUIBB	DERMOT MORRAH
York Herald	Somerset Herald
C. M. J. SWAN	R. O. DENNYS
Richmond Herald	Windsor Herald
J. P. N. BROOKE-LITTLE	A. C. COLE

Chester Herald
W. J. G. VERCO

Serjeant at Arms
STANLEY WILLIAMS

Usher	Usher
GROUP CAPTAIN PETER VANNECK	SIR RONALD BROCKMAN

Serjeant at Arms
RONALD HILL

Prince Charles's Equerry	Queen's Equerry	Queen's Equerry
SQUADRON-LEADER	LORD	LIEUTENANT
DAVID CHECKETTS	PLUNKET	JOHN SLATER, R.N.

Crown Equerry
LT.-COLONEL JOHN MILLER

Comptroller of Household	Treasurer of Household
IOAN EVANS, M.P.	CHARLES GREY, M.P.
Keeper of Privy Purse	Private Secretary
LORD TRYON	SIR MICHAEL ADEANE

Norroy and Ulster King of Arms
J. R. B. WALKER, LANCASTER HERALD

Lord Privy Seal	Lord President of the Council
LORD SHACKLETON	FREDERICK PEART, M.P.

Lord High Chancellor
LORD GARDINER

Black Rod	Garter King of Arms
AIR CHIEF MARSHAL	SIR ANTHONY WAGNER
SIR GEORGE MILLS	
The Earl Marshal	The Lord Great Chamberlain
DUKE OF NORFOLK	MARQUESS OF CHOLMONDSLEY

332

Sword of State		Cap of Maintenance
LORD MONTGOMERY		LORD SHEPHERD

QUEEN

PRINCE CHARLES

PRINCESS ANNE

Pages of Honour

ALEXANDER COLVILLE	CHRISTOPHER ABEL SMITH
JOHN MAUDSLAY	NICHOLAS BACON

Woman of the Bedchamber	Mistress of Robes	Lady of the Bedchamber
MARY MORRISON	COUNTESS OF	COUNTESS OF
	EUSTON	CROMER

Gold Stick in Waiting	Lord Steward	Master of the Horse
LORD	VISCOUNT	DUKE OF
MOUNTBATTEN	COBHAM	BEAUFORT

Lord in Waiting	Vice-Admiral of the U.K.
LORD HAMILTON OF DALZELL	ADMIRAL SIR PETER REID

Captain, Yeomen of the Guard	Captain, Corps of Gentlemen at Arms
LORD BOWLES	LORD BESWICK

	Queen's Principal	Queen's A.D.C.
Air A.C.D.	Naval A.D.C.	General
AIR CHIEF MARSHAL	ADMIRAL	GENERAL
SIR JOHN DAVIS	SIR JOHN FREWEN	SIR CHARLES
		RICHARDSON

Comptroller Lord Chamberlain's Office	Usher to Sword of State
LT.-COLONEL ERIC PENN	GENERAL SIR WILLIAM STIRLING

Field Officer in Brigade Waiting	Silver Stick
COLONEL A. I. D. FLETCHER	COLONEL H. S. HOPKINSON

Lieutenant, Yeomen of the Guard	Lieutenant, Corps of Gentlemen at Arms
LT.-COLONEL	BRIGADIER
VICTOR TURNER, V.C.	SIR HENRY FLOYD, B.T.

THE ROAD SHOW (p. 15)

EXPORTS TO BRAZIL:

	1964 £	1967 £	1968 £	1969–1st qr. £	% Changes
U.S.	136,895,000	199,107,000	295,250,000	48,042,000	−15·3%
W. Germany	32,501,000	69,099,000	95,009,000	24,042,000	+10·6%
Japan	10,447,000	19,825,000	42,514,000	12,328,000	+92·3%
U.K.	13,464,000	18,904,000	44,665,000	10,844,000	−10·8%

THE ROAD SHOW (p. 31)

The Queen was equipped before she began, with a list of times she was expected to be at various places, a skeletal plan of the tour that gives no indication of what happened, but provides easy reference to the scope of the activities. She and Prince Philip also collected a number of presents.

Friday, 1 November (Recife)

		Presents Received
4.30 p.m.	Arrive Recife Airport	Folder of children's paintings
4.40 p.m.	Depart Recife Airport	Wooden key
5.00 p.m.	Arrive Governor's Palace	Oil painting of ornamental gate by Lulla Gardoza Aires
6.15 p.m.	Depart Governor's Palace	
6.20 p.m.	Arrive harbour steps	3ft,-high pottery pot
6.25 p.m.	Arrive *Britannia*	L.P.s of local music
7.30 p.m.	Depart Recife	

Saturday, 2 November
At sea

Sunday, 3 November (Salvador)

7.30 a.m.	Arrive Salvador	Painting of horsemen
9.00 a.m.	Depart *Britannia*	Silver Balanganda
9.05 a.m.	Arrive Naval School	
9.10 a.m.	Depart Naval School	
9.25 a.m.	Arrive Anglican Church	
10.05 a.m.	Depart English Club	
10.10 a.m.	Arrive Governor's Palace	
10.40 a.m	Depart Governor's Palace	
11.00 a.m.	Arrive San Franciscan Church	
11.15 a.m.	Depart San Franciscan Church	
11.25 a.m.	Arrive Museum	
11.50 a.m.	Depart Museum	
11.55 a.m.	Arrive Market	
12.05 p.m.	Depart Market	
12.15 p.m.	Arrive *Britannia*	
12.30 p.m.	*Britannia* sails	

Monday, 4 November
At sea

Tuesday, 5 November (Rio de Janeiro)

10.05 a.m.	Depart *Britannia*	
10.15 a.m.	Arrive harbour steps	
10.25 a.m.	Depart Galeao Airport	
12.15 p.m.	Arrive Brasilia	Gold medal
12.35 p.m.	Depart Airport	Signed silver-framed photographs of the President and his wife
1.00 p.m.	Arrive Hotel Nacional	
2.25 p.m.	Depart Hotel Nacional	Gold Balanganda
2.40 p.m.	Arrive Palacio Alvorada	Oil painting of birds by Gauben Lima*
3.15 p.m.	Depart Palacio Alvorada	
3.20 p.m.	Arrive Supreme Court	Bound leather book on Brasilia
3.50 p.m.	Depart Supreme Court	Gold model of Brasilia Cathedral
3.55 p.m.	Arrive Congress	Two Oncas
5.05 p.m.	Depart Congress	
5.10 p.m.	Arrive Hotel Nacional	
5.30 p.m.	Press Reception	
8.40 p.m.	Depart Hotel Nacional	
8.45 p.m.	Arrive Palacio Itamarati Dinner	
10.45 p.m.	Reception	
12.30 p.m.	Leave Reception	

Wednesday, 6 November (Brasilia)

10.10 a.m.	Depart Hotel Nacional
11.40 a.m.	Arrive British Embassy
12.40 p.m.	Depart British Embassy
12.55 p.m.	Arrive Brasilia Airport
1.00 p.m.	Depart Comet
2.45 p.m.	Arrive São Paulo Airport
3.00 p.m.	Depart São Paulo Airport
3.20 p.m.	Arrive Ipiranga Monument
3.35 p.m.	Depart Ipiranga Monument
4.00 p.m.	Arrive Edificio Italia
4.25 p.m.	Depart Edificio Italia
5.00 p.m.	Arrive Governor's Palace
8.30 p.m.	President's Dinner Guests
8.45 p.m.	Dinner
10.30 p.m.	Reception
11.30 p.m.	Reception

Thursday, 7 November (São Paulo)

10.00 a.m.	Depart Governor's Palace	Gold key of São Paulo in leather box
10.15 a.m.	Arrive Burroughs Welcome	Book

10.45 a.m.	Depart Burroughs Welcome	Tiara
11.00 a.m.	Arrive Museum	Metallic picture on gold
11.50 a.m.	Depart Museum	Model of Edificio in metal*
12.05 p.m.	Arrive St Paul's School	Gold Cross brooch
1.05 p.m.	Depart St Paul's School	Rhino horn cup in case
1.20 p.m.	Arrive Airport	Carved wooden panel
1.25 p.m.	Depart Comet	
2.40 p.m.	Arrive Viracopos Airport	
2.45 p.m.	Depart Viracopos Airport	Gold plaque in leather case
3.15 p.m.	Arrive Institute Agriconomico, Campinas	
3.30 p.m.	Depart Institute Agriconomico, Campinas	
3.35 p.m.	Arrive Experimental Farm	White and gold coffee service
4.10 p.m.	Depart Experimental Farm	Desk ornament of tourmaline column, and semi-precious stones on rosewood base
4.35 p.m.	Arrive Fazenda	

Friday, 8 November (São Paulo)

11.30 a.m.	Depart Fazenda	Gold chalice
12.00 p.m.	Arrive Jockey Club	Gold and emerald bracelet
2.10 p.m.	Depart Jockey Club	
2.45 p.m.	Depart Varicopos	
4.00 p.m.	Arrive Rio de Janeiro	
4.15 p.m.	Depart by barge	
4.20 p.m.	Arrive *Britannia*	
5.00 p.m.	Depart by barge	
5.05 p.m.	Arrive Yacht Club	
5.55 p.m.	Depart Yacht Club	
6.00 p.m.	Arrive *Britannia*	
8.30 p.m.	Banquet	
10.30 p.m.	Reception	

Saturday, 9 November (Rio de Janeiro)

9.50 a.m.	Depart by barge
9.55 a.m.	Arrive Yacht Club
10.15 a.m.	Arrive Belvedere
10.30 a.m.	Depart Belvedere
10.50 a.m.	Arrive Gloria Church
11.00 a.m.	Depart Gloria Church
11.10 a.m.	Arrive S. Dumont Pier
11.15 a.m.	*Britannia*
12.05 p.m.	Depart *Britannia*
12.10 p.m.	Arrive Yacht Club
12.10 p.m.	Depart Processional Drive
1.15 p.m.	Arrive Museum of Modern Art

337

3.10 p.m.	Depart Museum of Modern Art	
3.30 p.m.	Arrive Ponta do Caju	Replica of plaque in gold and wood in wooden case
4.00 p.m.	Depart Ponta do Caju	
4.25 p.m.	Arrive *Britannia*	Gold medallion in case
9.45 p.m.	Depart *Britannia*	Stone statuette
9.50 p.m.	Arrive Yacht Club	Gold medallion in red leather
10.00 p.m.	Arrive Residence Reception	Book
12.00 p.m.	Depart Residence Reception Yacht Club *Britannia*	

Sunday, *10 November* (Rio de Janeiro)

10.05 a.m.	Depart *Britannia*	Oil painting of children**
10.10 a.m.	Arrive S. Dumont	
10.15 a.m.	Arrive War Memorial	Oil painting
10.35 a.m.	Depart War Memorial	Gold medallion in case
10.45 a.m.	Arrive Christ Church	Embroidered handbag
11.35 a.m.	Church Hall	Brooch, key-ring and two flags
11.50 a.m.	Depart Church Hall	Book
11.55 a.m.	Arrive Residence	Stone plaque*
12.10 p.m.	Favela	Wooden ship's wheel*
1.00 p.m.	Depart Residence	Portrait of the Queen carved in wood
1.10 p.m.	Arrive Yacht Club	
1.15 p.m.	Arrive *Britannia*	
4.30 p.m.	Depart *Britannia*	
4.35 p.m.	Arrive Yacht Club	
4.55 p.m.	Arrive Maracana Football Stadium	
7.00 p.m.	Depart Maracana Football Stadium	
7.20 p.m.	Arrive Yacht Club	
7.25 p.m.	Arrive *Britannia* Private Dinner	

Monday, *11 November* (Rio de Janeiro)

10.35 a.m.	Depart Britannia
10.45 a.m.	Arrive Galeao Airport
11.05 a.m.	Depart VC10

* Prince Philip
** Princess Anne

THE ROAD SHOW (p. 54.)

Medals to officials on a State visit are given at the beginning, so they can be worn for the duration. The following decorations were given to Brazilians by the Queen, most of them sent in boxes, by post. British Embassy officials have a personal prize-giving ceremony of their own, attended by the Queen.

President	G.C.B.
President's Household:	
Head of Military	G.C.V.O.
Head of Civil	G.C.V.O.
1	K.B.E.
3	C.V.O.
Brazilian Ambassador to Britain	G.C.V.O.
Ambassador Chermont	K.C.V.O.
One gentleman attached to the Queen	K.C.V.O.
Two ladies attached to the Queen	C.V.O.
Gentleman attached to Prince Philip	K.C.V.O.
Vice-President of Brazil	G.C.M.G.
Minister of Foreign Affairs	G.C.M.G.
Congress:	
President of Supreme Federal Court	G.C.M.G.
Two foreign affairs committee presidents	K.C.M.G.
Foreign Office:	
Secretary General	G.C.M.G.
Chief of Protocol	K.C.V.O.
1	K.C.M.G.
3	K.B.E.
1	K.C.V.O.
1	C.M.G.
4	C.V.O.
4	M.V.O. (4)
16	M.V.O. (5)
5	M.B.E.
Mayor of Brasilia	K.C.V.O.
Governor of São Paulo	G.C.V.O.
Governor of Guanabara	G.C.V.O.
British Embassy Staff:	
Ambassador	G.C.V.O.
2	C.V.O.
5	M.V.O. (4)

339

Miscellaneous:

C.V.O.	4
M.V.O. (4)	2
M.V.O. (5)	1
R.V.M. (Gold)	10
R.V.M. (Silver)	24
R.V.M. (Bronze)	39

THE ROAD SHOW (p. 63)

State visits by the Queen since she came to the throne:

Norway	24–26 June, 1955
Sweden	8–17 June, 1956
Portugal	16–21 February, 1957
France	8–11 April, 1957
Denmark	21–25 May, 1957
U.S.A.	16–21 October, 1957
Netherlands	25–27 March, 1958
Nepal	26 February–1 March, 1961
Iran	2–6 March, 1961
Italy	2–5 May, 1961
Vatican City	5 May, 1961
Liberia	23 November, 1961
Ethiopia	1–8 February, 1965
Sudan	8–12 February, 1965
Germany	18–28 May, 1965
Belgium	9–13 May, 1966
Brazil	5–11 November, 1968
Chile	11–18 November, 1968
Austria	5–10 May, 1969

THE ROAD SHOW (p. 67)

British exports to countries for years preceding and following visits by members of the royal family.

NORWAY £ $
1953	63,221,495	177,020,186	
1954	68,514,859	191,841,605	
1955	73,837,277	206,744,376	STATE VISIT, 24–26 June
1956	75,746,734	212,090,855	
1957	71,131,139	199,176,189	

U.S.A.
1957	273,357,000	765,400,000	STATE VISIT, 16–21 Oct.
1958	310,928,000	870,600,000	
1959	406,535,000	1,138,300,000	Chicago, 6 July
1960	354,535,000	992,700,000	New York, 9–10 June**
1961	320,964,000	898,700,000	
1962	360,142,000	1,008,400,000	New York, 7 June; San Francisco, 12–18 November**
1963	385,464,000	1,079,300,000	Washington, 24–25 Nov.**
1964	408,357,000	1,143,400,000	
1965	501,928,000	1,405,400,000	
1966	637,714,000	1,785,600,000	Variety Club Tour, 9–19 March;** Boston, 7 March
1967	610,678,000	1,709,900,000	
1968	856,041,668	2,054,500,000	

* The Queen
** Prince Philip

FRANCE
1965	186,613,000	522,382,000	3–4 July; 4–5 November**
1966	208,972,000	584,970,000	20–21 December**
1967	211,939,000	593,275,000	Normandy, 26–29 May*, 9 April, 20–21 April**

NETHERLANDS
1958	95,642,800	267,800,000	STATE VISIT, 25–27 March
1959	106,428,000	298,000,000	
1960	111,250,000	311,500,000	24–27 November**

1961	130,000,000	364,000,000	
1962	138,571,000	388,000,000	Amsterdam, 1–3 May
1963	154,071,000	431,400,000	
1964	180,464,000	505,300,000	
1965	173,464,000	485,700,000	
1966	174,642,000	489,000,000	

* The Queen
** Prince Philip

THE ROAD SHOW (p. 67)

BRAZIL	Exports	Imports
1967	£19,800,000	£26,500,000
1968 (first half)	£20,000,000	£19,700,000
1968 (second half)	£24,000,000	£17,300,000
1969 (first half)	£21,700,000	£25,900,000
1969 (second half)	£21,500,000	£24,800,000
CHILE		
1967	£13,300,000	£46,400,000
1968	£14,900,000	£56,500,000
1969 (first half)	£ 7,400,000	£32,500,000
1969 (second half)	£ 9,800,000	£39,600,000

House of Normandy			*House of Plantagenet*	
William I	1066–1087		Henry II	1154–1189
William II	1087–1100		Richard I	1189–1199
Henry I	1100–1135		John	1199–1216
Stephen	1135–1154		Henry III	1216–1272
			Edward I	1272–1307
			Edward II	1307–1327
			Edward III	1327–1377
			Richard II	1377–1399
				(deposed)

House of Lancaster			*House of York*	
Henry IV	1399–1413		Edward IV	1461–1483
Henry V	1413–1422		Edward V	1483 (murdered)
Henry VI	1422–1461		Richard III	1483–1485
	(deposed)			

House of Tudor				
Henry VII	1485–1509		Mary I	1553–1558
Henry VIII	1509–1547		Elizabeth I	1558–1603
Edward VI	1547–1553			

House of Stuart	
James I (VI Scotland)	1603–1625
Charles I	1625–1649 (beheaded)

COMMONWEALTH INTERREGNUM
1649–1660

Charles II	1660–1685
James II (VII Scotland)	1685–1688 (deposed)
William III	1689–1702
Mary II	1689–1694
Anne	1702–1714

House of Hanover	
George I	1714–1727
George II	1727–1760
George III	1760–1820

George IV	1820–1830
William IV	1830–1837
Victoria	1837–1901

House of Saxe-Coburg-Gotha

Edward VII	1901–1910

House of Windsor (from 1917)

George V	1910–1936
Edward VIII	1936 (abdicated)
George VI	1936–1952
Elizabeth II	Acceded 1952

ROYAL FAMILY INC. (p. 106)

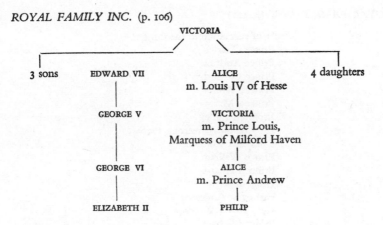

ROYAL FAMILY INC. (p. 102)

Much care is taken over the pedigree of the Queen's corgis, and there is a basic family strain in them:

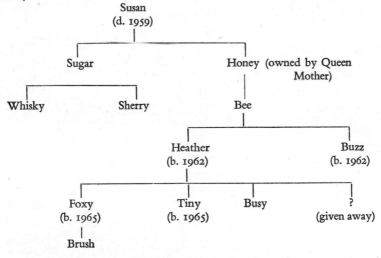

ROYAL FAMILY INC. (p. 121)

Order of succession to the throne:
Prince Charles
Prince Andrew
Prince Edward
Princess Anne
Princess Margaret
Viscount Linley
Lady Sarah Armstrong-Jones
Duke of Gloucester
Prince William
Prince Richard
Duke of Kent
Earl of St Andrews
Lady Helen Windsor
Prince Michael
Princess Alexandra
James Ogilvy

Speeches made by Prince Philip during the year:

6 November	Press Conference, São Paulo
13 November	Chamber of Commerce, Santiago
21 November	Gold Awards Presentation B.P.
21 November	R.Y.A. Annual Dinner
25 November	English-speaking Union ceremony, London
26 November	Dinner, Society of Industrial Artists and Designers, London
27 November	Medical Commission on Accident Prevention
27 November	A.G.M. Royal Society for Prevention of Accidents
27 November	Premiere of film *People+Leisure* =
16 December	Ashford Cattle Show – Lunch
17 December	Dinner, Anglo-Brazilian Society
18 December	Human Rights Year – Closing Ceremony
9 January	Highland Fling Exhibition
2 February	Gold Awards Presentation B.P.
6 February	Literary Lunch, *Yorkshire Post*
6 February	Opening of Minsthorpe High School
6 February	Literary Lunch, *Yorkshire Post*
6 February	Dinner, World Wildlife Fund
7 February	Opening, Sheffield Training School
10 February	Lunch, Master Mariners
11 February	Lunch, American and Canadian Chambers of Commerce
12 February	Lunch of Parliamentary and Scientific Committee
20 February	Installation of new Rector at Edinburgh University
21 March	Inauguration, Applied Science Building, Exeter University
24 March	Fleet Air Arm Officers Association – Annual Dinner
25 March	Dinner, British Institute of Management Council
26 March	Gold Awards Presentation, B.P.
28 March	International Student Conference, Chichester College, Opening Dinner
16 April	Royal Yacht Squadron, Annual Dinner
30 April	Oxford Centre of Management Conference
5 May	Open National Sailing Centre, Cowes
7 May	British Trade Council, Vienna
12 May	Dinner, Society of Licensed Aircraft Engineers
14 May	Royal College of Science, Students' Union Dinner
15 May	Guinness Awards Lecture

17 May	RAF Association Annual Conference
20 May	Prize-giving to nurses at Edinburgh Royal Infirmary
23 May	Lunch, Institute of Fuel
26 May	General Assembly, Church of Scotland
29 May	Presentation of C.I.D. Awards on Q.E.2
29 May	Visit to Shipbuilding Industry Training Board, Southampton
3 June	Inauguration of Gas Council Terminal, Norfolk
12 June	Dulwich College
24 June	Lunch, British Export Houses Association Dinner, Concrete Society
25 June	Machine Tool Industry Research Association
7 July	Simon Marks Educational Fund Dinner
9 July	Opening new building Borough Polytechnic
9 July	Athenaeum Club Dinner
21 July	Gold Awards Presentation, B.P.
24 July	Sovereign's Parade, Sandhurst

Speeches made by the Queen during the year:

30 October	Opening of Parliament
5 November	National Congress, Brasilia
5 November	Supreme Court, Brasilia
5 November	Itamaraty Banquet, Brasilia
6 November	São Paulo arrival
7 November	São Paulo Museum of Art
9 November	Governor's Lunch, Rio de Janeiro
11 November	Arrival Santiago
11 November	State Banquet, Santiago
12 November	National Congress, Santiago
14 November	Arrival, Valparaiso
17 December	Opening of Royal Mint, Llantrisant
25 December	Christmas Message
7 March	Opening of Victoria Line Underground, London
17 April	Opening of Cargo Terminal, London Airport
23 April	State Banquet, Windsor
1 May	Opening Ordnance Survey H.Q., Southampton
5 May	Statute of the Council of Europe Lunch, London
5 May	State Banquet, Vienna
6 May	Lunch, Vienna
7 May	Lunch, Vienna
8 May	Lunch, Innsbruck
8 May	Dinner, Salzburg
13 May	Presentation of New Colours, Royal Marine
20 May	Opening General Assembly, Church of Scotland, Edinburgh
20 May	Church of Scotland's Women's Guild
22 May	Opening of fruit market, Glasgow
23 May	Free Church of Scotland Assembly
28 May	Closing General Assembly, Church of Scotland
25 June	Presentation of New Colours, Grenadier Guards
26 June	Presentation of New Colours, Central Flying School, Little Rissington
11 July	Opening Poole General Hospital
15 July	State Banquet, President of Finland, Buckingham Palace
29 July	Presentation of Colours to Western Fleet, Torbay
4 August	Trinity House Lunch, Hull
4 August	Inauguration of new dock, Hull

INTERLUDES 3 (p. 161)

Informal lunches given by the Queen during the year:
19 December, 1968

The Queen
The Duke of Edinburgh
The Prince of Wales
The Princess Anne
Professor Asa Briggs (Vice-Chancellor, Sussex University; Professor of History)
Sir Matt Busby (Manager, Manchester United Football Club)
Mr Maurice Green (Editor of the *Daily Telegraph*)
Mr Andrew Grima (Jeweller)
Mr Frank Muir (Head of Entertainment, London Weekend Television)
The Lord Rothschild (Chairman, 'Shell' Research Ltd.)
Mr Victor Silvester (Ballroom Dance Orchestra)
Sir Michael Tippett (Composer)

13 February, 1969

The Queen
The Duke of Edinburgh
The Princess Anne
Dame Dorothy Vaisey (General Secretary, Society of Friends of the Poor and Gentlefolk's Help)
Mr John Brown (Publisher, Oxford University Press)
The Lord Geddes (President, Chamber of Shipping of the United Kingdom)
Mr Cliff Richard (Singer)
Sir Robert Somerville (Clerk of the Council of the Duchy of Lancaster)
The Lord Todd (Master of Christ's College, Cambridge)
Professor E. K. Waterhouse (Barber Professor of Fine Arts)
Mr Peter Willett (Racing Journalist)
Mr David Gallagher (Assistant Press Secretary)

5 March, 1969

The Queen
The Princess Anne
The Baroness Serota (Minister of State for Health and Social Security)
Dame Peggy Ashcroft (Actress)
Sir Donald Anderson (Chairman, The Peninsular and Oriental Steam Navigation Co.)
Dr Gordon Claringbull (Director, British Museum (Natural History))
Mr Richard Fleming (Chairman, Robert Fleming & Co. Ltd.)

Mr Andrew Forge (Head of Fine Art Painting, Goldsmith's College School of Art)
Mr Hammond Innes (Author and Traveller)
Professor David Keith-Lucas (President, Royal Aeronautical Society)
Mr Wynford Vaughan-Thomas (Director of Programmes, Harlech Television)
Major-General Peter Gillett (Secretary, Central Chancery of the Orders of Knighthood)

9 July, 1969

The Queen
The Duke of Edinburgh
Commandant Marion Kettlewell (Director, Women's Royal Naval Service)
Mr Malcolm Arnold (Composer)
Mr Gerald Benney (Silversmith)
Mr Charles Curran (Director-General of the British Broadcasting Corporation)
Mr William Davis (Editor of Punch)
Mr Robin Knox-Johnston (Yachtsman)
Sir Douglas Logan (Principal, University of London)
Mr W. B. Singleton (President, Royal College of Veterinary Surgeons)
The Lady Rose Baring (Lady-in-Waiting)
Major Randle Cooke (Equerry to the Duke of Edinburgh)

Advertising Budgets, 1968 Figures

	£
Unilever	15,683,600
Mars-Petfood-Dawnay	7,569,600
Government Departments	6,548,300
Imperial Tobacco	5,995,400
Proctor & Gamble	5,207,200
British Cocoa	4,913,400
Beechams	4,036,700
Gallahers	3,789,500
Carreras	2,787,300
Rowntrees	2,747,200
Kelloggs	2,578,700
Heinz	2,528,700
Spillers	2,374,600
Nestlés	2,325,500
Milk Marketing Board	2,323,300
Brooke Bond	2,123,400
I.C.I.	2,102,500
Colgate Palmolive	1,660,300
Gillette	1,573,700
Showerings	1,490,800
Bass/Charrington	1,482,400
Rank Hovis McDougall	1,430,400
Lyons	1,398,300
Cerebos	1,256,600
United Biscuits	1,217,800
Schweppes	1,112,700
British Leyland	1,094,700
Guinness	1,069,500
British Egg Marketing Board	918,700
Kraft	913,000
Fisons	905,500
Dunlop	836,900
Quaker	830,900
Bovril	755,300
Ford	730,900
Montague Burton	711,200
Tea Council	632,200
Butter Information Council	598,700
G.U.S.	523,800

ROAD SHOW (p. 261)

Medals presented by the Queen in Austria:

G.C.V.O.	3
K.C.V.O.	9
C.V.O.	13
K.C.M.G.	2
K.B.E.	4
C.M.G.	2
C.B.E.	12
M.B.E.	9
O.B.E.	5
G.B.E.	4
R.V.M. (B)	30
R.V.M. (G)	20
R.V.M. (S)	30
M.V.O. IV	16
M.V.O. V	9

THE ROAD SHOW (p. 255)

Presents received in Austria:
THE QUEEN

Two Haflinger ponies
Book 'Haflinger – a horse captures the hearts of the world' by Otto Schweisgut
Stamp Album
Two books of sketches
Four leaflets about 'Sights of Austria'
Four copies of 'Masterpieces of Kunsthistorisches Museum'
Book of prints from the Albertina Collection
Three copies of book on Crown Jewels
Silver reproduction of the Cellini Salt Cellar
Records of music from Vienna
Copy of piano score of 'Windsor-Klange' by Johann Strauss
Records of 'Die Fledermaus'
Books from Abbey of Klosterneuburg
Large painted wooden chest
Bronze cauldron
Two gold medallions
Album of prints 'Salzburg in Alten Ansichten'
Cut glass urn
Sketches of St Stephen's Cathedral
Large gold medallion
Book *Austria and the Anglo-Saxons* by W. Braumuller
Umbrella with tortoishell and ivory handle and picture of Spanish Riding School
Record of Austrian music
Two books on Piber Stud
Austrian cloth
Book *Romantic Danube*

PRINCE PHILIP

Mannlicher Schonauer rifle and case
Bronze statue of Margareta Grafin of Tyrol
Hunting dagger
Eumig camera and tape
Book of prints of military uniforms of the past
Case of pipes in wood
Book *Bernadotte*
Gold medal

PRINCESS ANNE

Super 8 cine camera in case and projector (Eumig)
Skis, boots and sticks
Austrian coat, blouse, skirt and socks
Table cloth
Book on Salzburg

PRINCE CHARLES

Ice pick

GOD v. SCOTLAND (p. 267)

The Queen's engagements in Edinburgh:

Monday, 19 May		Arrive in Edinburgh
		Evening Banquet
Tuesday, 20 May	10.30 a.m.	General Assembly Service at St Giles Cathedral
	11.30–12.30	Opening Ceremony of the General Assembly of the Church of Scotland
	3.40–4.00	Visit to mass meeting of the Church of Scotland's Woman's Guild
Wednesday, 21 May	9.30 a.m.	Communion Service at St Giles
	10.30–11.00	Visit General Assembly
	11.45–12.30	Investiture at Holyroodhouse
	2.55–3.55 p.m.	Visit to Youth and Community Centre, Clermiston
Thursday, 22 May	11.05 a.m.	Arrive Glasgow by train. Open new fruit market: Visit Lord Provost: Visit to William Collins & Sons: Visit to Scottish Design Centre
	3.50 p.m.	Leave Glasgow
	4.50 p.m.	Arrive Edinburgh
	8.00–	Performance of *The Gondoliers* by
	10.30 p.m.	Scottish Opera Company
Friday, 23 May	10.00–	Visit General Assembly
	10.55 a.m.	
	11.00–	Visit Free Church of Scotland General
	11.20 a.m.	Assembly
	3.00–	Tour Bruce Peebles Factory, East Pil-
	4.00 p.m.	ton, Edinburgh
Saturday, 24 May		No official engagements
Sunday, 25 May	10.55–	Morning service at St Giles
	12.00 a.m.	
	6.30–	Youth Service at St Giles
	7.15 p.m.	
Monday, 26 May	11.50 a.m.–	Order of the Thistle Service at St
	1.00 p.m.	Giles
	3.00–	Garden Party
	5.00 p.m.	
Tuesday, 27 May	10.00–	Visit General Assembly
	10.30 a.m.	

358

	10.35–	Visit Canongate Manse
	10.50 a.m.	
Wednesday, 28 May	2.40–	Visit to Liberton Secondary School
	3.40 p.m.	
	6.55–	Closing Ceremony of the General
	8.15 p.m.	Assembly of the Church of Scotland
Thursday, 29 May	11.30 a.m.	Arrives in Dundee by train. Visit to Camperdown Factory of National Cash Registrar: St Mary's Place Housing Development: Lunch at City Chambers: Douglasfield Works (Jute Industries Ltd.)
	4.00 p.m.	Leaves Dundee by car for Birkhall, the Queen Mother's estate, seven miles from Balmoral

GOD v. SCOTLAND (p. 273)

Overnight guests at Holyrood house between 19 and 29 May, 1969
        Mrs Harold Wilson
        William Ross, M.P.
        Mrs Ross
        The Duke and Duchess of Hamilton and Brandon
        Sir John and Lady Wheeler-Bennett
        Norwegian Ambassador and Madame Koht
        Earl and Countess of Wemyss and March
        General Sir Richard and Lady O'Connor
        Lieutenant-Governor of Nova Scotia and Mrs Oland
        Queen Mother
        Duchess of Gloucester
        Dowager Countess of Airlie
        Lord and Lady Reith
        Sir Alec and Lady Douglas-Home
        Sir James and Lady Robertson
        Earl and Countess of Mansfield and Mansfield
        Dowager Countess of Elgin and Kincardine
        Baroness Elliot of Harwood
        Lord and Lady Birsay
        Princess Alexandra, and Angus Ogilvy

THE ROYAL VAUDEVILLE (p. 291)

The twenty-one Princes of Wales from 1301

Edward b. 1284 (later Edward II)	1301
Edward the Black Prince (son of Edward III)	1343
Richard (later Richard II) son of the Black Prince	1377
Henry of Monmouth (later Henry V) son of Henry IV	1399
Edward of Westminster (son of Henry VI)	1454
Edward of Westminster (later Edward V)	1472
Edward (son of Richard III)	1483
Arthur Tudor (son of Henry VII)	1489
Henry Tudor (later Henry VIII) son of Henry VII	1503
Henry Stuart (son of James I)	1610
Charles Stuart (later Charles I) son of James I	1616
Charles (later Charles II) son of Charles I	1630
James Francis Edward, 'The Old Pretender'	1688
George Augustus (later George II) son of George I	1711
Frederick Lewis (son of George II)	1727
George William Frederick (later George III)	1751
George Augustus Frederick (later George IV)	1762
Albert Edward (later Edward VII)	1841
George (later George V)	1901
Edward (later Edward VIII)	1911
Charles Philip Arthur George (invested 1969)	1958

THE ROYAL VAUDEVILLE (p. 301)

Explosions preceding the Investiture

17 November, 1967	Temple of Peace, Cardiff
5 January, 1968	Snowdonia Country Club, Caernarvon
24 March, 1968	Inland Revenue, Cardiff
25 May, 1968	Welsh Office, Cardiff
27 May, 1968	Lake Vyrnwy emergency pipeline
28 June, 1968	Helsby, Chester water pipeline
9 September, 1968	RAF Pembrey, Carmarthen
2 December, 1968	Hagley, Worcestershire water pipeline
10 April, 1969	Chester Income Tax Office
15 April, 1969	Police H.Q., Cardiff
29 April, 1969	Electricity H.Q., Cardiff
30 June, 1969	Post box, Cardiff
1 July, 1969	Abergele, Denbighshire

THE ROYAL VAUDEVILLE (p. 309)

Processions to Caernarvon Castle for the Investiture Ceremony
Heralds
Representatives of Welsh Youth
Peers and Gentlemen who will take part in the Prince's Procession
Mayor and Council of Caernarvon
Officers and members of the Gorsedd of Bards and the National Eisteddfod
  Council
Mayors of Welsh boroughs
Chairmen and Clerks of Welsh County Councils
County Sheriffs
Members of Parliament for Welsh Constituencies
Church Representatives
Peers
Her Majesty's Bodyguard of the Honourable Corps of Gentlemen at Arms,
  followed by the Queen's Bodyguard of the Guard
Peers and Gentlemen who will take part in the Queen's Procession

Index

367

Public Order Act, the, 301

Quaker Oats, 109
Quant, Mary, 222
Queen Mother, the, *see* Elizabeth, Queen Mother
Queen's Award:
  for Industry, 140–1
  for Poetry, 87, 89
Queen's Flight, the, 19, 121, 191
Queen's Gallery, 214

RAF, 18–19, 34, 67, 189
Rainey, Jane, 311
Recife, 20 et seq.
Redgrave, Vanessa, 135
Reform Bill, the, 3
Reformation, the, 16, 183, 263, 265
Reilly, Sir Paul, 131
Reith, Lord, 273
Renshaw, Mickey, 167
Rhodesia, 151, 155
Rhodri Mawr, 290
Richard II, King, 291
Richard of Gloucester, Prince, 307
Rio de Janeiro, 11 et seq.
Roberts, Mervyn, 306
Roe, Captain Richard, 318
Rolling Stones, the, 158, 314
Rollo the Bold, 324
Roman Catholic Church, the, 32, 263, 266, 276
Roman Empire, the, 95
Ross, William, 268, 271
Rothschild, Eddie, 77
Royal Canadian Mounted Police, 285
Royal Company of Archers, the, 268
Royal Family (TV film), 25, 31, 212–15, 315
Royal Marine Band, the, 31, 56, 59, 136, 323
Royal Marriage Act, the, 223
Royal Mint, the, xiii
Royal Opera House, *see* Covent Garden
Royal Tournament, the, 284
Rumbold, Sir Anthony, 247–8
Rupert of Loewenstein-Wertheim, Prince, 125
Russell, Georgiana, 24, 46, 51
Russell, Lady (Aliki Diplorakos), 24, 51, 59
Russell, Sir John, 23 et seq., 39, 44, 50, 52

Sacher, Frau Anna, 256
Sahara, the, 20, 77
St George's Chapel, 107
St James's Palace, 187, 201
St Paul's Cathedral, 160
St Paul's School, São Paulo, 49
Salem, 114
Salisbury, Joan Countess of, 107
Salisbury, Marquess of, 179–80
Salvador de Bahia, 26 et seq.
Sandhurst, 106
Sandringham, xii, 94, 109, 134, 152, 186
San Francisco, 80
Santa Cruz, Victor, 69
Santiago, ix, x, 68 et seq.
Saragat, Pres. Giuseppe, 240–4
Scarbrough, Lord, 135, 145, 236, 239
Schönbrunn Palace, 249, 252–3
Scilly Isles, the, 175
Scotland, 262–76
Scottish State Coach, the, 267
Selby Abbey, 234–8
Selby Gazette & Herald, 234
Selective Employment Tax, 148
Sellers, Peter, 119, 125
Shetland Islands, the, 322
Shulman, Milton, 214
Siemens, 76
Sive, André, 33
Slater, Lt John, 81, 151, 168
Smuts, Field Marshal Jan, 157
Snowdon, Lord, xiii, 8, 95, 99, 119, 126–34 (life style), 297–9 (Investiture)
Snowdonia, 314
Soares, Lael Barbosa, 54–55
Sopwith, Sir Thomas, 323
South America:
  British trade with, 14
  Queen's visit to, 11 et seq.
Spanish Riding School, the, 253–5
Spectator, the, 93
Sporting Life, the, 98
Stamfordham, Lord, 154
Starkloff, Szuzui, 221
Steptoe and Son, 212
Stern, 207
Stevas, Norman St John, 93
Stewart, Michael, 71, 84, 241–2, 245
Stock Exchange, the, 283
Stockwood, Mervyn (Bishop of Southwark), 264
Storr, Paul, 143